Young Reds in the Big Apple

YOUNG REDS IN THE BIG APPLE

The New York YPA, 1923–1934

Jack Hodgson

EMPIRE STATE EDITIONS

AN IMPRINT OF FORDHAM UNIVERSITY PRESS
NEW YORK 2025

Cover: Members of the Young Pioneers of America, a children's organization affiliated with the Communist Party USA, picket in front of the Federal Building in Milwaukee to protest jailing of sixteen workers of a hosiery mill who violated a federal injunction against picketing, circa 1930. (Photo by Hirz/Archive Photos/Getty Images)

Copyright © 2025 Fordham University Press

All rights reserved. No part of this publication may be reproduced, stored in a retrieval system, or transmitted in any form or by any means—electronic, mechanical, photocopy, recording, or any other—except for brief quotations in printed reviews, without the prior permission of the publisher.

Fordham University Press has no responsibility for the persistence or accuracy of URLs for external or third-party Internet websites referred to in this publication and does not guarantee that any content on such websites is, or will remain, accurate or appropriate.

Fordham University Press also publishes its books in a variety of electronic formats. Some content that appears in print may not be available in electronic books.

Visit us online at www.fordhampress.com/empire-state-editions.

Library of Congress Cataloging-in-Publication Data available online at https://catalog.loc.gov.

Printed in the United States of America

27 26 25   5 4 3 2 1

First edition

CONTENTS

List of Abbreviations   vii

Introduction   1

Part I: A New Vision for American Communist Childhood

1. The JSYWL and YPA Regulations   13
2. Leo Granoff: Harlem's "Boy Trotsky" and YPA Tactics   20
3. Radical Recreations   31

Part II: Children of the Class Struggle

4. Pioneer Politicians and the CPUSA   55
5. Pioneers and Picket Lines   65

Part III: The School Struggle

6. Countering Capitalist Curriculum and Corporal Punishment   77
7. School Lunch Revolts   84
8. The Lenin Unit at PS 61   91

Part IV: Pioneers and Political Opponents

9. Periodical Culture, the Fish Inquiry, and the US Post Office   105
10. The Van Etten Camp Controversy   118

11. Bashing the Boy Scouts and the Campaigns to Free Harry Eisman   130

Conclusion   157

Acknowledgments   163

Appendices   165

Notes   171

Bibliography   189

Index   195

ABBREVIATIONS

ACLU	American Civil Liberties Union
ADS	American Defense Society
BAF	Better America Federation
BSA	Boy Scouts of America
CIA	Central Intelligence Agency
CPUSA	Communist Party USA (officially the Workers Party)
DAR	Daughters of the American Revolution
FBI	Federal Bureau of Investigation
ILD	International Labor Defense
IWO	International Workers Order
JKKK	Junior Ku Klux Klan
JRCs	John Reed Clubs
JSYWL	Junior Section of the Young Workers League (became the YPA)
KKK	Ku Klux Klan
LSU	Labor Sports Union

NSL	National Security League
NYPD	New York City Police Department
PAPD	Port Authority of New York and New Jersey Police Department
POA	Patriotic Order of America
PS	Public School (often used as a prefix)
SLC	School Lunch Committee
SLIC	School Lunch Inquiry Committee
SPCC	Society for the Prevention of Cruelty to Children
UCWW	United Council of Working Women
USLA	Unconditional Service League of America
WIR	Workers International Relief
YCL	Young Communist League
YPA	Young Pioneers of America
YWL	Young Workers League (became YCL)

Young Reds in the Big Apple

INTRODUCTION

OCTOBER 1928 WAS a big month for politics in New York City: Yankees superstar Babe Ruth took to the airwaves to endorse the Empire State's Democratic Governor Al Smith for the presidency while the eventual victor, Herbert Hoover, addressed a huge crowd at Madison Square Garden. In retrospect Hoover delivered one of the most ironic speeches in American history during which he claimed that only he could be trusted to safeguard the economy.[1] It was also campaign season for a host of minor candidates who were almost certainly destined to finish up as "also rans" in a series of down-ballot races. One such candidate was Robert "Fighting Bob" Minor, the Workers' Party candidate for United States senator from New York. On October 28 Minor made one of a series of campaign stops at Webster Hall on Manhattan's East 11th Street.

Before Minor spoke there were important rituals to observe. The crowd of up to one thousand stood in unison, raised their right arms, and gave their pledge of allegiance to the Red Flag: "I pledge allegiance to the workers' Red Flag and to the cause for which it stands. One aim, throughout our lives, freedom to the working class." Minor's speech was a disappointing flop and audience members were not shy in showing their disappointment. Some sought refuge in the lobby and others participated in impromptu games of tag or Ring-around-the-Rosie. They were mainly children from the Young Pioneers of America (YPA), a Communist Party (CPUSA) affiliate for youngsters aged roughly eight to sixteen. Their reaction reflected their youthfulness and Minor's political shortcomings.

As historian Theodore Draper summarizes, the famed radical cartoonist "struggled to transfer his genius from art to politics," and the same man who produced striking illustrations became known for boring and banal speeches.[2]

Pioneers had decorated the hall with banners bearing slogans such as "Fight the Boy Scouts!" and "Fight Anti-Labor Propaganda in Schools!" They identified as Communist and the CPUSA helped to facilitate their events, but the YPA often had its own child-focused working-class agenda. Pioneers frequently criticized the adult party and the Young Communist League (YCL), the Communist organization for youths under twenty-three, for not doing enough for the workers' children. Influential Pioneers often cared little for adult authority whether it came in the shape of capitalist schoolteachers or instructions from CPUSA headquarters. The keynote speaker that night was the YPA's own Jessie Taft, a fourteen-year-old pupil at Walton High School and a member of the local YPA executive committee. Unlike Minor, Taft received a rousing reception. She appealed to the audience of working-class children by focusing on the world they knew: New York City's overcrowded public schools.

Taft was a gifted public speaker whom the *Knoxville Journal* later described as one of the Soviet Union's "chief spellbinders" in the United States.[3] "Waving her arms around like a veteran of the hustings," Taft urged her fellow Pioneers to stick at what they termed "the school struggle." Pioneers faced disciplinary action, expulsion, and unwanted police attention because of their YPA membership and their efforts to recruit members at schools. Taft assured them that their punishments would ultimately be worth it, promising that one day they would be able to kick out unpopular principals and their "capitalist principles" from the schools. Taft also used her time at the rostrum to deliver "the workers' children's demands" to important figures in the adult party, singling out Minor and Herbert Zam, a CPUSA candidate for the state assembly. Taft put to them the "importance of workers' children and their activities" to the Communist cause and demanded that the adults work as hard for the youth as the youth did for the adults.[4] Taft's open dissent shows how the YPA functioned as a semi-autonomous and boisterous section of New York's wider radical community. It represented a new, more independent vision of Communist American childhoods that ultimately many Communists failed to get on board with.

American Communists launched their children's mass organization on May Day 1923 in Chicago. It was first called the Junior Section of the Young Workers League (JSYWL). In 1925 when the Young Workers

League (YWL) became the YCL, it was rebranded as the YPA and the headquarters were relocated from Illinois to the CPUSA's offices in New York's Union Square. The JSYWL and then the YPA's structure was based on the official Soviet state youth organization, the Vladimir Lenin All-Union Pioneers, an organization commonly known as the Young Pioneers. This meant giving the children as much control over their affairs as practically possible. Most Pioneers were the children or siblings of committed CPUSA members. The YPA's strength in New York mirrored the CPUSA's areas of strength—the Lower East Side, the Bronx, and parts of Brooklyn. A core contingent lived in the CPUSA's housing initiative, the Allerton Avenue Coops. Other youths were recruited by existing Pioneers and some children did come into the organization of their own accord. The ethnic makeup of the YPA varied across the country. Nationally and particularly in the Midwest it was dominated by Finnish Americans. In New York the largest group were Eastern European Jewish immigrants and their descendants. Despite this, most activities were conducted in English, reflecting the overarching desire to become the organization for the children of the American proletariat.[5]

Despite the YPA having grown steadily to a membership in the thousands adult Communists abolished the organization in 1934, closing a distinct children's organization. Some functions were absorbed into the YCL and the International Workers Order (IWO). The IWO had grown from a fraternity offering low-cost life insurance for workers to a broader organization with cultural activities for workers and their families. As Roger Keeran describes, the IWO's youth wing expanded on the YPA's recreational offerings with arts and crafts clubs, orchestras, drama groups, sports, and summer camping. But it differed from the YPA in that it tried to bind children to the values of their parents. A key difference was that the IWO envisaged children as students of the class struggle by placing them in so-called schools rather than as the active participants that the YPA model demanded. The IWO also differed in that it was segregated fifteen ways by ethnicity whereas the YPA had demanded full racial and ethnic integration as part of its staunch opposition to segregation and wider American racial politics.[6]

That formal end was not quite the end for the YPA, however as committed Pioneers had no intention of meekly ceasing their activities. They were accustomed to leading their own movement and engaging directly in the class struggle on their own terms. Youths who did not accept the CPUSA's decision continued to organize themselves as an unofficial YPA until they were old enough to join the YCL. Newspapers continued to report YPA activity in New York well into 1935. In May that year seventy-four children calling themselves the Brownsville YPA accosted Mayor Fiorello La Guardia on the steps of City Hall. As per the *Times Union,* they marched with protest placards, used an "amateur band" to draw attention to themselves, and demanded increased investment in playgrounds in poor neighborhoods, citing the fact that twelve children had been killed by automobiles while playing on Brownsville streets already that year.[7] In other parts of the country unofficial renegade YPA activism continued into 1936. Youths identifying as the YPA targeted a speech by Republican presidential nominee Alf Landon at the Los Angeles Coliseum. They distributed anti-Landon handbills and a cluster of young hecklers booed and hissed through his speech. One boy shouted in vulgar terms to accurately predict the scale of Landon's defeat. Another's impeccably timed "razzberries" permeated the scripted dramatic pauses in his speech, an apt representation of the electorate's view on a potential Landon presidency delivered two years after adults had officially closed the YPA.[8]

The YPA is a part of the history of American Communism. The historiography of what should be a fruitful area for historical inquiry has been reduced to a farcical caricature of extremes defined by bad-faith attacks and hyper-partisan scholarship. Two rival schools have been built on top of foundational scholarship by the likes of Theodore Draper. There is a traditionalist, liberal, vehemently anti-Communist school that has been dominated by John Earl Haynes and Harvey Klehr and a rival revisionist school linked to the New Left.[9] The fallout from Michael J. Carley's review of Klehr and Haynes's *The Secret World of American Communism* shows that it is only a mild exaggeration to say that one school considers the other Stalinist apologists for mass murder while the second school views its rival as Joe McCarthy's intellectual legacy.[10] The history of American Communism has always been written by people with a lot of skin in the game who are desperate to cast the main players as either deliberate villainous agents for pure evil or as noble working-class heroes motivated by a desire to fight economic and racial injustices. *Young Reds in the Big Apple* moves beyond this. Rather than debating the morality of those involved with the YPA it examines what its existence can tell us about the time it inhabited, ultimately leading to the conclusion that the 1920s was a period of continued Communist activism, continued efforts at repression in response, and that there was no genuine interlude between the two so-called Red Scares.

The YPA has received little scholarly attention in its own right, having previously been considered at monograph length once in Paul C. Mishler's *Raising Reds* (1999).[11] Even in works with tightly defined chronological and geographic boundaries like Mark Naison's study of Communism within Depression-era Harlem, the Communist children's movement, which was very active in Harlem, receives no serious consideration.[12] In *Raising Reds* Mishler offers breadth by analyzing the YPA alongside other Leftist youth movements in an exploration of American Communist adults' mission to create cultural environments for their children. *Raising Reds* is less concerned with the successes or failures of the YPA or the perspectives of the children who formed it. *Young Reds in the Big Apple* takes a different approach with an in-depth children's history of YPA activity in and around New York City, privileging the voices of historical children where possible. Young Pioneers were not passive beings beholden to the whims of adults but were political thinkers and actors in their own right. Working-class children were not merely victims of poverty and other social crises but had their own thoughts about their experiences and attempted to make change.

Britt Haas notes in *Fighting Authoritarianism* (2017), a history of student activism in New York's colleges, that historical literature relating to interwar youth activism is scant.[13] This is even more true when it comes to younger teenagers and children's activism. The historical profession has historically minimized children's efforts and abilities to shape the world around them despite the obvious fact that political opinions do not magically appear when a person reaches the age of majority. Brian Rouleau argues that children have been "hiding in plain sight" in the history of US foreign relations owing to adult historians' reluctance to acknowledge their capacity for and roles in diplomacy.[14] Rouleau is correct and the YPA is a perfect case in point. Pioneers took it upon themselves to act as miniature ambassadors for Communism and the Soviet Union in their schools and neighborhoods. They also engaged in transnational discourse with other Communist youth movements and a small number traveled internationally to engage in formal diplomacy with various Communist dignitaries in pursuit of their goals.

Reflecting the dearth of historical literature dealing with interwar radical youth activism, beyond Mishler's *Raising Reds* there are only glimpses of the YPA in adjacent historiographies. For example, Mischa Honeck's *Our Frontier Is the World* (2018), a history of the Boy Scouts of America (BSA) during the age of ascendancy, offers a tantalizing preview of the YPA in recounting its demonstration and subsequent riot against the BSA at a New York quayside.[15] There are also glimpses of the YPA in older Cold War–era histories looking back at Depression-era American Communism, but these works lack objectivity in their analysis. For example, Herbert Romerstein's *Communism and Your Child* (1962) describes one Pioneer as a "plague" on his local community.[16] The boy's own school principal described him as "inoffensive." Romerstein's pejorative language stems from a predetermined position that all involved in Communism, including children, were irredeemably bad actors by default. Individual Pioneers did many things, and the categorization of each action as good, bad, or something else is subjective. Romerstein's attitude is not unique. One only needs to scan published reviews of Mishler's *Raising Reds* to see that for some scholars anything short of a blood-curdling attack on American Communists and a thorough hunt for traitorous bogeymen is insufficient. For instance, Robert D. Cohen writes that "some might be surprised by the author's most positive view of the Communist Party and its allies."[17] *Young Reds in the Big Apple* aims to reconstruct the history of the YPA while moving away from the historiographical trend of moralizing the history of American Communism. Readers can make up their own minds as to who and what was good or bad.

Following this introduction, the first part of the book analyzes the vision for Communist childhoods that the YPA represented. The Pioneer movement wanted to renegotiate the relationship between Communist parent and child, claiming that parental authority came from a bourgeois concept of the right of the stronger and demanding that children be taken seriously as friends and comrades within Communism. The JSYWL/YPA ideal of a politically active Communist child was exemplified in 1923 New York by eleven-year-old Leo Granoff. A case study of Granoff, who was arrested by the NYPD's radical bureau, highlights the YPA's tactics in New York. Although anti-Communists frequently worried about secretive Communist tactics and alleged underhanded infiltration plots, the truth is that following the Granoff affair the YPA preferred bold public protest, sought to manufacture mini martyrdoms for their movement, and engaged in deliberately inflammatory press-seeking behavior. The second part of the YPA vision for childhood revolved around asserting children's right to leisure in a rejection of child labor. The YPA provided cheap unsegregated recreational opportunities including organized sports, musical theater, and summer camping. Even while having fun, the YPA embodied opposition to American gender norms and racial politics.

The second part of *Young Reds in the Big Apple* examines how Pioneers attempted to live up to the Pioneer vision and become changemakers in their communities. "The school struggle" meant different things to different children. Some Pioneers focused on challenging anti-Communist and imperialist curricula; others challenged corporal punishment, poor school conditions, and overcrowding; and others attempted to use public schools as an organizing base for growing the Pioneer movement. Although there was no clearly defined grand school strategy, in part because school-based activism was dependent on the whims and priorities of individuals willing to risk punishment, the YPA flourished in certain schools such as PS 61 in the Bronx. Outside of schools, Pioneers proved themselves within the CPUSA by contributing to the *Daily Worker* and giving speeches at Communist cultural and political events. Pioneers carved a unique niche for themselves in local industrial disputes. Rather than learn about the class struggle in Socialist Sunday school classrooms the Pioneer model demanded that children be active on picket lines. Many were and they gave particular attention to helping the children of striking workers. This all typified the YPA's vision for an American Communist childhood where children were active participants in the class struggle.

The third part of the book details how various political opponents worked to counter the YPA, ranging from members of Congress to anti-Communist children and even extremists including the Ku Klux Klan (KKK). Following the Fish Inquiry (controversial congressional investigations into Communism), the US Post Office refused to deliver the YPA's periodical *Young Pioneer* (originally named *Young Comrade*). Several hundred Pioneers burst through lines of mounted police to occupy Manhattan's main post office. A replacement publication titled *New Pioneer* was launched. Pioneers faced physical danger primarily from police officers and became entangled in regular skirmishes with the NYPD. At the very least police were more than happy to become involved in physical altercations with youths, deploying their nightsticks, fire hoses, and other weapons, while on other occasions there appears to have been deliberate planned extrajudicial violence perpetrated against children. Sometimes with the blessing of law enforcement members of the KKK, the Patriotic Order of America (POA), and the American Legion violently targeted YPA summer camps. Whenever they perceived being targeted, Pioneers frequently fought back, seeking to work confrontation to their advantage. The YPA's international networking capabilities are best shown in its coordinated response to Pioneer Harry Eisman's imprisonment at a New York reformatory. Following protests in several American cities and Pioneers wooing authorities in Moscow, Eisman was granted Soviet citizenship and left with a hero's farewell.

The history of the YPA is clearly an eventful one—but what to make of it? The 1920s was as John Chalberg points out a decade of juxtaposition. Politically, Calvin Coolidge might be considered one of its standard-bearers. F. Scott Fitzgerald might be cast as one of its cultural icons. Thus, one titan of the Twenties was a tight-lipped, tight-pursed New England puritan and another a non-puritan writer who escaped the Midwest for the relative Babylons on both coasts.[18] Continuing this theme of juxtaposition, on one hand the Twenties can be regarded as a return to normalcy between two World Wars and two Red Scares. As William Carleton argues, there was a new passion for conformity and "100-percent Americanism."[19] On the other hand, rather than a rejection of political extremes the 1920s was a decade during which the KKK flourished; both the Communists and the Klan launched their children's wings in 1923. The sustained relative success of the JSYWL and the Junior KKK (JKKK) does not align with a return to normalcy unless one considers radicalism and extremism the norm for American history.

So how radical was the YPA? When assessing the Communists in Buffalo in 1919 and 1920, William H. Siener comments, "Radicalism is sometimes in the eye of the beholder. It would require great effort to see the Radicals of Buffalo as a threat to the Republic, but the effort was made."[20] The same can be said of the YPA. Its members advocated for a workers' and farmers' government, gave fiery bombasts, and took part in rowdy public demonstrations. They occasionally engaged in premeditated violence. But they remained a relatively small group of Communist children. Assessing how radical the Young Pioneers were is dependent on how much value one places on method and how much value one places on intent. Consider briefly the YPA group in Cleveland. In December 1929 twenty-one YPA members, including a six-year-old, brought a city council meeting to a halt after forcing their way into the chamber. This bold disruptive method of protest accompanied a relatively meek demand for subsidized streetcar tickets for children traveling to school.[21] It seems farfetched to portray these types of campaigns as Revolutionary Communism. It took a great deal of effort and at times complete unmitigated buffoonery to construe these children as urgent threats to the United States, but officials who made such claims often saw a personal benefit in doing so.

The Pioneers remained a vociferous but relatively small organization of children and adolescents and for the most part their major achievements in terms of forcing change were few and far between. Part of the YPA's historical importance is in the reactions it drew from others. One part of the view of the 1920s as the return to normalcy that Warren G. Harding promised is that it was a period between the two Red Scares. A traditional narrative in the history of American Communism is that there was a first Red Scare often defined as spanning 1919–1920 only and then a second Red Scare after the Second World War.[22] Yet the YPA was born, rose to a certain level of prominence, and died during that alleged interlude. That original narrative has recently been challenged to an extent with works such as Robert Justin Goldstein's edited collection, *Little "Red Scares": Anti-Communism and Political Repression in the United States, 1921–1946*.[23] The idea of "little Red Scares" however appears to sorely underestimate the intense public vitriol, press hyperbole, extrajudicial suppression, intimidation, and violence that characterized reactions to the YPA in New York, 1923–1934, which are detailed extensively in this book. Of course, the American public had not forgotten the bombings of 1919–1920. New Yorkers would not have forgotten the 1920 Wall Street bombing that killed thirty people. Fear may have subsided somewhat; the Red Scare may have passed a peak, but the idea that this first Red Scare ended neatly is implausible.

Murray B. Levin, a former Communist and a political scientist, defines a Red Scare as a period of "nationwide, anti-radical hysteria" resulting from a "mounting fear and anxiety that a Bolshevik revolution" was imminent and threatened "the American way of life," particularly "church, home, marriage," and "civility."[24] Levin's characterization of a Red Scare focuses on one element, the fears of anti-Communists. But there is another vital component to a Red Scare which is action. There is no visible Red Scare if fears are not acted upon. A Red Scare, it is suggested here, includes sensationalized press coverage, counterprotests including inflamed rhetoric and violence from the public or political opponents, and efforts at suppression from authorities, including the possibility of a willingness to engage in violence or extrajudicial conduct. YPA children encountered all of that in their daily lives in New York City. Therefore, a Red Scare state existed in and around the city to a fluctuating extent throughout the 1920s and into the 1930s.

Young Reds in the Big Apple is an intimate history of the YPA in and around New York City, 1923–1934. It examines how a network of Communist children and adolescents operated within the city to challenge the adult authority of teachers, cops, Santa Claus, and American capitalism. It provides biographic details for previously obscure activists who were part of the JSYWL and YPA's alternative vision for a Communist childhood that rejected parental authority. Political protest and an important right to play dominated their activities as Pioneers strived to show that they were "always ready" in the cause of the working class. They took up causes including school lunch provision, playground-building, child labor abolishment, and fighting racial prejudice. For doing so, as well as vociferously and sometimes violently calling for a "workers' and farmers' government," they were subject to expulsion from school, surveillance, and police brutality from authorities who also refused to act when Pioneers were subjected to orchestrated violence from opposing adult organizations such as the KKK. The history of the YPA shows that radicalism did not suddenly appear only to be quashed by a concerted effort of government and public in a swift return to normalcy; rather radicalism was a constant of the early twentieth-century political milieu. The history of the YPA proves that there was no true interregnum between the two commonly recognized Red Scares.

Part I

A NEW VISION FOR AMERICAN COMMUNIST CHILDHOOD

Chapter 1

The JSYWL and YPA Regulations

Origins and Ethos

THE JUNIOR SECTION of the Young Workers League (JSYWL) officially commenced operations as the Communist Party USA's (CPUSA's) mass organization for the children of the proletariat on May Day, 1923, in Chicago. In 1925 the JSYWL became the Young Pioneers of America (YPA), and its headquarters relocated from the Windy City to the Big Apple amid a wider reorganization of Communist groups in the country. The YPA could trace its roots further back than 1923 as it recognized itself during its tenth anniversary celebrations in 1933 by paying tribute to those behind the growth of Communist and Socialist Sunday Schools across the United States during the 1910s. In *Wilshire's Magazine* in 1910, Kenneth Thompson described the operations of a Young People's Socialist League Sunday study class. The twenty-nine enrolled children elected officeholders, including a chair, secretary, and treasurer. They received a balanced offering of recreational fun like picnics in the park and teaching on Socialist and Marxist principles. The lessons were "carefully worked out" so that "the class struggle is always before the children." Supporters like Thompson argued that Socialist work among children was one of "the most important branches of the party work" because he found that children's minds were open, willing, and eager to learn about the Socialist movement and its philosophy.[1] According to historians Kenneth Teitelbaum and William J. Reese, the Socialist Sunday School movement of the early twentieth century represents the most obvious, formal, and widespread children's educational endeavor undertaken by American Socialists. Working-class radicals provided children with formal education on the weekend that disputed public school capitalist curriculums. To opponents these schools were "schools of nonsense" and to supporters they were exciting, potential "rebel factories."[2] But for some on the American Left they did not go far enough or offer the Communist child what they needed.

A sign of change came in 1921 when students from various Socialist and Communist Sunday Schools organized troops of so-called famine scouts who worked to facilitate aid for famine-hit Russia. These youths were not satisfied with classroom-based learning about Marxism and wished to actively contribute to working-class causes. These children viewed themselves as active participants in a movement, not merely students of an ideology. It was in that spirit that JSYWL was founded. Members of the Junior Section, who were often simply referred to as "the Juniors," not only learned about radical philosophy but were expected to take part in action; the JSYWL reconceptualized the Communist child not merely as a student but as a comrade in the class struggle.

Early supporters of the JSYWL emphasized to adults on the Left that it was something more important than a childcare solution or a study class. Prominent Young Workers League (YWL) member Nat Kaplan was chosen to act as the Juniors' director. He addressed Communist parents via the *Daily Worker* and told them that a "new relationship" was needed between parents and children. He insisted that it was time adults treated children as "friends and comrades." Kaplan and his young membership accused American Communist parents of hypocrisy by arguing that parents wielded "nonsensical discipline over the child by virtue of the economic and physical domination of the adult." Kaplan insisted that adult-child relations in American society were defined by the "bourgeois conception" of "the right of the stronger." In essence, through a young adult spokesman in Kaplan the Juniors were declaring their personal autonomy and the right to wage their own youth-focused class struggle. True Communists, they told parents, would refrain from "castigation," would never deprive a child of a meal as a punishment, and would ensure they did not stifle the "class struggle activities of the young."[3]

Early issues of the YPA's first periodical, *Young Comrade*, included various letters from children detailing why they joined the organization. A boy named Peter who gave his age as eleven-and-a-half lamented the long hours his father worked at a steel mill in Bethlehem, Pennsylvania. Shift patterns meant that they sometimes went days without seeing each other.

He was convinced that the very structures of society needed to change if a boy and his father were deprived of each other's company. To end his letter, Peter confidently declared that one day "we will wipe capitalists off the earth." Eleven-year-old Ruth Miller informed *Young Comrade* about her Communism, which was inspired by the plight of her best friend at school, a boy named Walter. Walter was always hungry, she wrote, visibly undernourished, and inadequately clothed for winter. Miller was profoundly upset by his circumstances and believed that workers needed to be better compensated for their labor to improve conditions for working-class children.[4] These children's testimonies are worth reflecting on. Child Communists were framed as anti-American enemies of the nation who had been tainted and corrupted by scheming adults to become adversaries of their fellow children. From these letters it is evident that children who joined the YPA considered themselves to be Americans and found the motivation for their politics from desires to improve the childhoods of the working class. Wanting to improve one's country is not unpatriotic in principle. Peter and Ruth Miller were not, as opponents would have had the public believe, enemies of other American children.

The YPA found themselves making similar arguments over children's place in society and Communism in the 1930s as the JSYWL founders had made in 1923, which shows that few adults were convinced by it. Writing for the *Daily Worker* in 1930 from inside a reformatory, fifteen-year-old Harry Eisman argued for the political importance of the child. He suggested that Communists adopt his slogan, "Workers' children have no bread! Working parents must vote Red!" and called for the CPUSA to pay greater attention to youth. In Eisman's view, "in previous elections many workers have thought that children have nothing in common with politics." He asked, "When a worker because he is unemployed comes home with the news 'No more money to buy bread,' doesn't that affect his children more than himself?" Answering his own question, Eisman concluded, "Therefore, we see that the workers' child is as much if not more affected by politics as the adult after all."[5] The JSYWL and then the YPA represented a new vision for American Communist childhood, a vision that challenged traditional age-based power structures in wider society and within the microcosm of the home by accusing Communist parents of exercising fundamentally capitalistic control over children. As David Macleod summarizes, many parents on the Left did not want more juvenile independence and, as the 1930s developed, began to favor ethnic programming, meaning that even among Communist adults the Pioneer model only ever attracted minority support.[6]

Regulations and Structure

The JSYWL and then the YPA expected Pioneers to abide by a series of rules that were more vague ideals to aspire to than concrete expectations. In an article in a 1928 edition of *Young Comrade* the ideal meant striving to "follow in Lenin's way."[7] The YPA's motto was "For the cause of the working class—Stand Ready! Always Ready!" The ending, "Always Ready!" became something of a slogan for Pioneers. Children deployed the phrase in their writings and rhetoric to indicate their membership without saying as much. Others uttered it in defiance when addressed by the judge at court. By being "always ready" the Pioneer was an active participant in the class struggle rather than simply a student of Communist teachings. The rules made clear that Pioneers were always trying to learn because "knowledge is power in the struggle of the working class." They also placed significant emphasis on recruitment, indicating that a good Pioneer paid attention to and took an "interest in the lives of other children around them with the ultimate goal of drawing them into the Pioneers." For the full rules, see Appendix A.

The Pioneer organization was led by the National Pioneer Bureau, headquartered in Union Square, at the top of the organization. District Pioneer Bureaus oversaw operations across relatively large areas. For example, District 2 consisted of New York, New Jersey, and Connecticut. In large cities with a good number of Pioneers, such as New York, Philadelphia, and Baltimore, there was a city-wide executive layer of leadership too. Pioneers elected one another to these positions of authority at city- and district-wide conventions. Similar to the Boy Scouts of America (BSA), local Pioneer troops were established within neighborhoods or occasionally around individual schools. Troops were divided into squads of eight children who were grouped together based on their age. These squads each elected a squad captain to serve for a six-month period. By design this structure gave children leadership opportunities and opportunities to organize among themselves. Guidance issued to Communist adults instructed them in block capitals: "DO NOT INFLUENCE THE PIONEERS IN ANY WAY IN THEIR SELECTION OF THE SQUAD CAPTAINS." After all, the Pioneer model demanded it be child-led.[8] The children's chosen squad captains formed the troop's leadership council alongside the adult troop leader who was assigned by the local bureau and usually came from the local YCL contingent.

Financially, Pioneer troops incurred costs to offer what grew into a considerable recreational program alongside political meetings and activities.

By 1932 troops were expected to offer exhibits, concerts, hikes, educational outings, games, and songs. Many spent money producing their own leaflets to place in schools or at playgrounds. Pioneers paid ten cents to the national bureau every six months and dues to their local troop; however, the children themselves decided on the amount of the dues. Regulations also stated that "children of the unemployed, striking, or very poor parents should be exempt from all dues." This meant that troops were almost always financially dependent and relied on sponsorship from adult organizations. More often than not, local YCL branches sponsored Pioneer troops. Sometimes trade unions, ethnic workers' clubs, the IWO, and JRCs sponsored Pioneer troops. Sponsoring organizations provided money and helped facilitate activities, transportation, and meeting venues.[9]

The level of broader adult Communist control of the YPA is something that must be pondered. Of course, Joseph Stalin did not direct fourteen-year-old Joe Grossman to launch a petition against cafeteria prices at PS 109 in 1928. But did anyone? It is very easy to assume that adults control and direct the activities of children. But the YPA, since its foundation as the JSYWL, stood in opposition to the "adult domination" of the child. Pioneers like Jessie Taft made very public criticisms of the CPUSA. The YPA ultimately had the closest ties to the YCL, which sponsored troops and provided troop leaders—troop leaders who were outnumbered by child squad captains on democratic troop leadership councils. But even YCL control, which does not appear to be the case anyway, would not amount to full adult control. Of the YCL Britt Haas writes that "American youth activists were protective of their autonomy and vigorously resisted adult efforts to control their organization's platform."[10] Put simply, the CPUSA did not fully control the YCL, which in turn did not fully control the YPA.

Growth, Demographics, and Reputation

Within one month of joining the YPA a new Pioneer took part in a ceremony of acceptance before their troop. They took the Pioneer Oath by which they confirmed they would "stand ready in the cause of the working class" and received their membership book and red bandanna. Most children who joined the YPA were the children or siblings of committed card-carrying CPUSA members. Areas of Pioneer activity in New York City correlated strongly with the CPUSA's areas of strength in the Lower East Side of Manhattan, the Bronx, and parts of Brooklyn. For example, Pioneer Irving Shavelson was the son of militant Communist activist

Clara Lemlich. Other Pioneers came from families of so-called pinks who, although not Communists, were sympathetic to criticisms of American capitalism, such as trade unionists or Socialists. Pioneer Saul Wellman, for instance, had Socialist parents who took him as a young child to see Eugene Debs speak. Other children were brought into the Pioneers. For example, Black Pioneer Leslie Boyd quit the BSA for the YPA, citing racial segregation in scouting. Notorious Pioneer Harry Eisman, an orphan, took advantage of living practically independently to devote himself fully to YPA activities.

The childhood of Murray Bookchin (1921–2006), who went on to become a noted environmentalist, Left-Libertarian social theorist, and philosopher, typifies how children growing up adjacent to the American Left and in urban poverty could easily be persuaded to join the YPA. Bookchin grew up in the East Tremont part of the Bronx. He did not have a good relationship with either of his parents but had a strong bond with his grandmother, a Russian social revolutionary. He joined the YPA not long after her death in 1930 after a boy he estimated to be two years his senior knocked on his door hawking copies of *New Pioneer*. The seller held up a copy: "It tells young people the truth about what's going on in America . . . that Washington was a drunkard, and Jefferson owned slaves." With the Depression biting it was likely somewhat comforting for impoverished youngsters to hear that the sources of their problems were not down to their families but were instead attributable to an evil rich ruling class. The boy told Bookchin, "Rockefeller, Vanderbilt, the Goulds own the American economy." The solution, the *New Pioneer* suggested, was for American workers to overthrow this system to create a socialist paradise.[11]

The magazine seller invited Bookchin to the next weekly meeting of the East Tremont YPA, which took place at an International Workers Order (IWO) building on East 180th Street. A few older teenagers stood by, but Bookchin noticed how the children ran the meeting as much as possible. It was called to order when a boy yelled, "Comrades and fellow workers! This meeting of the Young Pioneers will come to order!" The first part of meetings at Bookchin's troop was always educational or political. He recalled Pioneers discussing "the glorious Soviet Union," "the economic crisis in the United States," cases of injustice including that of the Scottsboro boys, and analyzing popular culture such as talking about racism in films like *Tarzan the Ape Man* (1932). The meeting then moved on to something more practical or fun like making protest placards, playing games, or watching films like the 1923 Russian propaganda film *Road to Life*. Bookchin contributed most to the YPA's more philanthropic efforts, especially helping evicted families. He recalled that the first time he was hit by a police officer's club was when he was carrying a family's furniture back into an apartment building as a landlord attempted to evict them.[12]

The ethnic makeup of the JSYWL/YPA varied across the country. Nationally and particularly in the Midwest the organization was dominated by Finnish Americans. In Los Angeles there was a significant Latin American contingent. In New York City and Philadelphia there were Italian American Pioneers. The YPA in New York was dominated by Eastern European Jewish immigrants and their descendants. Although many Pioneers' first language was either Finnish or Yiddish, most meetings and publications were in English, reflecting that desire to become the movement for children of the American proletariat. New York arguably became the YPA's stronghold, but there were undeniably strong presences in Baltimore, Chicago, Philadelphia, and Los Angeles.

The apparent growth of this Communist children's movement was a concern for self-designated patriotic organizations like the American Defense Society (ADS). ADS director R. M. Whitney feared that it aimed for "mass growth" in preparation for a "class struggle." By 1924 Whitney had identified twenty-three JSYWL troops across seventeen cities, including five troops in New York. He estimated the membership to total 1,200. By 1928 the YPA claimed a similar number in New York City alone. Ultimately gauging the exact size of the YPA is difficult because both Pioneers and their adversaries frequently exaggerated their size to shore up their respective political legitimacies. During its early-1930s peak in New York the YPA was capable of filling large venues—including Webster Hall and the Central Opera House—with members and supporters.[13] From the size of the YPA in New York City, and the reactions to its presence, it is evident that the late 1920s and 1930s was not a time without radicalism or a time without fear of Communism.

Chapter 2

Leo Granoff

Harlem's "Boy Trotsky" and YPA Tactics

Establishing the JSYWL in Harlem and Granoff's Arrest

DURING SPRING 1923 ten-year-old Leo Granoff arrived in Harlem with his widowed mother. The pair had spent the previous four months living in northeastern Pennsylvania's coal region. The Granoffs' spell in the Keystone State had a profound impact on Leo. Having witnessed children his own age and younger heading off to work down mine shafts, he developed an ardent opposition to child labor and any person responsible for a system he deemed fundamentally immoral. In New York Granoff was enrolled in the public school system and first attended PS 171. His mother found work at a nearby textiles shop, and they settled in cramped accommodation near a drugstore on Lexington Avenue. Granoff took his burgeoning political views and absolute opposition to child labor with him to school where he befriended Harry Fox, a boy who spent some of his evenings working in a fur factory to supplement his family's income. Listening to Fox talk of the poorly ventilated, dimly lit factory and of how the strong smell of camphor made him vomit served to strengthen Granoff's views.

The America that Leo Granoff saw around him and the America that his teachers spoke of in their lessons did not match. How could he live in a truly free country when children were forced into dangerous work environments because greedy bosses did not pay their parents a livable wage? How could there be freedom if workers' children's prospects were constrained by the structures of society? This all seemed very unfair and Granoff wanted to do something about it. His first calling point was the Young Workers League (YWL) where he was told he was too young and that unfortunately there was no branch of the new Junior Section in Harlem. Undeterred, Granoff promptly recruited seven classmates and marched into Communist Party USA (CPUSA) headquarters, demanding to be able to establish a Junior Section of the Young Workers League (JSYWL) branch in Harlem. This much we know because after he had risen to a position of prominence Granoff authored an article for both the *Daily Worker* and *Young Comrade* laying out his motivation for starting a branch and encouraging other children to do the same.[1]

By October 1923 New York was overcome with baseball fever as the Yankees claimed their first World Series title by defeating their then cross-city rivals, the Giants. Meanwhile, Leo Granoff was doing his best to spread Marxism among the children of Harlem. He remained the *de facto* leader of Harlem's JSYWL and had succeeded in growing the membership beyond the original octet. Granoff became known locally as a somewhat eccentric child who spent a lot of his time on street corners loudly advocating for child labor abolishment and criticizing the evil perpetrated by "de bosses." Some suspected him of egotism and overconfidence. He also developed a habit of giving adults unsolicited advice on their love lives. Others suspected he did not like being home alone when his mother went out. Perhaps the two appraisals are not mutually exclusive. In public spaces Granoff distributed Communist literature that he collected from Union Square. He "preached his various isms" to anybody who would listen and became known for his catchphrase, which he delivered in boyish working-class vernacular: "Freedom is only fer de rich."[2]

Granoff's distinctive brand of Communist streetside preaching soon caught the attention of the NYPD's radical bureau, which locals commonly referred to as the bomb squad. On a cold November 1923 night Granoff made his way home from a JSYWL meeting to find that he was locked out. He had forgotten his key and his mother was out enjoying a night at the theater. The Harlem Juniors were rehearsing for a musical production, so he carried song sheets to "The International" and "The Solidarity." Granoff opted to shelter from the cold by waiting for his mother in the nearby drugstore. There it became apparent that he had been followed by Patrolman Thomas Donegan, Detective Louis Herman, and Lieutenant James Gegan. They instructed him to turn out his pockets, revealing the song sheets and a red JSYWL membership card. When Herman asked if he was a Communist, Granoff shrugged his shoulders casually and replied "Sure, I'm a Communist." He was immediately arrested.[3]

Newspapers reported the NYPD's arresting Granoff with a great deal of Red Scare sensation. According to some journalists, the police had saved the city or perhaps even the country from a deadly insurgent threat by locking up an eleven-year-old who was waiting for his mommy. The most ridiculous reports appeared in the *Sun-Globe,* which described Granoff as an "avowed anarchist leader" and told readers a "revolt" had only narrowly been averted. News of Granoff's arrest spread far beyond New York. He made the front page of the *San Francisco Examiner* and his photograph appeared in the *Los Angeles Times.* Texans, Californians, and Floridians all read of the NYPD's heroic discovery of a "dangerous cell" of "young Reds." Jessie Henderson's serialized column "Seven Days in Little Old New York" appeared in a slew of small-town newspapers with updates from the Big Apple and included the allegation that Granoff was an aspiring "boy bomber."[4] He and his acolytes were certainly up to something—radical literature distribution and Communistic singing for the most part—but they had certainly not escalated to bomb-making.

The JSYWL's adult director Nat Kaplan issued a statement condemning the NYPD's actions. Kaplan, who would be better known as Nat Ganley after changing his name because of union blacklisting, decried the "stupid attack made by the bomb squad on Leo Granoff." Invoking the Red Scare, he asserted that it "brought to mind the Palmer Raids of 1919," which he insisted had been "thoroughly repudiated by the American public." Others made Red Scare comparisons too. For example, the *Des Moines Tribune* declared that "the Red Scare had a revival in New York." Kaplan's statement posed a question to the authorities; he asked whose interests they were serving by seeking to prosecute a boy who wanted to abolish child labor. He likely did not expect a reply. The question was a rallying call for the wider JSYWL. It framed Granoff's activity as being in defense of the children of the proletariat, casting his arrest as an attack on all who opposed child labor and the JSYWL as a collective. He presented the NYPD as enemies of all working-class children and agents for the wills of capitalist bosses.

Granoff received offers of moral if not practical support from New York and beyond. The Chicago JSYWL wrote to encourage their New York counterparts, "Comrades, we are firmly behind you." The Chicagoans also explained that in their minds Granoff's arrest had confirmed their suspicions that they did not live in a "free country" but instead in one controlled by capitalists who punished working-class children for holding "class views." His friend Harry Fox told the *Daily Worker,* "We are going to fight this thing to the limit," and a protest meeting was held at the Harlem

Educational Center on East 116th Street where children sung "The International" and took turns to speak in support of Granoff.[5] These reactions typified the problems authorities would continually encounter over the next decade whenever they acted against the JSYWL or YPA. Any attempt at punishment appeared to immediately validate the notion that authorities were on a mission to persecute class-conscious children; so rather than suppress the YPA, any attempt at punishment provided a rallying call and inspired a fresh wave of activism.

Grumbles from Communists were not going to deter authorities in New York from pursuing their case against Granoff. None of his possessions were illegal, nor had he been observed breaking any laws, criminal statutes, or ordinances. Instead Granoff appeared at Manhattan Children's Court to answer an allegation of child delinquency. These types of proceedings demonstrate the immense power of the state and the adult over the child. Minors could find themselves removed from their home and institutionalized without being accused of breaking any law. The aim of bringing the case against Granoff was likely twofold: to thwart his Communist organizing in Harlem and to discourage any similarly minded youths. These aims rested on a successful case, however, and a botched case had the potential to be highly embarrassing for the radical bureau; it would also legitimate Granoff's activities.

Granoff at the Children's Court

Leo Granoff appeared at Manhattan Children's Court on November 28, 1923, wearing a smart but well-worn suit. One journalist remarked on how the "Boy Trotzky whose dark doings in Harlem" had been uncovered by the NYPD was "not so much a terror to meet." They explained that "to begin with he's only eleven years old, a little shaver with snapping brown eyes and unkempt black hair that blows in a Communistic wave over his head." Granoff was not the terrorist boy bomber reports had made him out to be but instead a "dreamy-eyed boy with a sensitive and mobile face," who it seems possessed that unquantifiable but incredibly useful quality of charisma.[6]

The appointment of the Children's Court's chief judge, Franklin Chase Hoyt, was likely hugely beneficial to Granoff's cause. Prior to the 1967 Supreme Court case *In Re: Gault* juvenile delinquency hearings were not expected to follow due process and children were not considered to have full constitutional protection. Individual judges operated with wide-ranging discretion. Hoyt was a veteran of the bench who had heard over 10,000 delinquency cases. He came from a family of esteemed jurists—his grandfather Salmon Portland Chase served Abraham Lincoln's administration prior to becoming the sixth Chief Justice of the United States. Chase was not a man to care for controversy, something which he later demonstrated in serving Franklin D. Roosevelt's administration despite being a lifelong Republican. During his early career Hoyt had consistently advocated for the creation of a children's court. He contended that children deserved hearings conducted by "a very human judge" who understood that they were not yet fully matured and was mindful of the damage to their long-term prospects that proceedings could do. In his 1922 book *Quicksands of Youth* Hoyt meditated at length on the vulnerability of juveniles and lamented how misguided or mischievous youngsters who had the will and potential to be "good citizens" could be set on track for a life of crime if saddled with a felony record or accommodated with more "experienced" criminals in institutional settings. Because of this, Hoyt was known to both his most enthusiastic supporters and biggest detractors as "the bad boy's friend."[7] He would not send Granoff to a reformatory only because the radical bureau asked him to.

The main argument put forward to support the notion that Leo Granoff was a delinquent child was his regular organizing of JSYWL meetings in Harlem. The radical bureau contended that he willfully corrupted other children, many of whom had come to see him as "something of an oracle." When asked about the JSYWL, Granoff first claimed that it was "just an athletic club for the children of the workers." When asked about membership requirements he stated that there were "no bourgeoisie allowed," describing them as "children of the rich parasites." His answers illustrate that he was, as alleged, a vociferous and committed Communist. When asked if he would continue "disseminating Bolshevism" to other children, Granoff assertedly replied, "Yes." But in describing Granoff as a "menace to the United States," detectives certainly overplayed their hand and engaged in the type of hyperbole that irked Hoyt. The accused boy let out a childish giggle, apparently amused by the idea of himself menacing the whole nation, and the case against him began to appear irreparably overblown and farcical.[8]

Prosecutors put to Granoff that anybody in the United States could become a millionaire if they put their minds to it, and he responded sarcastically, "Well, when I gets to be a millionaire, I shall buy you a pair of skates." The boy lost his patience at being repeatedly described as delinquent, shouting, "I haven't done anything wrong!" By the letter of the law, he was of course correct. This was the start of what journalists described as "an extraordinary burst of rhetoric." Interrupting proceedings he asked, "Gee, do they pinch a man in this free country for saying what he thinks?"[9] This was not a serious attempt to invoke First Amendment rights. Indeed, the Supreme Court did not recognize that children had such a thing until 1969. Even if a little sulkily, Granoff drew attention to the hypocrisy of his accusers who sought to punish his political beliefs while insisting to him that he lived in a free country.[10]

Even the judge was not spared from Granoff's fiery tongue. When Hoyt asked why he had been out so late at night he could quite easily have explained that he was locked out. Instead, he questioned the line of questioning and launched into an angry tirade against American courts' attitudes to child welfare. "Why don't you worry about the children in factories who have to work all night?" When Hoyt did not answer, Granoff continued, citing recent Supreme Court cases, to complain that the courts did not "look out for the kids" as he thought they should. The *Daily Worker* told how Leo "talked about the repeal of the child labor law by the Supreme Court and wanted to know who was to protect the kids when the courts wouldn't."[11] When Hoyt arrived that morning, he likely had not expected to be grilled on the recent Supreme Court decision in *Baily v. Drexel Furniture Co.* (1923). Even the capitalist press praised Granoff's ability to argue his case and his knowledge, which included the concept of *habeas corpus*. The *Indianapolis Times* simply observed, "Leo is a bright lad."[12] As a noted child welfare advocate, Hoyt likely disagreed with the Supreme Court's rulings in *Bailey* and the preceding *Hammer v. Dagenhart* (1918). The *Social Service Review* agreed with Granoff too, stating "because of a vote of 5 to 4," the court had "followed an outworn social philosophy and sentenced an army of little children to be disinherited citizens of our democracy."[13]

Those presenting the case against Granoff had succeeded in drawing a series of sensational reactions from him. For his part, Granoff had demonstrated that he was indeed a committed Communist, but his activism was framed as stemming from his opposition to child labor rather than something overtly sinister. His beliefs came from a sense of generational solidarity with America's other children rather than a hatred of their Americanness. His goal was to save children from the dangers of working in mines and factories. He was not the want-to-be boy bomber that journalists had made him out to be.

Granoff's mother's voice and even name were strangely absent from proceedings. While few people put stock in her insistence that "Leo is a good boy" who helped lots around the home, nobody sought to blame her for her son's politics. She stated that she herself was not a Communist or a member of any political organization, but she defended her son's right to be what she called "a free thinker." Assistant school principal Nancy B. Kirkman testified. She recalled one incident in which Granoff had interrupted his teacher's lesson about the preamble to the US Constitution to ask classmates if they thought it "just" under the Constitution that children were made to work in mines in Pennsylvania. Other than that, she told the court that Granoff was an "unusually intelligent" child and a well-behaved student. She furnished the court with his latest report. His teacher had graded his conduct as an "A," and he was topping several of his classes. Kirkman directly repudiated the suggestion that he was a "problem child." She stated that, in her view, the best thing was for him to continue attending a school where he was academically flourishing. Given Hoyt's well-known reluctance to institutionalize a child for a first-time problem and Kirkman's testimony, it is unsurprising that Granoff walked free from court, albeit on probation. He was instructed to update the court with his school reports, and his mother was advised to provide "better guardianship" to keep him out of trouble—advice that was frankly useless to a single, widowed, working mother.[14]

Repercussions of the Granoff Affair

Hoyt's decision was not the end of the Granoff affair as it prompted outrage from anti-Communists who were appalled to see Granoff free to continue his JSYWL organizing with the added benefit of publicity and new nicknames from the press, including "Little Boy Red," "Harlem's Boy Trotsky," and "the eleven-year-old Lenin of New York." Etta V. Leighton, the National Security League's (NSL) spokesperson described the case as a "tragedy" and expressed her fear for the welfare of the country when "the Leo Granoffs of this world" grew up and attained the vote. In a letter to the *Standard Union,* she labeled him a "pathetic victim of the enemies of childhood." Similarly, New York's *Daily News* adjudged it most regrettable that "a bright small boy whose faith in Santa Claus should just have left him" had seen the "sweetness" of his youth "soured and warped by the vinegar and acid of Communism." Granoff's critics viewed childhood as an ideally apolitical stage of the life cycle defined by innocence and a belief in fantasy. Granoff also saw himself as a defender of childhood, representing the JSYWL's different ideals of childhood. To him childhood should be defined by material security and play but too often was defined by poverty and premature employment.

The Granoff affair caught the attention of journalists who capitalized on evident public interest in his case. In Granoff they found a boy who reveled in all this attention. Through Nat Kaplan he issued a statement inviting reporters to his home for a post-trial press conference. The *New York Times* described a slightly surreal scene of reporters bundling into the Granoffs' cramped accommodation while his mother was at work and Granoff welcoming them "as gravely as Tchitcherin receives the foreign correspondents in the Kremlin." He indulged them in his opinions on all manner of things, including Communism, "the burning political issues of the day," and the concept of "free love," something which he claimed to support in principle but did not believe was yet "practicable" in society. He justified his politics by reference to his mother's wages and perceived hypocrisy among self-proclaimed patriots:

> It says in the Constitution: free assemblage, free thinking, and these things are for the bourgeoisie and the parasites. . . . My mother works in a shop and other men and women do and they do not get enough pay, and the bosses who do not give it to them preach this patriotism. . . . History is just patriotism. Why, they even made a God of Rockefeller and put ideas in children's heads. Yep, I'm opposed to war, that is a certain kind of war. The World War, for instance, where only the workers fought and not the rich. I don't believe in force. But if we have to use force to get a Communist government, I'm all for it.[15]

Following Granoff's *New York Times* interview, the opinion pages of local newspapers and publications from further afield were filled with ideas on what needed to be done about Harlem's Boy Trotsky. In the *Buffalo Courier* Heywood Broun, who in 1930 ran for Congress as a Socialist, insisted that the entire affair was much ado about nothing. Broun compared Granoff's childhood wish to be a Communist revolutionary to many children's unfulfilled childhood ambitions to be engine drivers. Just as those children ended up in different professions, Broun considered it likely that Granoff would mellow. Even if he did not, Broun suggested that this would not be a huge problem, saying he would join the ever-present minority of John Smiths who neglected to vote or did "foolish" things with their votes.[16] The *Standard Union*'s editors suggested the whole situation was highly amusing. They claimed that "Leo is essentially a boyish boy, judging from his interview; he is frankly intent on having a good time." Since his arrest, which they described as "comic," the *Union*'s editors suggested he had been having a "gorgeously good time" by taking delight in aggravating the so-called "super patriots" and eliciting "heavy artillery" from the security leagues. They concluded that ordinary members of the public who had "enough boy spirit" left inside them could have "just as fine a time" as the boy at the center of it all, by "contemplating the spectacle of the menace of a Little Boy Red who toots his own horn."[17]

Others were more inclined to agree with the NSL's Etta Leighton. She compared Granoff to pollutants and employed the language of infectious disease to portray him as a danger by claiming that his "boyish body" housed darker forces: "We pass laws to prevent the poisoning of child bodies by impure foods, but here is a poisoned mind infecting the minds of other children."[18] An anonymous letter sent to Brooklyn's *Tablet* expressed fury that Granoff had "earned the distinction of a private interview." The letter writer suggested that he needed "substantial application of the rod" and that his "defiance should be whipped out of him." As he showed no remorse, they suggested a public flogging was needed because otherwise he would continue to spread Bolshevism among youths and make it hard for public schools to do their job to "inculcate high American ideals." The letter writer stated that the thought of taxpayers funding his continued education all while "a rat basks in hero worship" was enough to make an upstanding citizen physically sick. The writer was mistaken about many things. They spent considerable time advocating that corporal punishment needed to be legal in New York's public schools when it already was. As for the accusation that Granoff "imagines himself as a little Napoleon," it is safe to say that Trotsky and Lenin were much higher up on his list of potential idols.[19] The letter writer was certainly correct to suggest that Granoff was enjoying the media attention he was receiving, and that fellow young Reds were growing in their admiration for him as a result.

Amid the hubbub of supposedly serious national organizations issuing statements about the disciplining of an eleven-year-old boy, Granoff continued to organize his local JSYWL troop. His anti-child-labor courtroom tirade influenced the burgeoning New York JSYWL city executive, which strengthened the rhetoric in its flyers. The organization now recruited youngsters by telling them to join Leo and stand against the "men who fatten on the blood of the children who are put to work."[20] Every Saturday afternoon in Harlem he addressed a JSYWL meeting, giving typically flamboyant speeches to larger audiences than ever before. Harlem's other "little Communists" flocked to hear "revolutionary defiances roll from his boyish lips." The radical bureau's attempts to bring Granoff under control had backfired spectacularly. Keen to try to reassert authority, its officers were sent to "observe" meetings of Granoff's "band of juvenile Reds," which now boasted a dedicated core of "boys and girls all under the age of fourteen." Officers continued tracking Granoff. The *Daily Worker* joked that he "needs never to go home alone anymore" as "three to six policemen are always on his tail." The officers' presence did not bother Granoff or his audiences in the slightest. Much to the crowds' delight, he launched into what was now his tried and tested material: "De bosses pay my mother a starvation wage den preach patriotism. Bah! [spits disgustedly on the floor] Down with the capitalists and the paraseets!" When the police reported some children's attendance to their parents, their families "expressed amazement at the political philosophies of their offspring."[21] Granoff may have succeeded in recruiting children from families who were not Communists, or these parents could have been in the know and feigned shock when the police came knocking on their doors.

Wider opportunities from across the Communist movement beckoned for Granoff, and he wrote essays for *Young Comrade* and the *Daily Worker*. He was invited to give speeches at other Communist events and received further praise in the Communist daily later in 1924 for his "great speech" as the "star orator" at a YWL Liebknecht memorial meeting. Granoff was held up as an "example of the Junior Section membership which promises some opposition to the present system." He established the playbook for the YPA's forerunner, the JSYWL. His spell of wider notoriety soon ended, but Granoff remained celebrated within his own circles. Nearly two years after his arrest his name was brought up in a speech by Herbert Zam, a YWL leader in New York, who described the arrest of three of his associates as a "repetition" of Granoff's arrest.[22] Granoff's case was the one that the subsequent arrests of youngsters was compared to and became the reference point at the start of what New York's youngest Communists perceived as a campaign against them by the NYPD. Granoff remained a committed JSYWL/YPA organizer. He viewed his JSYWL group as part of an international Communist children's movement. In late 1924 he and his group's secretary, a diminutive newsboy known by his nickname "Scamp," exchanged letters with Pioneer Group Four of Perm, Russia.[23] He was congratulated in the *Daily Worker* in 1926 after leading a successful subscription drive. His strengths and interests leaned toward writing and public speaking. Having graduated to the YCL in 1931 during his senior year, he was elected to Thomas Jefferson High School's student council as a Communist candidate, much to the displeasure of school authorities.[24] He viewed himself as a Communist intellectual rather than an on-the-ground demonstrator and took to authoring longer theoretical articles in periodicals as he got older, often co-authoring these pieces with fellow New York Pioneer Thelma Kahn.

The case of Harlem's "Boy Trotsky" Leo Granoff has huge significance for any historical understanding of JSYWL and YPA activity in New York City. Though his wider fame subsided, Granoff's arrest and the subsequent fallout defined his comrades' tactics in the city for the decade to come. The first lesson they learned from the case was that even hostile mainstream press coverage designed to condemn them was more a friend than an enemy to them. In fact, the New York JSYWL even wrote to *Young Comrade* in the aftermath and declared "the best part of the Granoff case was that the juniors got over $20,000 worth of free publicity in the capitalist papers."[25] Press-seeking behavior became a YPA staple. Children offered to pose with their protest placards for photographers or would loudly sing "The International" when arrested in public spaces. YPA protests often involved horns or using household objects like dishpans as improvised instruments. They made a habit of seeking out local journalists to feed them deliberately inflammatory sound bites, which were almost guaranteed to be published. These comments were not simply childish exuberance but were calculated and deliberate acts committed with an end goal in mind. Some members emulated Granoff by treating the courtroom as their own performance stage. Dramatic and likely planned outbursts were designed for the benefit of their movement, to rally their supporters and to provoke the press, rather than help their individual cases. The YPA's brazen, loud, and disruptive behavior dared the authorities to strike back. From the Granoff case, the YPA had come to realize that this was not always a bad thing. They recognized that any attempted sanction from school authorities, the police, or the courts could be easily transformed into the latest case of their oppression, creating a mini martyrdom for the movement to rally around. These patterns of behavior became the bread-and-butter tactics of the YPA in New York City and can be observed time and time again in the following chapters. Furthermore, by embracing bold, loud, publicly disruptive, attention-grabbing tactics, the YPA generated publicity that helped fuel a fear of Communism and perpetuate a continued Red Scare.

Chapter 3

Radical Recreations

Parties, Religion, and Radical Theater

IN MANY WAYS Leo Granoff fulfilled the Junior Section of the Young Workers League's (JSYWL's) vision for children to become active participants in the class struggle through his organization of fellow youth in Harlem and his unyielding opposition to child labor. The other important component of life in the JSYWL and then the Young Pioneers of America (YPA) was leisure and recreation. In opposing child labor, the YPA emphasized its view that play and fun should be rights rather than privileges in childhood. This second aspect of the Juniors' and Pioneers' vision for Communist American childhood was frequently referred to in children's own writings submitted to *Young Comrade*, which as a collection offers a rare and untapped archive of working-class literary juvenilia. Poetry proved to be a particularly popular format. See, for example, the following poem titled "The Workers' Children," which was submitted by eleven-year-old New Jerseyan William Gershonowitz in 1924:

The Workers' Children
The workers' children work and slave,
For whom? For whom?
The big fat boss,
And the capitalists too.

> The Workers' children have no play,
> Why? Why?
> Because they have to eat to live,
> And so, they have to work not play.[1]

We know quite a lot about Gershonowitz because he was a prolific correspondent with *Young Comrade*. Like Leo Granoff in Harlem, Gershonowitz established his own JSYWL troop in Paterson, New Jersey, and took on additional responsibilities because he did not have a Young Workers League (YWL) member to assist him. He kept *Young Comrade* updated with his efforts to plan events, entice his friends to defect from their local YMCA-sponsored youth programs, and learn new games to keep his fellow Juniors amused. In his poem Gershonowitz took aim at the greed of capitalist bosses using degrading imagery of gluttony and fatness. As it was for Leo Granoff, the very existence of child labor was proof of an immoral, unjust society which put children to work not because it was beneficial but because of economic necessity: "They have to eat to live." The tragedy of this for Gershonowitz was that workers' children "have no play" and were thus denied the experience of childhood he believed they should have been entitled to.

During the YPA era as the Pioneers' organization steadily grew, it offered more and various recreational opportunities to members, often in association with local John Reed Clubs (JRCs). Between 1929 and 1935 the JRCs consisted of local chapters for journalists, artists, writers, and intellectuals; the aim was to expand Communist influence within the arts.[2] The YPA's recreational program became an important selling point for the organization, as is reflected by one of the Pioneers' "favorite yells" that was printed in *Young Comrade* in November 1927:

> This is Little Johnny (or Rosie) Red.
> Did you hear what Johnny (or Rosie) said?
> Johnny's (or Rosie's) never tired of telling,
> Asking, talking, shouting, yelling,
> To the children he (or she) may meet,
> "Join the Pioneer Group today:
> With your comrades work and play."[3]

The chant alluded to the multifaceted and gender inclusive nature of the YPA. Children could shout about "Johnny" or "Rosie" Red as boys and girls were equal as members and leaders in the organization. The YPA strove to be relevant in all aspects of its memberships' lives. As the rhyme suggests, being a Pioneer was not just about work but also involved a duty to play among one's comrades. There were many aspects of a YPA troop gathering that were already recreational in nature, including the Communist songs and short plays members practiced and then performed.

In 1935, after adults had officially closed the YPA, several YPA troops in New York City attended a protest organized by the Conference for Playgrounds in East New York, Ocean Hill, and Brownsville. The two keynote speakers, Dr. Maxwell Ross, chair of the Democratic Party in the State Assembly's 23rd district, and youngster Isaac Seigmeister, withdrew after several "units" of YPA marchers refused to abandon Communistic placards. The YPA's Harold Klein chaired the mass meeting in their absence and approximately 3,000 youths paraded down Pitkin Avenue, Brownsville. As they moved, they chanted, "more playgrounds, less accidents," a reference to increasing collisions between automobiles and children playing on the streets, and "We have the bat, we have the ball, and we have no place to play at all!"[4]

Pioneers believed that all children should have time to play and stood against the economic barrier of cost, the racial segregation of leisure spaces, and the Jim Crow structure of American sports. At times Pioneers protested racial inequality directly. In 1932 African American Pioneer James "Jimmy" Ford was arrested alongside a group of white YPA friends as they demonstrated on the steps of the newly opened Bronxdale public swimming baths, which were open only to white bathers.[5] The rest of the time, simply by providing their own unsegregated leisure opportunities the YPA rallied against American racial politics and rigid gender norms. In the YPA girls played baseball with the boys rather than softball on a separate field, and children of all ethnicities took part in activities together, juxtaposing the practices of larger capitalist youth organizations like the YMCA and Boy Scouts. Even when playing games, the YPA partook in an alternative vision to the segregated America they lived in. Other leisure offerings were explicitly political. For example, in 1934 around 500 Brooklyn YPA members made an "educational visit" to the Soviet freighter *Kim*, which was moored at Pier 9 on the North River. They boarded the vessel in groups of twenty for a guided tour under suspicious surveillance from a half-dozen NYPD and PAPD (Port Authority) police officers.[6]

As the YPA grew in New York City, it began to make more concerted efforts to provide recreation outside of its meetings and specifically political activities. The YPA grew to the extent that it supported a series of YPA-affiliated single-interest clubs, including rather obscure ones such as a group of artistic soap carvers and a group of model aircraft enthusiasts.

Beyond social company the advantage of these clubs was that children could share resources, such as the expense of soap or model aircraft supplies. Getting hold of equipment to support these clubs was a constant problem, but Pioneers were not shy in asking adult Communists to help them. For example, in November 1933 the *Daily Worker* included a small notice asking for any surplus lumber or old tools to be donated to aid a New York YPA woodworking circle.[7] Over time, the YPA's recreational offerings grew to include performing arts, parties and functions, organized sports, and summer camping. Each of these reflected its politics, being unsegregated and unmistakably Red in nature.

When the Great Depression really began to bite, the YPA in New York City continued to place an emphasis on leisure, combining it with more philanthropic initiatives. In 1932 it worked with the Workers International Relief (WIR) to establish a children's hub on West 53rd Street that served a predominantly Black neighborhood. Attendees received free Communist political education and had access to a recreational program. Children there were encouraged to take part in International Workers' Day demonstrations and to protest for public schools to provide for lunch and shoes for the children of the unemployed. In the WIR's newspaper, *Workers Life*, Preva Glusman and Morris Colman praised the offerings of the "real Pioneer centre," which included an arts and crafts circle, a dance group, a theatrical group, and a football team. Children were given copies of *New Pioneer* and had the chance to paint, sew bandannas, carve soap, and learn new skills. Glusman and Colman also reported that a Native American had organized a bow and arrow team among regular attendees.[8]

In collaboration with JRCs, the YPA provided significant performing arts opportunities. The Communist children's movement was a part of the wider Communist amateur theater scene, which thrived in New York City. For December 1933 the YPA offered a Red alternative to Christmas pantomimes by performing Harry Alan Potamkin's *Strike Me Red* at four venues across the city. The choice was likely influenced by Potamkin's death that July. Despite not being a CPUSA member, he was afforded a formal Red funeral in recognition of his "revolutionary" work as a Marxian writer and critic. Potamkin lay in repose prior to his funeral to allow "workers and artists" to file past his plain pine coffin, which had been adorned by a Red Flag and black drapes. Owing to Potamkin's "devoted, ardent support" of the Young Pioneers, six "workers' children" stood guard as mourners paid their respects.[9]

The production of *Strike Me Red* was directed by Brooklyn-born Jewish theater performer Will Lee, who is best known for his role as the grocer in the long-running children's television show *Sesame Street* until his death in 1982. The operetta consists of a series of short sketches detailing aspects of the class struggle, all in rhyming verse. Admission cost five cents at shows at the Manhattan Labor Lyceum, the Finnish Hall in Harlem, Fulton Street in the Bronx, and the Brownsville Lyceum. The cast included seventy boys and girls, including African Americans. The *Daily Worker* exclaimed, "Boy! Do they sing! The songs are swell." The production returned for a second run in 1934 at City College auditorium on Lexington Avenue.[10]

The YPA's musical theater and performing arts programs focused on education, entertainment, and enjoyment, but they were still part of a deliberate wider CPUSA arts campaign. Leading American Communists wanted to foster a working-class literary and arts movement through the likes of JRCs and the cultural magazine *New Masses*. Pioneers performing Potamkin operettas played a part too. Film, dance, and sports were all pastimes, but they all had the potential to boost recruitment and foster class-conscious attitudes. "Dance must be used to teach workers' children that they belong to the working-class," declared one dance teacher. As Sally Banes explains, "Children could be won over through dance to join the revolutionary movement and, in particular, the Young Pioneers of America."[11] Some children liked baseball. Others liked comic strips.

Figure 1. Young Pioneers of America's production of *Strike Me Red*, 1934. Box 2, Will Lee papers, American Heritage Center, University of Wyoming.

Others liked to sing and dance. The point was that if the YPA was ever to be an organization for the children of the American proletariat, it had to cater to a variety of interests.

The holiday season presented a challenge for the YPA. It viewed Thanksgiving as a celebration of imperialism and Christmas as a celebration of capitalist excess. As it did with performances of *Strike Me Red* during pantomime season, the YPA attempted to offer children Communistic alternatives rather than tell them to miss out on all the fun. Offering Communist alternatives to Christmas meant that the YPA was often branded as atheist and hostile to religious people. The membership in New York included many Jews, some of whom actively practiced their faith, as well as a significant number of atheists. Religion within the YPA and American Communism is a little more complicated than generalizations of atheism suggest. Italian American Pioneers in particular sometimes came from Catholic homes. Although Communist leaders strongly rejected organized religion and Catholic leaders strongly rejected Communism, there were Communist Catholics in the United States, many of whom formed the Catholic Worker Movement which had a significant presence around Mott Street in New York's Chinatown.[12] American Communists' attitudes toward religion varied and, in some cases, what is frequently deemed hostility toward the concept of religion was in fact a hostility to capitalist religion.

Around Christmas time various YPA troops, sometimes in conjunction with nearby Young Communist League (YCL) groups, provided alternative parties and events. The press frequently labeled them as "anti-Christmas" parties, although Pioneers rarely if ever used this language themselves.[13] Rather than constituting direct attacks on Christmas, such events focused on the material inequalities between rich and poor at Christmas time. For example, at a YPA so-called anti-Christmas party held at a Ukrainian Workers' Hall in Rochester the program included two short playlets. The first, titled "The Scab," was designed to show the importance of solidarity on the picket lines, and the second, "Who Filled My Stocking?" tackled the difficulty poor parents faced filling Christmas stockings. A December 1930 *Young Pioneer* comic strip emphasized this point by depicting a working child who appears to be selling newspapers and a second child boasting about what his father will buy him for Christmas, telling the first "you won't get nothing" because "your father is out of work." In response, the newsie accuses the other child's father of being a "slave driver" and provides an additional "present" by way of an uppercut to the chin.[14]

The most infamous so-called anti-Christmas party took place on Christmas Day 1930 in New York City. Depending on estimates, somewhere between 1,200 and 3,000 children descended on the Central Opera House. After being threatened with losing their licenses by the city, the respective managements of both the original Irving Plaza venue and the Opera House canceled their contracts with the Pioneers to host the event. When the Pioneers turned up regardless, the manager and a small cluster of NYPD officers decided against trying to prevent their entry. The jam-packed event opened with a circus-style "freak parade" where children could boo and throw projectiles at their favorite enemies. Eighty actors-for-a-day trooped across the stage, including a child holding a sign that read "child labor" and adult imitations of President Herbert Hoover; the pope; New York City Mayor Jimmy Walker, or "Jimmy the Jackass" to use YPA parlance; and former NYPD commissioner Grover Whalen, who was known as the "New York Napoleon" to Pioneers. Around 700 Pioneers participated in a "snake dance," and a popular party game involved Pioneers using toy clubs to knock paper police hats from each other's heads. As a finale, a lucky group of children were chosen to destroy a Christmas tree. Instead of being topped with a traditional star of Bethlehem, the tree was decorated with a large dollar sign. The *Middletown Times Herald* summarized that youngsters who had attended the anti-Christmas party had likely had just as good a day as all the children who had celebrated Christmas and that both would also spend Boxing Day recovering from their exertions.[15]

The 1930 Christmas Day event was more an attack on the commercialized celebration of capitalist Christmas than it was on Christmas itself, but the perception of such events was never going to be good. Any so-called anti-Christmas party would fit neatly with a wider belief that all forms of Communism were at threat to white Christian America. Historian of religion Gene Fein describes a "for Christ and country" brand of American anti-Communism that was present on the streets of New York City and naturally lent itself to antisemitism.[16] To the editor of the *Wisconsin State Journal* the YPA were "anti-American" because they were an "atheistic" group. Typical of press coverage of the YPA, Brooklyn's *Tablet* repeated Congressman Carl G. Bachmann's warning that the YPA "taught hatred of God." This coverage was epitomized by the *Indianapolis Star's* allegation that the YPA was in a "pact with hell to help provide the cross upon which to crucify Christian civilization." Social commentator Gilbert H. Parkes insisted the YPA was launching a "relentless war against all forms of religious beliefs," that it was "not sufficient" for them to be "irreligious," so instead they were "anti-religious." Wisconsin's *Sheboygan Press* accused the YPA of "extreme sacrilege" and stated that they were destined to find out that "after every enemy of the Christian religion has turned to dust, the elevating Spirit of God and Jesus will still remain."[17]

Despite this perception of American Communism including the YPA as staunchly atheist, a perception that was based on the reality that many Communists were openly hostile to religion and that the unofficial Soviet state policy favored atheism, the YPA appears to have been more institutionally agnostic. Jewish cultures and traditions remained a prominent part of the lives of many of the New York Pioneers, and some continued to be synagogue-attending Jews. Children at YPA meetings in some areas were known to exchange Purim gifts, for example. As the 1930s progressed Pioneers increasingly allied themselves with local rabbis in opposition to the rise of Nazism. In Binghamton, New York, for example, Rabbi Julian Griefer noted the "special significance" of 1933 Purim celebrations during which the local YPA group participated alongside the wider Jewish community, remarking on the rise of antisemitism, which Griefer attributed to "Hitler and his Nazis."[18] Of course, none of this Judaism was deemed the right type of religious faith by the YPA's critics, who espoused a "Christ and country" type of anti-Communism, but it nevertheless demonstrates that the depiction of the organization as staunchly atheist across the board is not strictly true.

In the 1930s the YPA was open to certain forms of Christianity. *New Pioneer* was launched in 1931. It was edited by Myra Page with several prominent Christian Communists on the editorial board. Joining CPUSA leader William Z. Foster and party co-founder Max Bedacht on the panel among others were Grace Hutchins and Bishop William Montgomery Brown. Hutchins was a well-known labor reformer, journalist, and strike supporter but also self-identified as a feminist, a pacifist, and a Christian. She co-authored *Jesus Christ and the World Today* (1922) with her life partner the Marxist academic Anna Rochester. Bishop Brown had faced a heresy trial in the Episcopal Church, the first to do so since the Reformation, owing to his support of pacifism during the First World War and a willing engagement with the works of Karl Marx in his writing. Brown believed that Communism and Christian moral teachings were complementary and wrote *Communism and Christianism* in 1920. He circumnavigated the heresy proceedings by accepting an ordination as bishop of Arkansas in the Old Catholic Church, meaning that his position in apostolic succession could not be challenged by his former church.[19] The vast majority of American Christians would have rejected Brown's and Hutchins's claims to Christian identities and faith, but the fact that these self-identified Christians were welcomed onto *New Pioneer*'s editorial board shows that Pioneers were accepting of forms of religion if they did not preach against Communism.

The only real barrier to acceptance was one of class, as Leo Granoff told the Manhattan children's court when he stated, "No bourgeoisie allowed." Granoff, alongside fellow New York Pioneer Thelma Kahn, pondered spirituality in a lengthy *Young Comrade* essay. In their nuanced consideration they explained that their objection to religion in the United States was not born out of opposition to spirituality but to religious institutions' relationships with working-class people. They resented a focus on "Bible Studies" because they felt it was used as a distraction from pressing concerns; they wrote, "We fail to see how knowing the Bible improves the condition of the working class." Religious leaders who preached on morality and advocated for spending on new religious buildings, they argued, should have been more concerned with the "many children" in the "great city of New York" who lived in "crowded tenement housing." At no point did they attack workers or children of faith. Granoff and Kahn accused religious leaders of hypocrisy, suggesting that if the teachings of their faiths were truly observed, they would be obligated to do more for the city's impoverished children. They theorized that religion had the potential to be a force for good but had been co-opted by anti-Communists and manipulated to the point where it was "like an opium to keep the working classes contented." Attempts at forced religious instruction at school were evidence to Granoff and Kahn of a conspiracy to use faith to dissuade people from engaging in the class struggle. To them this all displayed American capitalists' willingness to "work contrary to their constitution" to suppress Communism.[20] Granoff and Kahn attacked religious leaders who failed to do enough to help their congregations improve desperate living conditions and were highly critical of the conditions working-class children endured under capitalism, but they ultimately expressed an agnostic attitude toward spirituality and religious teachings.

Organized Sports

Organized sports were one of the YPA's most successful leisure initiatives alongside its summer camp programs. Sporting competition developed organically at the behest of children themselves as the membership increased during the 1920s. This benefited Pioneers' physical health and fostered teamwork, although the main priority was often competitive fun. In 1926 various New York City YPA troops competed in an indoor soccer league. The first match took place in at the Harlem Workers' Center gymnasium during which Harlem's "very strong" team defeated Brownsville's by seventeen goals to eleven. R. Greenburg provided a match report for

Young Comrade on the "dandy game," during which they recognized the potential for sports as a recruitment tool: "Thru sports we will be able to get many new members."[21]

The YPA was not alone on the American Left in embracing soccer. The Labor Sports Union (LSU) operated an adult soccer league, which in 1928 comprised three divisions encompassing thirty-two teams from traditional Communist strongholds in predominantly northeastern industrial cities. The secretary of the New York league Emil Austin considered it an "athletic vanguard" for the CPUSA. Sports were an enjoyable pastime, but Austin considered them imperative for maintaining physical fitness in anticipation of a potential revolution.[22] One surprising aspect of the YPA's soccer initiative is that it received little assistance from older Communists. The YCL considered sports vital for its own members. Like the YPA, the YCL used their organ *Young Worker* to update members about each other's latest sporting endeavors. Contrary to some older, dogmatic members of the American Left, younger Communists tended to recognize the wide popularity of sports among American workers and viewed sports as something good that was subjected to capitalist exploitation. Barney Mass, a YWL organizer in St. Louis, argued that team sport itself by its very nature could be used to introduce workers to Communism, based on its emphasis on working together for a collective good.[23] Despite this obvious consensus between the YPA and organizations of older Communist youths and adults, the YPA was largely left to its own devices when it came to sports until around 1928. What took place happened thanks to the will and enthusiasm of Pioneers. For example, in 1927 five Brownsville Pioneers, Herbert Righthand, Albert Schneider, Benjamin Bushlowitz, Meyer Hartman, and Bimbo Greenburg, laid down a challenge via *Young Comrade*. The quintet had been playing basketball together and considered themselves a good team; so they challenged anyone to try to beat them.[24] With Pioneers and the YCL displaying appetite for sporting competition and the LSU's expanding Communist sports programming, it made sense for the LSU to start facilitating youth sports in cities.

The LSU united numerous unions and political groups on the Left, including the CPUSA, through sports. Participants belonged to different organizations but were united in opposition to Jim Crow athletics and frequently criticized American sporting bodies for being profit-driven, jingoistic, and religious. According to historian William J. Barker, the LSU offered sporting opportunities as part of an "alternative vision" for sport in society.[25] Only a limited number of people ever subscribed to this alternative; however, it was important to those who did. Children and the YPA were never the LSU's priorities, but the LSU was happy to help establish youth leagues in places like New York where their adult competitions boasted strong attendance. From 1928 onward the New York YPA competed against other children and on many occasions against different local YPA branches under the LSU's umbrella. These other children were not always Communist, but they and their parents were sympathetic enough to allow them to share a sports field with the YPA. Non-YPA teams were often made up of children whose parents were part of the same trade union or were members of an ethnic workers club, like the Finnish Workers' Cooperative or the Slavic Workers' Club. Pioneers primarily competed in basketball and baseball championships but also took part in track and field, soccer, and swimming contests.

Sporting success did not always come the Pioneers' way. In January 1929 a YPA basketball team suffered a heavy 48–26 loss against a team from an all-Black high school, who formed the Colonials Athletic Club. Magnanimous in defeat, *Young Pioneer* praised the winners for their "splendid pass work and basket shooting." The Pioneers too were praised because they "took their defeat in the way young worker sportsmen and Pioneers should," though it was hoped that with more practice the team's fortunes would improve.[26]

Defeat did not put the YPA off basketball, and they contributed five of the founding ten members of the LSU's Eastern District's inaugural junior basketball conference. The cost of a basketball (two dollars) and the need to hire indoor practice facilities during the depths of winter limited wider participation. Nevertheless, organizers were particularly pleased by the participation of two girls' teams. *Young Comrade* kept readers abreast of the competition's progress. Due to the participation of numerous YPA teams their various squads were given nicknames. A match between the "Sea-Gulls" and the "Kaytees" in Brooklyn in March 1929 attracted a crowd of more than two hundred children. According to the match report, the spectators had to "fight even harder" than the players "to keep themselves from pitching in to the exciting game," which ended in a Sea-Gulls victory by a single point margin. The same day the YPA's own "Staten Island Spartans" showed "unusual talent" and commendable resilience in defeating the Wing Foot Athletic Club after conceding the first nine points of the game.[27]

Participation in LSU sports gave the YPA children who played or turned out to watch a source of enjoyment. It also gave them an air of legitimacy by competing with teams from a wider section of the community who supported their ideals of equal participation on the grounds of race and gender. In this regard the LSU's and YPA's very public challenging of Jim Crow sports should not be diminished as insignificant. Some saw this as a positive: The *Chicago Tribune* described an unsegregated LSU tennis tournament as delivering a "blow to racial prejudice."[28] Pioneers taking part in racially diverse junior LSU events in New York City undoubtedly hoped to do the same.

In New York City Black children were able to compete against other children in school athletics, but they did so in an atmosphere contaminated by hatred and at significant risk to themselves. The YPA and LSU provided a venue for Black children to participate in the knowledge that they were not only eligible according to the rules but actually welcomed and safe. A horrific unsolved murder that rocked Harlem's ethnically diverse community including the YPA proved the necessity for that: In April 1929 thirteen-year-old African American Henry Clarke was murdered by an unidentified white youth or youths. Clarke suffered a brutal attack during which his skull was shattered by a rock after he had won the 100-yard dash at the New York Board of Education's athletic meet. Prior to the race Clarke had received threats and was told that he should not win. His grieving mother Odessa Clarke organized a vigil. She was joined in speaking there by a representative of the Harlem Inter-racial Club, Leo Grant, Williana Burroughs from the American Negro Labor Congress, and the YPA's representative Harry Eisman.[29] Eisman spoke of the evil that condemned Black children like Clarke to live in borderline uninhabitable, racially segregated housing and prevented them from doing things that all children should be able to try to do—such as in Clarke's case win a race. Eisman characterized Clarke's death as a lynching and expressed a hope that it would prompt change, conveying the New York YPA's condolences and its commitment to fighting against racial prejudice. Clarke's murder reveals the truth that although Black student athletes were free to participate in New York athletics at this time, it was not safe for them to do so. The YPA provided children with a safer unsegregated sporting environment.

When summer came around, Pioneers swapped the basketball court for the LSU's baseball leagues. *Young Comrade* encouraged its readers to retrieve bats and balls from winter hiding places in anticipation for the season. American Communists in the 1920s very much took to baseball, America's pastime. For example, on August 10, 1924, in the Bronx's Pelham Bay Park there was an exhibition baseball match between teams from the adult Workers Party and the YWL. Communist vice-presidential candidate Benjamin Gitlow captained the main party's side while the New York party secretary Harry Winitzky umpired, having learned to do so when incarcerated at Sing Sing prison. The JSYWL were not left out of the fun. The Juniors had a picnic in the park and competed in athletic events, including a sack race and three-legged race, before watching the big game.[30] By 1930 the Pioneers were keen competitors in the LSU's youth baseball conference. According to an enthusiastic *Young Pioneer* correspondent, that season started "with a bang" for the YPA's Wing Foot Athletic Club, as a "whopper" of an opening game ended in victory "in front of a crowd of kids."[31]

In addition to baseball, summer played host to regular LSU and YPA track meets. In 1930 before the LSU championship for children across the whole of New York City, the YPA aimed to "mobilize children from all parts of the city" through a series of local track meets.[32] One particularly successful "block meet" was held by the Brownsville and Bensonhurst YPA. *Young Pioneer*'s praise of the event was not tied to athletic performance but came because interest in the games was "very high," and "many outside children [non-YPA members] were drawn into the event." Furthermore, "many children gave their names to participate in the next meet." In Coney Island the "street races" attracted a crowd of seventy-five local children who watched the twenty athletes take part in heats and then a grand finale. Three boys who had hoped to compete but were unable to due to their work commitments selling confetti at the ongoing Coney Island Mardi Gras sent their apologies alongside a statement of intent to compete at an upcoming LSU swimming contest, declaring anyone who wished to beat them would have to be "faster than a fish."[33]

After the Coney Island races, Pioneers from different troops' sports squads, the Superior Athletic Club, and the oddly named Midgets, played a spontaneous game of punch ball. This impromptu street game shows how athletic events brought youths together through competitiveness and provides important insight as to the backgrounds of the children involved. Punch ball is referred to by the late evolutionary biologist and baseball enthusiast Stephen Jay Gould as the "canonical recess game." It is like baseball but dispenses with more expensive equipment, being played without a bat, a pitcher, and a catcher. The batter either bounces or tosses a small rubbery ball into the air, commonly a Spaldeen or Pensie Pinkie, and punches it into play with a volleyball style hit with their hand. Unlike baseball, stealing bases and bunting are both prohibited. Punch ball featured in the 2010 PBS television documentary *New York Street Games* and has historically been associated with the city's poorer, working-class Jewish neighborhoods where children could not afford standard baseball equipment. Brooklyn-born duo the baseball hall-of-famer Sandy Koufax and United States senator for Vermont Bernie Sanders have both spoken publicly about playing the game, Sanders doing so during a return to his childhood neighborhood during his 2016 campaign for the Democratic presidential nomination.[34] The playing of the game by different groups of YPA children in New York was a result of their shared play culture with working-class, predominantly Jewish, immigrant communities and is a small detail that provides great insight into the children and cultures of the YPA in New York.

The keen appetite among YPA members for organized sport is demonstrated by their arranging inter-YPA soccer matches and issuing one another challenges to compete. Fun and competition were the chief motivators. For some members the YPA's LSU partnership presented significant opportunities. The June 1931 issue of *New Pioneer* summarized the progress made in Brooklyn, congratulating both the Wingfoot Athletic Club for triumphing at an athletics league hosted at the Vanguard Community Center and a member of the YPA's Kaytees Athletic Club, who had achieved qualification to the Spartakiad—a Soviet supplement and rival to the Olympic Games.[35] The spontaneous membership-led nature of many YPA sporting initiatives undermines the interpretation of a the YPA as a cultural environment created by Communist adults for their children. Young members were active participants, leading their own activities, rather than simply doing what adults decided. Regarding organized sports, the YPA were already playing competitively before the advent of the LSU. With the advent of the LSU, the New York YPA were happy to use the opportunities of competitive swim meets, basketball conferences, track and field meets, and baseball championships that it provided through its Eastern Division's junior section. The benefits were numerous: LSU offered affordable leisure and an easy opportunity to interact with nonmembers who were likely to be somewhat sympathetic to their politics. The sports on offer were quintessentially American. This was not only Communist youth recreation but distinctly American Communist youth recreation that reflected the YPA's aim of being a group for the children of the American proletariat.

Summer Camping

The first modern American summer camps opened in New England during the late nineteenth century. Early camps often responded to anxieties about boys growing up in an increasingly modern industrialized society. The first private camps catered exclusively to boys from wealthy families and sought to be a counterbalance to the supposed femininity of their increasingly refined urban and suburban homes. This frequently involved putting them to work, making them cook their own food and complete tasks like gathering firewood. This back-to-basics experience in the woods, supplemented with a great deal of pioneer-era nostalgia, was promoted as a cure for an apparent boyhood masculinity problem. Early summer camps were therefore intended to be fun but were also purposely controlled environments intended to benefit boys' health, development, and masculine potential to the benefit of the nation. Summer camping proved popular, and religious groups and organizations such as the YMCA and the Camp Fire Girls cemented middle-class access to summer camping. Charity camps then expanded access further by funding summer vacations for working-class urban children, often in the hope that an escape from polluted, cramped urban environments would be good for their health.[36]

During the interwar period, summer camping became an increasingly professionalized industry. At larger camps being a camp director became a year-round job rather than an ad hoc summer vocation. Purpose-built camp environments were designed to appear rustic and wild but were carefully controlled, designed spaces. This shift occurred transnationally: The camp environment was co-opted by all manner of forces each hoping to use it to mold the next generation. In Germany the Hitler Youth used camps to instill Nazism in whom it hoped would be governable, patriotic Nazi youths.[37] In the Soviet Union Pioneer summer camps aimed to help produce loyal Communists. The Boy Scouts in Britain, North America, and elsewhere hoped to produce governable patriotic young citizens. And the YPA utilized summer camps to encourage budding young revolutionaries. As the historical popularity of religious summer camping shows, camps have long been recognized as a fertile ground for community building, cultural transfer, and ideology-based living. Summer camping was always about fun, but it was never seen as a trivial pursuit. For example, in 1913 *Good Housekeeping* sold camps to parents as "schools of fun and fellowship." In the 1920s the Teachers College at Columbia University praised camps for teaching children important lessons that schools did not. Through "character-building" summer camps on all sides of the political spectrum hoped to be able to shape the next generation.[38] The high stock placed in summer camping meant that YPA camps came under intense scrutiny. If camping was a powerful tool for patriots and Christians, those groups would also see camping as a powerful tool for Communists.

Communist summer camps were, as Paul Mishler examines in *Raising Reds,* one of the ways that American Communist adults attempted to create Communist cultural environments for their children.[39] Two caveats need to be applied to that analysis. First, Pioneers enjoyed some success in selling summer camp experiences to nonmembers, so-called "outside" children. Second, the YPA's summer camping in New York, much like its earlier organized sports events, were initiated from below by youths themselves. Only later did Communist adults seek to administer a camping program from above. The Pioneer camping environment was therefore shaped in part by children. In early 1925 the JSYWL citywide executive committee in New York was chaired by fourteen-year-old Morris Spector and included Esther Gross, Martin Gross, and Harry Eisenman. Eisenman should not be confused with Harry Eisman, who features so heavily in the New York YPA's history. Eisenman was several years older and by the time Eisman rose to prominence he had graduated into the adult party and was most notably active in the Plumbers' Union. The quartet appealed to adult Communists to fund a Pioneer summer camp via a *Daily Worker* notice. They had already arranged for a summer encampment for "over twenty children" at Camp Nitgedayget in Dutchess County but needed funds. They explained, "We are working-class children and cannot afford to pay the amount Camp Nitgedayget charges us." They suggested a Communist "junior camp fund" to facilitate children's summer camps separate from intergenerational summer communes. The group argued that summer camps could be a "splendid thing" which "can help us in organizing working-class children."[40] Spector and his peers on the city executive committee were intent on summer camps being fun and serving explicit political purposes.

During the mid-1920s when the YPA was exploring summer camping, some in the YCL continued to advocate for a different approach, favoring formal environments like Communist summer schools. Sixteen students attended one in Chicago in 1926, and 140 youngsters completed four- to five-week programs in Waino, Wisconsin; Waukegan, Illinois; and Winchendon, Massachusetts. That same year almost 800 children attended YPA summer camps in Chicago, New York, and Boston. Youths and their families clearly favored the YPA's summer camp initiative. Furthermore, CPUSA and YCL administrators continued to disparage younger children within the YPA age bracket. Oliver Carlson, director of the YCL's Winlock summer school in 1927 argued that "the boy or girl of 14, 15, or 16" who was "still in school" and had not "been forced to shift for himself" had yet to "feel the pressure of the class struggle." He concluded that "to such a one the class war and all other theories cannot be duly appreciated." Pioneers would argue that young children felt the pain of working-class poverty as acutely as their working parents. The fact that older Communists in charge of Communist youth programs continued to minimize youths' place in American Communism explains continued tension between the YPA and older Communist groups.[41] Based on attendance, the YPA's summer program for Communist youth proved more popular than the school program favored by Carlson, and within a few years a growing number of Communist adults supported YPA children's summer camps.

Summer camping became an integral part of YPA culture. Camps were held in New York, California, Michigan, Illinois, Pennsylvania, and the New England states. They were typically staffed by young women in their late teens or early twenties who were members of the YCL and volunteered with the WIR. What had started for New York Pioneers as an excursion organized by Morris Spector quickly became a professionalized camping program. Camp leaders in New York attended a mandatory presummer training program in the city, and strict safety protocols were put in place. For example, children took part in a swim test and were graded on their swimming proficiency. Those who could not swim received one-to-one attention in shallow water to help them learn. Training literature emphasized to camp leaders that "leaders must realize that the safety and lives of the children are in their care."[42] Especially regarding water safety and lifeguarding, the Pioneers' camps went above and beyond the common industry standards at the time.

Some campers attended Pioneer summer camps locally, but many were bused from cities to rural locations. These camps' dedication to Communist ideals was a major selling point for Communist parents, but the camps served other families too. Reflecting the YPA's race and gender ideals, its summer camps served boys and girls of all races together, a sharp contrast to other camping programs. Rules were put in place to ensure diversity at Pioneer summer camps. A national communiqué from the Pioneer Bureau in New York City instructed, "We must ensure that the children in the camps do not all come from one nationality, such as Jewish or Finnish." It added, "It is especially important that in every district with a Negro population we must send as large a number of Negro children as possible."[43] Unsegregated camping attracted some Black youths. Rather than being sold on Communism, they were convinced by the YPA's opposition to racial injustice. In 1929 Leslie Boyd wrote about his defection from the Boy Scouts to the Pioneers in *Young Comrade*. As a scout, he explained that he was "not permitted to be with the other children, because I am a Negro." Whereas "in the YPA camp we are all the same, white children and Negro children. I like the camp for that reason. I know they are really my friends."[44] For Boyd and other youths like him the inherent racial discrimination in American capitalist society and its children's institutions drove them toward Communism and the YPA.

Cost was another factor. BSA summer camps were much more affordable than exclusive private camps but still cost around $16.00 for a two-week camp session in the late 1920s. YPA summer camps operated on a nonprofit basis, and prices therefore fluctuated depending on the costs incurred locally. In the Midwest YPA camp fees were as low as 25 cents per day but in Los Angeles, where hiring campgrounds and paying staff were considerably more expensive, the price rose to $6.00 per week. Camp organizers were under strict instructions to keep costs at the "very minimum" and that they should charge less than "the amount necessary for the upkeep of the child." That deficit was filled by annual fundraising campaigns. Furthermore, up to half of the campers were "children of the unemployed" whose camp costs were fully subsidized by the national bureau's camp fund. Although Pioneer summer camps were a cheap option, they were not free for all, placing a financial burden on some aspiring attendees. For example, New Yorker Harold Bell wrote in a letter to *Young Pioneer* that because he "had no money" he had "got a job for the first part of the summer" in order to pay the cost of going to camp during the second part.[45] For Bell, Pioneer camp was worth saving up for. So, what did a typical day look like? The organizers' guidebook suggested the following daily schedule:

7:00. All up, dressed, and washed.
7:30. Morning exercise; salute to flag.
7:45. Breakfast.
8:15. Clean-up; inspection.
9:15. Work period.
11:00. Circles.
12:15. Dinner.
12:45. Rest.
14:30. Swimming.
15:30. Milk & cake/crackers. (Double portion for undernourished children.)
16:00. Sports.
18:00. Supper.
18:45. Evening program.
20:30. Younger children to bed.
21:00. Older children to bed.
21:15. Lights out.[46]

YCL members charged with operating Pioneer summer camps, some of which catered to over one hundred children, received extensive guidance. They were told that campers "should not get the feeling that they are rushed from activity to activity" because that may "destroy a good camp spirit." The guidance also suggested giving the children short "free periods" for half an hour just before dinner and just after supper. The schedule was very similar to the timetables in place at most other summer camps although activities were adapted for the YPA's mission. Campfire skits (one of the evening programs) and flag assembly were typical Boy Scout camp fair, but in the YPA camp the flag assembly was held around a red camp banner or even a Red Flag. Campfires involved obligatory marshmallow toasting, but the entertainment consisted of YPA playlets like "The Scab," and the songs were Communist favorites like "The International." Leaders also read younger children bedtime stories, but these came from Hermynia Zur Mühlen's *Fairy Tales for Workers' Children* (1925) rather than the originals.[47]

The "work period" at a YPA camp involved children in groups working on large projects over a two-week camp session. Every child was expected to take part, although leaders were instructed that this was "according to the physical abilities of each child." These projects were supposed to be educational in a social, collaborative way. Guidance instructed leaders to take part as a foreperson and ensure that they never behaved like an observing boss. One work project called "water works" tasked a group to build a small dam in a creek or stream. Campers were told to lift the water level, dig out the mud, and build a wall around to hold the water. Leaders had to be on the lookout for any fish, frogs, salamanders, snakes, or turtles to point out to the children and educate them about nature, especially as city-dwellers could have been unfamiliar with these creatures. This activity was also an opportunity for the leader to discuss capitalist control of public utilities and the conditions workers faced building damns or other public infrastructure projects in the United States. Similarly, arts and crafts projects allowed leaders to talk about conditions in the needle trades and textiles industry, and carpentry projects allowed leaders to talk about the building trades. Camp garden projects allowed leaders to talk about the estimated two million child laborers working in agriculture.[48] Each of the recommended projects related to a major industry and lent themselves to Communist critiques of American capitalism.

The "circles" period consisted of a different selection of activities each day, and the campers had a free choice in what circle they joined. These ranged from using milk and lemon juice to write secret codes to nature study to soap carving or pottery. Organizers were also told they could eliminate circles on one day to teach first aid, something "every Pioneer should know." There was some flexibility for individual camp organizers too. For instance, they were encouraged to choose one night to let the older children stay up late and take them on a nighttime hike to see the stars. Sports were a significant part of the YPA camp program and were competitive, with campers working in designated squads to win points for victory in each game, many hoping to be part of the triumphant squad at the end of the week. Pioneer M. K. described the sports at a New York YPA camp, writing how playing together was not only fun but also taught campers to "stand together" and "fight together," fostering a spirit that could be transferred from camp games to the "labor struggles" of the outside world.[49]

Helen Weiss described her YPA camp experiences in Dutchess County, New York. In addition to playing basketball, volleyball, and baseball, Weiss also attended classes named "the fundamentals of Communism," "American history," and "revolutionary heroes." A fascinating detail of Weiss's account is her description of the camp's geography. Tents were arranged in a U shape around the camp office, which was known by campers as "the Kremlin."[50] The Kremlin was both physically and metaphorically at the center of the camp universe and the seat of its power and ultimate authorities. This less than subtle symbology placed the Kremlin as the ultimate authority for Communist children looking toward it from all angles around the world. Opposite to "the Kremlin," campers at some YPA summer camps were also known to christen the lavatory facilities as "the White House."

It is easy to understand why such summer camps proved controversial to the surrounding local communities. The *Pittsburgh Post-Gazette* described summer camps as "one of the most sinister projects of Communists."[51] Sections of a speech given by a member of the Daughters of the American Revolution (DAR) to a women's rotary club and subsequently reprinted in the *Indianapolis Star* typified fears. DAR supporters worried that the YPA was "out to capture childhood" by drawing children into its ideology through "songs and games." The YPA's teachings were scary to many people. These fears offer a portrait of American society. In this case the DAR representative said that the YPA would teach children hatred but gave the example that "they boast [that] they offer social equality to all races."[52] In a nation where racial bigotry was enshrined in law, the YPA was accused of "hatred" by providing an unsegregated camp environment. Capitalist opposition to the YPA was frequently rooted in a defense of racial segregation, white supremacy, and hostility to immigrants. At the annual convention of the Daughters of Union Veterans of the Civil War in 1929, *Young Comrade* and the YPA were denounced as examples of "what the foreigners are doing in our midst."[53] At times strong opposition to what the YPA stood for moved beyond rhetoric and translated into direct action. It is very easy to view this through the lens of American anti-Communism but given the presence of Black and Jewish immigrant children, the violent episodes uncovered later in the book cannot be separated from racial and religious hatred.

The chair of DAR's national defense committee, Mrs. William Sherman Walker, testified to the Fish Committee about her and her organization's worries over YPA summer camping. Some of her evidence was believable. Although there does not appear to be a YPA record of it, it is quite possible that children at such camps may have renamed the classic game of "hide and seek" to "hunt the capitalists." If the lavatory was "the White House," it was not beyond them. Some of Walker's allegations appear farfetched, bordering on the ridiculous, and make ready comparisons with the hyperbole that surrounded the Leo Granoff affair. There is no evidence to support her claim that children at YPA camps were being taught "how to assume leadership in military movements." It seems unlikely that the young YCL women who acted as camp counselors were well versed in that field themselves. Likewise, classes on "how to incite riots" and how to "conduct street fighting" do not fit in with the YPA camp program.[54] Despite its inaccuracy it was this type of testimony from self-designated patriots that shaped how YPA summer camps were perceived. These sensationalized fears were amplified by the press and politicians, and this was not without consequences. The YPA's opponents engaged in acts of violence and intimidation perpetrated against the children attending these camps.

Part II

CHILDREN OF THE CLASS STRUGGLE

Chapter 4

Pioneer Politicians and the CPUSA

Morris Spector and Pioneer Speechmakers

DURING THE LATE 1920S and early 1930s the Young Pioneers of America (YPA) enjoyed the best of both worlds. It was afforded a degree of autonomy which allowed Pioneers to decide their agendas locally at squad and troop levels. They participated in a democratic process at citywide and district levels to select leaders and vote on policy resolutions. Pioneer activities were also supported and funded by older Communists, most typically the Young Communist League (YCL). The YPA was an accepted part of New York's wider radical community. As such, Pioneers were invited to participate in Communist political and cultural events. They regularly participated in events hosted by the United Council of Working Women (UCWW), which in turn supported Pioneer troops. For example, Pioneers provided entertainment, including "songs, dances, playlets, and rhymes," for a UCWW celebration of International Women's Day in 1935 at the Pythian Temple in Jamaica, Queens. Opportunities afforded to Pioneers extended beyond providing entertainment and extended to writing for the adult Communist newspaper, the *Daily Worker*, and contributing to Communist Party USA (CPUSA) political campaigning and events.[1]

In July 1928 fourteen-year-old Pioneer Harry Eisman spoke at a CPUSA rally in the Bronx that served to launch Rebecca Grecht's candidacy in the upcoming state assembly elections. Grecht was a perennial Workers' Party candidate and a well-known personality on the Left, having originally risen to prominence as an on-the-ground agitator during labor disputes. Described by the press as a red-haired woman with a "round face of determined countenance," Grecht had led a 1923 "celebration of the Russian Republic" in Paterson, New Jersey, and returned there during the 1926 Passaic Strike, during which she earned a reputation as a "fiery speaker." In March 1928 she was arrested and charged with sedition in Burgettstown, Pennsylvania, after she had made a speech to striking coal miners during which she allegedly encouraged them to attempt to overthrow the American government. Weeks prior to the campaign launch, Grecht served two days in a New York jail after refusing to pay a $10 fine which she had incurred because of her part in a demonstration at the J. P. Morgan building on Wall Street alongside Robert Minor. To Eisman this all made Grecht the ideal candidate, and he endorsed her as a true fighter in the class struggle in an accomplished, enthusiastic speech. Eisman's school principal later said of him, "He is an excellent speaker; he can speak from a soap box as well as any debater that any of us heard."[2] Grecht was an accomplished activist with links to figures at the very top of the party and had previously run for office in 1925. Eisman being chosen to help launch her campaign says something about him and the position of the YPA in New York. At least to fellow Communists his voice and a YPA endorsement mattered.

Eisman's speaking at Grecht's campaign launch was not a one-off event; appearances by well-known Pioneers who held leadership positions within the organization were commonplace at Workers Party political rallies and cultural events. The most significant example occurred in 1925 at a Lenin memorial meeting held at New York's Madison Square Garden where American Communists commemorated the former Soviet leader a year after his death. Fourteen-year-old Morris Spector, who was the YPA's elected city organizer for New York and is not to be confused with the Canadian Communist of a similar name, was given the opportunity to speak. Spector, who had been born in Winsted, Connecticut, to two Russian immigrant parents, was described by the *Standard Union* as a "quiet-appearing lad, with distinctly Kalmouk" features. The Kalmyks are a Mongolian population in Russia and Kyrgyzstan whose ancestors migrated from Dzungaria in Northwest China. Journalists made sure the public were aware that he was a visibly distinguishable racialized other. His teachers and principal at PS 149 in Brownsville were apparently surprised to hear of his appearance at the event. They claimed to have previously been unaware of his Communistic views and described him as a "good and well-behaved" student who was "fond of his books."[3]

Spector wore a neat gray knickerbocker suit with a soft-collared white striped shirt and a plain tie. He was introduced by Benjamin Gitlow, the Communists' candidate for vice president in 1924 and 1928 and for governor of New York in 1926, to an audience estimated to number around twelve thousand people. Spector's performance at the rostrum stole the show as his impassioned delivery contrasted with his unassuming natural demeanor. In the *Daily Worker* Anna Thompson praised him for providing the event's "climax," and the mainstream press, although strongly critical of the event, praised the "silver-tongued" Spector, saying that his speech was "forceful dynamite." Spector used his opportunity to memorialize Lenin, to extol Leninism, and to promote the YPA's youth-oriented brand of Communism:

> In Lenin, the toiling masses of the earth saw promise of a time when the blood and bones of little children shall no longer be coined into yellow gold to feed the greedy. . . . When then the flower of working-class youth shall no longer be slaughtered for the dirty gains of the capitalists . . . when the oppression and exploitation shall have vanished from the earth. When man shall no longer tremble before his fellow man. Comrade Lenin is dead. But Leninism still lives—will live forever. Ours is the duty of mobilizing the working-class children under the leadership of the Communists. Ours is the task of enrolling the masses of the working-class children into the class struggle. Brothers, Comrades, Young Leninists of the World! Close your ranks, forward to the struggle. Remember our slogan: "Always Ready!" Down with the capitalist oppressors of the working-class children! Long live the young Leninists of the world! Long live Leninism![4]

Spector focused his eulogy to Lenin on the class struggle as seen by YPA children. His powerful rhetoric contrasted with his meek appearance. Spector framed his personal activism and that of the Pioneers across the city that he was elected to organize as being specifically in defense of children and a certain ideal of childhood. His strong metaphorical language decried child labor, which appears to have been his main criticism of the capitalist reality he lived under: "the flower of youth" being "slaughtered for the dirty gains." Spector strove for a post-revolution world where "the blood and bones of little children" were no longer "coined into yellow gold to feed the greedy." He later articulated these views further by writing an article for the *Daily Worker* as a sixteen-year-old arguing that capitalism "forced" parents to "send their children to factories and mines" so families could survive. City children should instead spend their summers, he suggested, "at a camp or a farm for a vacation" in a just world. Of course, it was under Spector's leadership that YPA children in New York city began organizing their own summer camp.[5] Spector was not speaking at Madison Square Garden just to make friends and even criticized the adults in the Communist movement for not doing more, not working harder to combat child labor, at one point telling the crowd, "We are doing our part. You do yours." He was there to make his point with the hope of forcing some kind of change, using his eulogy for Lenin to put forward a vision of a different Communist movement and an improved America for working-class children.

The greatest compliment paid to Spector's Lenin memorial speech is the significant reaction it provoked from his political opponents. A patriotic flag rally took place three weeks later at Carnegie Hall, and one of the organizers' expressed aims was to combat the rhetoric of the "Boy Bolshevik" Spector. These anti-Communists also sought a juvenile orator of their own. Thirteen-year-old Bertram J. Stern, a teacher's son, derided Spector as a "traitor" in a fiery riposte. Stern's speech was broadcast on local radio and won praise for his patriotic tribute to the United States and its flag.[6] Thus, the huge ideological debate between capitalism and Communism and the adversarial relationship between supporters of the United States and supporters of the Soviet Union was reduced to two rousing speeches by New York schoolboys in knickerbocker suits. The decision to pitch boy against boy in this battle of the speeches recognized that young people had the potential to reach and persuade their peers in ways that adults talking down to them simply did not. Furthermore, the very act of responding recognized Spector and Young Pioneers like him as being worth taking seriously.

Following Spector's Lenin memorial speech, moves were made to establish a patriotic rival to the YPA. Columbia University student Howard Gutman and Herbert C. Worth, a lawyer who provided counsel to the city, established The Unconditional Service League of America (USLA). Their group was intended to cater to a similar age group, youths aged fourteen to twenty. Fifteen-year-old Erasmus Hall High School student Harold M. Miller of Brooklyn was installed as its chair. Miller's selection was motivated by a desire to "combat" the "Red doctrine" of Spector and the Pioneers with somebody of a similar age.[7] The USLA ultimately failed to get off the ground. It seems that even to patriotic opponents of the YPA "unconditional service" was an ineffective rallying call and unattractive proposition. Nevertheless, attempting to start a rival group shows a certain level of concern among anti-Communists and a belief in the power of youth organizations to shape the next generation of American citizens.

As an elected leader of the YPA movement in New York City, Morris Spector made very little effort to obscure his politics or the extent of his role in the YPA, making his school's claimed ignorance seem implausible. His YPA branch met at Pitkin Avenue on Saturday afternoons and boasted fifty members. A measure of Spector's popularity and dedication is that he also served on the district's executive committee as well as being city organizer for New York. The confident and very public nature of his activities belied the fear of "infiltration" of schools by Communists via secretive or underhand tactics. Spector and the YPA rarely favored secrecy. Perhaps taking a leaf out of the playbook left by Leo Granoff, who by this time was a schoolmate at Spector's high school, Spector happily spoke to a *Standard Union* journalist following his controversial speech. Like Granoff a few years earlier, he sought to justify his politics as a stand against what he considered societal ills, saying "we want to abolish the evils that exist at present . . . child labor and the capitalistic impositions of the rich upon the poor." Anti–child labor views were not unique to Communism, but Spector's idea of how abolishment would be achieved certainly was: "by means of revolution." Although he hoped that it could occur "as peacefully as any revolution can be carried out," Spector expected and was happy to accept violence as part of the process, qualifying his statement by saying "by bloodshed if necessary."[8]

If Spector's words were designed to provoke, they achieved exactly what he intended. Criticism came his way from publications in New York and beyond. Some even came out in support of child labor simply because a Communist like Spector was opposed to it. Brooklyn's *Tablet* opined that the public school system was responsible, accusing it of being too lenient toward children who damaged property, committed crimes, or in Spector's case espoused anti-patriotic views. Morris Spector was cited by the editors as the reason for their opposition for the proposed public college in Brooklyn, as they wrote, "Every time we would be paying taxes to educate the likes of him, we would get a cramp." Of course, the editors did not suggest exactly what school authorities should do with a pupil like Spector who on the face of it studied hard and behaved well in school but outside of school participated in radical politics.[9]

The press in Michigan seized upon the Spector story. The *Grand Rapids Press* and the Port Huron's *Times Herald* were particularly enraged and accused Spector of "sedition." Ignorant of the fact Spector already worked at a fruit shop, they suggested the child labor he opposed as the ideal punishment or cure for his Communism. They argued that the "enforced spare time" and the "idleness of after school hours" allowed Spector to spend his time "gobbling up all the 'Red' literature obtainable and peddling it to his school friends." Making a prediction that aged as well as unrefrigerated milk, they concluded that when faced with a choice between more and more Morris Spectors and "honest child labor industry for boys of fourteen, giving them a sense of the meaning of saving and the value of work," the nation would decisively back the *status quo* and that opposition to child labor from well-meaning adults would quickly subside.[10]

Reaction by sections of the press to Spector's words typified what the *Daily Worker* termed "rabid hostility to mild reform." It accused capitalist bosses and journalists of instructing people to hate a child for backing a "proposal to deprive employers of the power to rob and kill children for profit." The press furor which surrounded Spector therefore emboldened the YPA and its supporters, cementing opinions that capitalism was inherently anti-child and that American capitalists worked to suppress working-class children who expressed dissatisfaction. According to Communists, this "vicious attack" by the "courtesan press" on Morris Spector proved that "thinking workers' children" were "not wanted by capitalism." Spector's opposition to child labor saw him "hated like a scarlet woman by the Protestant press and like a heretic to the Catholic organs." To Communists Spector's speech showed "the intellectual capacity of children" and disproved the capitalist proverb that stated that "child[ren] should be seen and not heard." Spector's speaking to the *Standard Union* succeeded in provoking a press retaliation which in turn served to consolidate the strength of feeling among his comrades. He himself was both seen and heard in the following years, chairing citywide conventions in his capacity as organizer and being invited to give subsequent speeches following the success of his Madison Square Garden address. For example, the Young Workers League (YWL) invited their junior comrade to speak at the Stuyvesant Casino, advertising him as an attraction in the *Daily Worker* by telling readers they did not want to "miss out" on hearing from "Morris Spector, who spoke at the Lenin memorial." Years later in 1928 Spector, having graduated from the YPA through to the YCL, remained a regularly advertised speaker at Communist events in Brownsville.[11]

Celebrating Workers' May Day

May Day was perhaps the most important day in New York Communists' cultural calendar, and the YPA took part alongside other party affiliates. In 1899 the Marxist Internationalist Socialist Congress met in Paris to establish the Second International and passed a resolution to hold a "great international demonstration" in support of an eight-hour working day. May 1, traditionally Spring Festival Day in much of Europe, was chosen by the American Federation of Labor to commemorate the anniversary of the 1886 strike, which culminated in the Haymarket Affair. Pioneers of the 1920s and 1930s read in *Young Comrade* about the events at Haymarket Square in Chicago, where a previously peaceful demonstration ended in an unknown person detonating a dynamite bomb and the police opening fire. Four demonstrators and eight officers were killed.[12] During the earlier *Young Comrade* era of the children's Communist periodical Pioneers were encouraged to "celebrate Workers' May Day" and were encouraged to think of it as a "great holiday for the workers" akin to the Fourth of July. By the post-1928 *Young Pioneer* era of the publication the rhetoric had grown much stronger. Rather than take a holiday Pioneers were expected to take part in demonstrations and cultivate disruption. The YPA's job was to organize as big a school strike as possible, and in April 1928 Pioneers were warned not to "scab," equating school attendance on May Day with crossing a picket line.[13]

The CPUSA and others on the American Left encouraged as many workers as possible to put down their tools for May Day, and the Pioneers encouraged school pupils to put down their pencils and textbooks. They displayed posters in and around their schools telling children to observe International Workers' Day and providing the necessary logistical information. A poster found on the hallway walls of New York's Thomas Jefferson High School was subsequently exhibited in Congress. The various meeting points for children across the city's boroughs shows the spread of YPA presence in New York (see Appendix B). After arriving at the meeting points, children were escorted by members of the YCL to join the main CPUSA parade at Madison Square Garden.[14]

Pioneers responded to instructions to strike from school on May Day either by heading straight to the meeting locations or by holding pickets at their schools beforehand, hoping to either convince their classmates to join them or create a spectacle. Both the NYPD and school authorities took dim views of this behavior. On May Day 1928 Walton High student Jessie Taft and a quartet from the Bronx's PS 61—Harry Eisman, Milton Kaplan, Miriam Rosenfeld, and Boris Saltzman—were arrested together on their way to Madison Square Garden. The ILD (International Labor Defense) provided them with legal representation, assigning Jacques Buitenkant as counsel. Given that they had been doing exactly what the adult editors of *Young Comrade* had told them to do, it only seemed fair that adults aided the quartet who were all bailed at the children's court. Eisman's bail was set at $100, since he was a regular customer. The ILD paid Eisman's bail, and ultimately, they were all given a warning for truancy. Anyone who hoped that a slap on the wrist would deter them from similar activities in the future would be left sorely disappointed.

Eisman and Taft were arrested together again the following May Day, this time alongside two of Eisman's regular associates, Saul Wellman and Bernard Kaplan. This turned out to be the first of many arrests for Wellman, who after being expelled from school was able to devote himself to full-time Communist activism in his teens. After organizing a Long Island truckers' strike in the 1930s Wellman was injured twice in Europe fighting fascism. He was injured in the Spanish Civil War's Ebro Offensive as part of the Lincoln Brigades and then hurt once again at the Battle of the Bulge as a rifleman in the US Army's 101st Airborne division. After relocating to Michigan, Wellman chaired the state Communist Party there, led the national party's auto industry strategy, and was convicted in a 1954 Smith Act trial. He subsequently campaigned extensively for Civil Rights and contributed to the New Left. By 1980 Wellman had transitioned from a derided figure to a celebrated one, and the Michigan State Senate passed William F. Kelly's resolution honoring his life work in "trade unions, civil rights, and peace movements."[15] Wellman was joined in the Lincoln Brigades by another New York YPA alumnus, the novelist sometimes known as the American Orwell, William Herrick. Herrick regularly attended YPA meetings and summer camps as he grew up in Bronx cooperative housing.[16] Of course, not every YPA child grew up to be an influential adult Communist or even a Communist at all, but Wellman and Herrick typified what supporters of the junior section hoped it could be, a producer of new young leaders.

Jacques Buitenkant was again assigned to defend Eisman, Kaplan, Wellman, and Taft. Ever the opportunist, Eisman secured himself an op-ed in the *Daily Worker* after his arrest and used it to criticize the conditions he and his co-accused encountered in custody. Due to their ages, after being processed, the group was moved from the police station to the SPCC (Society for the Prevention of Cruelty to Children). Eisman objected to being treated "like a real convict" and being made to change into blue prison-style boiler suits when in his mind all he had done was express his political views. He took a dislike to SPCC employees, or guards, as he called them, giving him "lectures on how to behave" and complained about the food, describing a "disgusting cup of so-called milk" and an evening meal of "two thin slices of white bread" followed by the bland combination of plain pasta noodles and a naked hot dog.[17] The others were permitted to go home either later that evening or the next morning, but Eisman was held at the SPCC until he appeared at the children's court later in the week. Using the same tactics Leo Granoff had put to good use in 1923, Eisman made sure that his court appearance was anything but forgettable.

All four children faced charges of parading without the required city permit, and Eisman faced an additional charge of outraging the public decency, owing to a grossly offensive protest placard that police attributed to him. The hearing was very quickly derailed when Eisman began shouting and gesticulating toward a police sergeant, accusing him of "cooking up" false charges as he made his way to his place in the courtroom. When asked to account for his actions on the day, Eisman unbuttoned his shirt and began exhibiting various bruises to the court. He accused several patrolmen who were not present at court of assaulting him. The judge adjourned the trial, and the patrolmen in question were compelled to attend the court. Each of the three backed one another up in testifying that Eisman had not been assaulted. This, of course, did not account for the boy's injuries.[18]

Buitenkant engaged the court in a drawn-out defense of Eisman's placard-related charge. Eisman admitted to having known what the placard said but insisted that it was not his. Buitenkant pointed out that the police officers knew what the placard said too, at which point Eisman interjected and demanded they all be arrested too, claiming there to be as much evidence against everyone else in the courtroom as there was against him. Buitenkant, with or perhaps despite Eisman's "help," managed to convince the judge that there was simply no evidence to connect the placard to the boy and that the vague suspicions of officers were not enough. As for the issue of the permit, the judge stated that the children were technically guilty but said that he "wouldn't like to fine children" in relation to a law that had been designed to apply to adult political parties. Before letting them go he gave them some advice, telling them to "go and play in the park" in the future and that in his view children should not become entangled in labor disputes.[19] The judge's idea of childhood and of distinctly adult laws enabled Pioneers to escape punishment in this case, but the YPA would nevertheless disagree with his notion that children should be apolitical. The YPA ideal of childhood too held that childhood should be about play but contended that due to the material circumstances of working-class children, they had to engage in politics and advocate for change rather than spend their days in parks.

International Workers' Day disruption was not solely the preserve of Taft, Eisman, and their close friends. May Day 1931 in Coney Island ended up being particularly eventful. Eight so-called "juvenile radicals" targeted

PS 100 on Sea Breeze Avenue. Early in the morning they daubed slogans on the sidewalk and on the school building itself, including "Be a Communist," "Join the Young Pioneers of America," "Down Tools," and "Workers' Children Strike on May Day." With this done, they stationed themselves around the school where they distributed circulars telling children: "Lay down your books and join the line of children of the unemployed at Union Square." Schoolgirl Roy Birozy, thirteen, was arrested for handing out the literature. Two older girls, Dora Cooper, sixteen, and Sadie Berger, seventeen, were arrested and hauled before a magistrate following a complaint by Raymond Jacobs, thirteen, who alleged they beat and chastised him after he refused their instruction not to attend school. "Boos and yells of derision" attracted the attention of the school's custodian John J. Esposito to a cluster of school strikers. When he urged them to move on, the group of youths, "set about and pummeled him." Solomon Leofrowitz, thirteen, Ethel Zamos, fourteen, Jacob Cohen, sixteen, and seventeen-year-olds David Perisky and Leo Demzeloss were arrested alongside their branch's YCL nineteen-year-old assistant Jack Kliede. Zamos and Leofrowitz were referred to the children's court and the others were all bailed by the magistrate at the Coney Island Courthouse, apart from Cohen and Perisky, the apparent main assaulters of Esposito, who were held on $500 bail bonds.[20]

International Workers' Day was a prominent part of American Communists' political and cultural calendar, part protest and part celebration. YPA children were encouraged to take part in this so-called workers' holiday, and many of them did so with zest and enthusiasm. The YPA's periodical was one of the driving forces of children's participation in Communist May Day activities. Pioneers attempted to pressure peers into joining them, condemning children who did not stand alongside them as "scabs." From a recruitment perspective this failed, as fellow schoolchildren were irked by being harangued and called names while on their way to school. May Day school strikes remained the preserve of the YPA's more committed membership, many of whom had no qualms whatsoever with assaulting school staff who stood in their way or being punished for their truancy or actions on the day. For members like Harry Eisman, disciplinary or legal consequences were another welcome publicity opportunity and provided chances to write for the Communist press or put on a show in a courtroom.

Chapter 5

Pioneers and Picket Lines

Anti-Imperialism and Rose Plotkin

THE VISION OF the Young Pioneers of America (YPA) for American Communist childhood demanded that Pioneers were active participants in the class struggle. Pioneers were expected to have a significant presence on picket lines and to take interest in labor disputes and other protests in their vicinity. *Young Comrade* spread awareness about ongoing disputes and provided a space for Pioneers to report on their own activities and express their opinions. In 1927 Pioneers in New York responded with gusto to *Young Comrade*'s urgings to protest American military intervention in Nicaragua. The January 1927 edition asked readers, "Now do you know what the American government has done?" It told them: "It has sent war ships and sailors to Nicaragua to help the reactionary and labor hating Diaz." Later Pioneers read that normal "American boys" were to be sent to "fight against the Nicaraguan people" on the orders of "American bankers." November 1927's edition informed them that "Nicaraguan natives" were "slaughtered" as "Yank tyrants feasted on colonial loot."[1] Similar to Communist rhetoric surrounding the Great War, the situation in Nicaragua was sold to Pioneers as another example of imperialist military intervention and another case where working-class young Americans were dying in a conflict created by wealthy elites.

In July 1927 the All-American Anti-Imperialist League organized a demonstration on Wall Street. Leading local and national Communist

Party USA (CPUSA) figures such as Robert Minor and Rebecca Grecht formed a picket line outside the J. P. Morgan building on July 4th. They were joined by Pioneers, including Rose Plotkin who at thirteen had earned a reputation as one of New York's "most active Pioneers." Minor and Grecht were both jailed after refusing to pay fines imposed for causing a public disturbance. Plotkin was already something of a veteran activist. She first gained recognition as a Pioneer in Chicago when she was nine. She spoke at the 1924 Illinois district convention on the relationship between publicity and punishment. She recalled being sent home from school for challenging her teacher's criticisms of Communism. The *Daily Worker* accused the school of persecution, and the Chicago Junior Section of the Young Workers League (JSYWL) held a protest meeting that was attended by 150 children who unanimously passed a resolution supporting "comrade Rose" and "any comrade who gets into trouble for trying to learn the truth about our class."[2] Although less sensational than the Leo Granoff affair in New York, this was another early example of punishment by authorities leading to publicity and a rallying moment for the children's Communist movement.

At the 1928 Wall Street demonstration Plotkin was arrested by—in her words—a "big husky policeman." She had been distributing anti-imperialist handbills and chanting Communist slogans calling for the "independence of American colonies" and against "America's war in Nicaragua." Because of her age Plotkin was taken to the SPCC (Society for the Prevention of Cruelty to Children) after being arrested, and she was held there for over a week before appearing in court. Authorities refused to release her from the SPCC despite the ILD (International Labor Defense) filing a writ of *habeas corpus*. Plotkin did not approve of the SPCC accommodations, joking that "prevention" should be removed from the name and wrote in *Young Comrade* that "SPCC" was merely a "very posh" name for a jail. Although Minor and Grecht served a few days in jail for their presence at the demonstration, the consequences were more severe for Plotkin. At the children's court Magistrate Samuel D. Levey ruled that Rose's older sister Fannie Plotkin, who served two days in jail for her presence on Wall Street, was no longer a suitable guardian. This meant that the younger Rose was sent to La Porte, Indiana, to live with other relatives.[3]

The Plotkin sisters were convinced that authorities had "cooked up" the situation to remove Rose from New York because "the bosses' government doesn't want to see workers' children take part in demonstrations." Children attending a Workers International Relief (WIR) summer camp in Wingdale, New York, took a day out of their summer vacation to hold a protest march against her treatment. The Pioneers cried foul, alleging a stitch-up, citing the fact that authorities had arranged Rose's court appearance to coincide with Fannie's two days in jail, which meant that she was not accompanied by her older sister. Despite these apparent underhanded tactics to rid New York of Rose Plotkin, authorities did not manage to cut her off from the Pioneers in the city. She arranged for her new address to be printed in *Young Comrade,* and although she admitted that being forced to move to what she called a "hick town" was an inconvenience, she insisted that it would not stifle her spirit. She assured her fellow Pioneers that it made her want to "carry on the work" and "go further with renewed vigor." As committed an activist as Plotkin was, the New York YPA was well enough established to carry on without her, and what authorities actually achieved in moving her to Indiana was the creation of a small YPA cell in La Porte. The *Daily News*'s celebration that "Red Rose" had been sent away proved a tad premature. Although authorities did have the power to reassign Rose Plotkin's guardianship, they did not have the power to permanently banish her from New York. She visited the city from Indiana and was arrested there once more in August 1929 while taking part in demonstrations at a cafeteria workers' strike.[4]

Whether in Illinois, New York, or Indiana Rose Plotkin was determined to be an active Communist child. Authorities could inconvenience her but were unable to cut her off from her YPA contacts or fully stop her activism. Plotkin was an exemplary YPA member in this sense from the Communists' perspective. She organized among her peers and took an active part in the wider movement by protesting alongside adult activists at demonstrations about the issues of the day. YPA children took part in local or sometimes not particularly local labor disputes, as Plotkin did at the cafeteria strikes. Many of them wanted to be active participants in the class struggle, acting as the Communists they wished to grow to be or like the Communist adults and historical figures they idolized. YPA participation in working-class causes was something of an expectation for the membership but they were not content in participating and instead carved themselves a unique role, specific to children, in the event of a labor dispute.

Labor Disputes

Pioneers in New York read in *Young Comrade* and then *Young Pioneer* children's perspectives on such notorious strikes as the textiles strike in New Bedford, Massachusetts, the Passaic strike in New Jersey, and the Loray Mill strike in Gastonia, North Carolina. Pioneers fade into the background at such events but were often there and involved. For example, YPA children in Lawrence, Massachusetts, joined the picket lines and held their own demonstrations during the 1931 mill strike there. Police detained sixteen boys who belonged to the YPA, ages eight through seventeen, for deliberately creating a disturbance after they took to the street singing with "dishpans, horns, and other noise making devices."[5] Singing and improvised amateur bands were frequent Pioneer attention-grabbing protest tactics.

Across 1924 and 1925, Joseph Alukonis, who was a ten-year-old Paterson, New Jersey, Pioneer, provided regular *Young Comrade* updates on a silk strike. That was a lengthy and bitter dispute during which Paterson's mayor Colin M. McLean courted and received backing from the KKK after calling for the deportation of foreign-born strikers. Such threats failed to quell local workers' activism, and the 1924–1925 silk strike was quickly overshadowed by the 1926 Passaic textile strike. Alukonis attended public meetings and demonstrations to compile his reports. He heard from Grace Hutchins, a high-profile reporter and labor reformer; Herbert Moore "Harry" Wicks, founding member of the CPUSA; and the Right Reverend Paul Jones, a prominent Socialist forced to resign as Episcopal Bishop of Utah due to his pacifist beliefs in 1918, the same beliefs for which he is now venerated in the American Episcopal Church. Alukonis adjudged Wicks the best speaker and admitted there were "a few others whom I have forgotten." As for law enforcement, he sarcastically commented that "a few people were treated with so much kindness by the police that they had to go to the hospital." These child's-eye reports, both humorous and brutally honest at times, also speak of the impact of the dispute in the wider community. For example, on one occasion Alukonis led his classmates, many of whose families were involved in the strike, out of their classroom on a "strike" of their own in response to their teacher's disparaging strikers as lazy.[6]

Pioneers in New York City never had something quite like the New Bedford or Paterson strikes, but they did their best to support local labor disputes whenever they arose. In 1927 a New York Pioneer with the initials C.E.W. updated *Young Comrade* on the Furriers' Strike and a Bakery Strike in Brooklyn. As well as supporting picket lines, Pioneers sought to find and engage with the children of striking workers, viewing this as a special duty of their own. They joined the furriers' demonstration at City Hall and distributed a pamphlet, "Furriers Children." Eighty children staged a demonstration in solidarity with the striking bakers in Brooklyn, drawing the attention of a crowd of local youngsters to whom they distributed a four-page leaflet, "The Fighting Little Baker." C.E.W. concluded the report by reflecting that interacting with pickets was a good way to "grow influence" and that seeking out the children of striking workers appeared to be an easy way to increase membership.[7]

The following year transportation workers faced a 10 percent pay cut, and Leo Granoff, now sixteen and still an active member, offered his opinion in April's *Young Comrade*. In a piece overflowing with sarcasm, he opined that the situation was due to "poor traction millionaires" who felt they were "starving and not making enough for a few more Rolls Royces."[8] In May 1928 Harry Eisman informed the readership that New York Pioneers had been active in a local fruit clerks' strike by "helping" on the picket lines. The demands of the strikers on that occasion were for their bosses to reduce their working week from seven to six days and their daily hours from twelve to ten. Despite being "pelted by apples and potatoes" (it is unclear by whom) and being "chased by cops," Eisman concluded that he and his friends had helped a "whole lot." He expressed particular pride in managing to organize "the children of the strikers and their friends" to play their part and contribute to the dispute.[9]

Police and truancy officers scrutinized Pioneers on picket lines. Rose Plotkin was correct that city authorities did not want children attending political demonstrations or being present on picket lines. Truancy officers could intervene as soon as a school-aged child was seen, whereas at least in theory it would take a little more to attract NYPD attention. Harry Eisman occupied a significant amount of truancy and NYPD officers' time. He was put on probation by the children's court in 1929 after being adjudged to have caused a disturbance at a dressmakers' strike. After being dragged from the picket line, Eisman and fellow Pioneer Leonard Levann drew attention to themselves by loudly singing "The International" as they were taken toward a police wagon. When a school superintendent attempted to take Eisman and Levann to task over their truancy and arrests, Eisman did not feign contrition. Instead, he boastfully admitted to having been "real active on the picket line" and justified his actions by stating that he wished to organize more protests against the "sweatshop system" of New York's garments industry.[10]

Eisman's and Levann's punishment did not deter other New York Pioneers from joining strikes. Later that year three boys, Leo Shapiro, Morris Rosenblaff, and Sam Sliptzen, were arrested for taking part in the cafeteria workers' strike demonstration alongside the returning Rose Plotkin. Shapiro, Rosenblaff, and Sliptzen's defense was orchestrated by the ILD. *Young Comrade* told readers that they should not be intimidated by the "terrorist methods" of the bosses or "police brutality" and to continue making their presence felt on picket lines in order to show solidarity with striking workers and their children.[11] Although authorities attempted to dissuade Pioneers from taking part in workers' demonstrations, Pioneers received encouragement from their periodical. Perhaps more important, Communist adults were willing to provide them the same ILD legal assistance that arrested adult demonstrators were entitled to.

Covert Philanthropy

The youth-focused Pioneer movement was particularly conscious of how extended strike action could be detrimental to striking workers' children. New York Pioneers undertook a range of philanthropic activity to help offset the hardships encountered by families. Following the 1927 Columbine Massacre in Colorado where six striking miners were shot and killed by police, the YPA emphasized supporting striking miners and their families. This included working with other sympathetic youth and adult organizations. The YPA participated in a New York children's relief conference that was attended by around 250 delegates representing over 90 different youth organizations. The conference heard from Eddie, the son of a striking miner, and he told the hall that the workers were "fighting coal companies and the state police." If arrested, strikers were held in barracks that Eddie described as "a chicken coup, only bigger," and the hardships of the strike meant that "sometimes we don't have dinner." Eddie put the blame for this on "the scabs," who by continuing to work were "taking the food out of our mouths."[12]

Stories like Eddie's resonated with Pioneers who formed miners' relief clubs at PS 147 and PS 149. Even these charitable efforts were not tolerated by teachers. One Pioneer complained that a teacher had confiscated their miners' relief leaflets and instructed all the children to donate to the Red Cross rather than directly to striking workers.[13] In their drive to suppress YPA activities in schools, authorities and teachers often made it rather easy for the YPA to present themselves as the so-called good guys. Nevertheless, some members realized that the toxicity of their proud Communist brand was hampering their fundraising efforts, and the solution was to establish shadow organizations under different names. A.B. informed *Young Comrade* readers how they had established an organization of "Miners Relief Scouts," no doubt taking advantage of connotations from the term "Scouts." Under this name they were successful in earning the support of their neighborhood's local women's committee and signed up thirty children who collected donated clothes and sold meal tickets.[14]

Pioneers established various subgroups dedicated to miners' relief, such as the Miners' Relief Scouts. In New York City Pioneers established the Children's Committee for Miners' Relief, which held collections and events at various schools, advertising their presence with flyers. Tell-tale YPA language still appeared, and Miners' Relief Scouts activities would likely still be condemned as radical. Nevertheless, the YPA had dropped their explicitly Communist brand in the hope of boosting fundraising. Pre-collection flyers informed children that miners' children "fight side by side with their fathers, even though they are beaten up by police and are prevented from picketing by injunctions" and that "their fight is our fight." They finished with the plea: "Tomorrow a committee will be stationed in your school with collection boxes. Bring some money to help feed the starving miners' children. Every little helps."[15]

This miners' relief effort was a tried and tested approach that Pioneers had also used during the Passaic strike two years prior. Then, fundraising was done by selling meal tickets for the benefit of strikers' children. The YPA's New York leadership committee met and passed four resolutions. The first was to begin a "special relief campaign" immediately. The second was to give free subscriptions of *Young Comrade* to any child who wanted it in Passaic. Third, they ordered that a special Passaic strike edition of *Young Comrade* to be distributed far and wide. Last, Pioneers were instructed to carry out "energetic" work to organize the working-class children of Passaic and introduce them to the Young Pioneers. As Pioneer Sylvia Gudisman recorded in *Young Comrade*, the Brownsville YPA was particularly active and sent some representatives to Passaic where they attended public meetings and performed the play "School Days" for the local children.[16]

In addition to fundraising for children who were affected by labor disputes, the YPA also paid keen attention to the jobs that were often filled by child workers. In the long-term they advocated for the total abolishment of child labor but recognized the positive impact any incremental change might have on some children's lives. In the short-term they sought to support child workers attempting to organize among themselves and advocated for improvements to their working conditions. They had some success in engaging with messenger boys, newspaper sellers, and ferry bootblack boys. Of course, the newsies of the city had a longer history in organizing than the YPA, staging, among others, a famous strike in 1899. Decades later some newsies were convinced that their newsboy unions were not as radical as they once were and joined the YPA. Some even flourished in the organization. A newsboy became district chair in Philadelphia, and an Italian American newsboy was elected to the New York YPA's district executive committee at the district's 1929 convention.[17]

Pioneer conventions reflected the YPA's desire to conduct itself as a serious political entity. Adult Communists supported the children's movement's mimicking the procedures of adult political movements, hoping Pioneers who graduated from the YPA into the YCL and eventually the CPUSA would be prepared to seamlessly slip into their operations as a result. The 1929 YPA convention in New York City proved eventful. Previewing the event in the *Daily Worker*, Harry Eisman praised the "many victories" the YPA had secured, particularly in the "school struggle." He claimed that the YPA had delivered twelve school bulletins and now boasted groups in twenty-six New York schools. Eisman praised a list of students, making sure to include his own name, from PS 61 and PS 89 who had faced disciplinary sanctions for their school-based activities. The three-day convention opened with what Eisman described as a "big concert." He said it was so much fun that those in attendance would surely never forget the day.[18] Akin to many political party conferences, a YPA convention was part self-celebration, part party, and part serious business.

On the first day of the 1929 convention a battalion of NYPD officers forced their way into the hall. Somewhat ironically officers took exception to a banner reading "Down with Police Brutality" and tore it away from the walls. Pioneers booed and hissed at officers who arrested seventeen nonvoting YCL convention stewards and nine Pioneers. Disruption or intimidation appear to have been the main aims as the arrested Pioneers were all high-profile members of the YPA and were released without charge the next day. They were Jessie Taft, Harry Eisman, Saul Wellman, Bernard Kaplan, Frank Baillinson, George Gorchoff, Abraham Malakin, Irving Shavelson, and Louis Levy. Upon their release they wasted no time in returning to the convention's second day where they received a standing ovation from the other fifty-six nominated delegates and thirty-seven alternates.[19]

It appears that the NYPD targeted Pioneers for arrest who were particularly active, popular within the movement, and had significant connections to wider American Communism. By this stage Eisman was developing something of a cult following and had worked with Kaplan to create a "Lenin Unit" within their school. Taft was a popular YPA leader. Brownsville's Irving Shavelson came from a radical Communist family. His mother, Clara

Lemlich, was a leading figure in the International Ladies Garment Workers Union. As a young worker, she led various strikes culminating in the 1910 New York garments industry strike. Shavelson was ever-present at YPA activities in the city during the late 1920s although he did not quite achieve the same level of notoriety as some of his contemporaries. He changed his name to Irving Velson and in the 1930s married another former Pioneer, Ruth Yonkelson. Velson was active in the shipbuilders' union and ran for the state senate as an American Labor Party candidate. Velson served in the US Navy during World War II but in 1951, 1953, and 1956 was called to Congress to testify over his Communistic activities and potential Soviet espionage within the US military. Velson refused to answer questions and invoked his Fifth Amendment rights against self-incrimination. Decades after his death in 1976, decrypted Soviet communications were made public which appeared to show that Velson was "Nick," the code name of a Soviet military intelligence asset who had passed on information on weapon technology.[20] As a youngster, Shavelson was from a typical background for a Pioneer, but it is unusual that he was implicated in Soviet espionage during World War II.

As was the case with newsboys' union members joining the YPA in New York and Philadelphia, it often took only one youngster to become involved with the Pioneers for their fellow young workers to become interested too. For example, fourteen-year-old New York Pioneer Carl D. P. described working as a bootblack (shoeshine) on a ferry. The bootblacks worked from 7 a.m. to 8 p.m., seven days a week, earning around a dollar a day. A real bone of contention was Sundays when the ferry's adult porters had the day off and the bootblacks were expected to pick up the slack by completing the porter's duties as well as their own despite receiving no compensation from the ferry companies for doing so. Carl announced his intention to form a union among the bootblack boys hoping to demand better pay, an hour's lunch break, and no extra porter's work.[21] A similar note appeared in *Young Comrade* from Moey, a Pioneer and representative of the messenger boys employed by the Western Union Telegraph Co. Moey complained that the boys who worked there were forced to work overtime without extra pay and contrasted those experiences to the company's head Newcomb Carlton who "makes 15 million." A group of boys had decided they were "willing to organize" and were hoping to demand a lunch hour, an end to unpaid overtime, a 44-hour working week, and for the company to equip them with "rubbers and raincoats" seen as they were expected to work in any weather conditions.[22] Such demands, particularly the raincoats, had the potential to be hugely beneficial for the children's health but were clearly not the demands of the radical Communists that the YPA was made out to be and liked to claim to be. At least in the short-term, they displayed elements of realistic pragmatism, supporting incremental material improvements to working-class children's lives.

Part III

THE SCHOOL STRUGGLE

Chapter 6

Countering Capitalist Curriculum and Corporal Punishment

Public School Conditions

NEW YORK CITY'S public schools hosted the city's Young Pioneers of America (YPA) contingents during term time, and Pioneers were keen to use their schools as venues for networking, activism, and recruitment. YPA guidance stated that "the main struggle of the children is in the school. The method to be used in the school is the United Front. We aim to unite all children in the school in the direct struggle for partial demands in every possible form."[1] Pioneers had a conflicted relationship with the public school system. On one hand, the YPA supported expanded public education, being totally opposed to both child labor and separate private schools for children from wealthy families. On the other hand, they bitterly contested what they saw as teachers' abusive treatment of children in public schools and capitalist curriculums. Literature distributed by the YPA in Minneapolis–St. Paul explained this position succinctly, stating that "while we realize the bias of public school education today, still it is better than none at all."[2] Private schools were viewed with deep suspicion by the YPA but also served as proof that better resourced and safer school environments were possible. *Young Comrade*'s adult editors informed their readers that capitalists had "created two kinds of schools": private schools where the children of the rich were taught "to rule over the workers" and public schools where working-class children were taught to be "willing workers and slaves."[3] The YPA had many grievances with the public school system in New York City. These criticisms were sometimes material, such as complaints about overcrowding or the lack of affordable school lunch provisions. On other occasions, however, they were ideological with protests centered on the content of lessons that they deemed to be overly patriotic, suspiciously religious, or hostile to Communism.

A number of children took to grumbling about various aspects of their school lives by writing to *Young Comrade* or *Young Pioneer*. Some went a step further and attempted to translate this discontent into action. They seldom enjoyed much success, as teachers and school authorities were keen to harshly punish any activity associated with Communism, often enlisting the help of the NYPD's radical bureau to help do so. The YPA believed that its members were engaged in what they called "the school struggle," and this appears to have been an organizational focus for them in New York since their formative years. For example, at a citywide convention in 1925 under Morris Spector's chairmanship the 160 delegates passed a resolution by Spector and city secretary Esther Gross which "emphasized the necessity for more school work and for a greater participation in the school struggle."[4]

School was a major topic in just about every issue of *Young Comrade*, *Young Pioneer*, and *New Pioneer*. The "Into the Schools" section usually comprised at least one page but often more. Mainly children's letters were printed, which detailed various aspects of their school life. Some were happy to let off steam to a sympathetic readership by telling of their latest irritations with their teacher, their lessons, or school leadership. Others went a step further and used the section as a forum for sharing ideas on how to achieve change or at the very least ferment agitation. Through what is almost a decade's worth of collected children's anecdotes there exists an untapped archive of child's-eye perspectives on conditions in public schools in New York and beyond. Of course, these letters were written by Communist children and were selected for publication by adult Communist editors. But this context does not automatically delegitimize the testimony of those letter writers, especially regarding accounts of brutal corporal punishment or unsafe and overcrowded school buildings. Historically, children have shown a great affection for diligently recording complaints about their teachers, but these letters should not be dismissed out of hand as typical childish moans or displays of adolescent attitude. Many of them, even in distinctly juvenile language, engage with complicated issues such as pondering on what the duties of a teacher should be or to what extent wider global politics should influence the curriculum in their classroom.

A common area of concern in letters submitted to the YPA's periodical from New York schoolchildren had to do with unsanitary or unsafe school environments, not politics. The first two decades of the twentieth century had seen a significant growth in the number of children enrolled in public schools, and the city's educational infrastructure had failed to keep up. By the time of the YPA, overcrowding and dilapidated buildings were widespread problems. In certain sections of the city, particularly poorer neighborhoods with higher proportions of immigrants, double occupancy classrooms had become common practice, meaning that two classes were forced to share the same space. At this time pupils' academic attainment fell significantly across the city, and only 42 percent of New York's students passed the eighth grade.[5] In 1927 children who attended PS 63, the Thomas Jefferson High School in Brooklyn, wrote to *Young Comrade* with a collective set of complaints, which they were addressing to the school's administration as part of a walkout. Their chosen slogan of "more schools, less firetraps" is nothing short of a damning indictment of the condition of New York's public schools. Pupils worried that over one thousand students now attended a school with only three exits and that a fire or even a false alarm would lead to a deadly crush. They also called for "better ventilation," "sanitary conditions," and felt the need to demand "a seat for every pupil."[6]

Even complaints that were clearly not purely Communistic in nature, relating to basic matters of health and safety, were routinely ignored, especially when it was the YPA making the complaint. For instance, Pioneer Anna Schlopak expressed her frustrations in *Young Comrade* that her complaint about a classroom with a broken heating system had gone unresolved. Schlopak described the room as "very cold," observing "my teacher and the children are suffering from head colds." Pioneers and other children refused to attend until it was fixed. Their school strike was more about their health than it was Communism.[7] Failing to act in these circumstances made it very easy for the YPA to appeal to their peers and make the argument that school leaders were "against the interests of the children." Punishing YPA children who raised these types of concerns only appeared to legitimize the YPA as an organization to other children.

In April 1928 pupils at PS 109 in Brooklyn attended a mass meeting called by the YPA to discuss their safety concerns. Students complained that they felt unsafe after the school had reopened a previously abandoned annex for teaching and that the lunchroom was an unsanitary damp basement. Teachers responded by calling the police who arrived to break up what they determined was an "unpermitted gathering." As far as authorities were concerned, these children had absolutely no rights of assembly or expression. This heavy-handed approach allowed the YPA to accuse the capitalist authorities of the police and teachers of not caring about working-class children's safety. It was just about the best local recruitment boost a burgeoning YPA cell could hope for, and it did not deter committed organizers either. Indeed, the PS 109 pupils wrote to *Young Comrade* to declare that "the police can't scare us" and to encourage others to challenge their schools over unacceptable conditions.[8]

Calling in the police was not the only school disciplinary tactic that the YPA disapproved of. Pioneers criticized the "tyranny" and "brutality" of teachers who used corporal punishment to maintain classroom discipline. To them, teachers' using corporal punishment typified "the bourgeois right of the stronger." New York Pioneer James Rosen argued in *Young Comrade* that corporal punishment needed to be made illegal. Rosen recounted an incident from a recent gym class. One of his friends had been guilty of "talking to his neighbor," and the teacher had smacked him in the face with such force that it knocked one of his teeth out. Bleeding from the mouth, the boy began to cry, but the teacher humiliated him further, verbally berating him for being a "baby" about it.[9] These types of physical assaults by teachers were a reality of the classroom in New York in the 1920s though public opinion on the use of corporal punishment was hardly uniform. Teachers' use of corporal punishment was banned in the Empire State's public schools only in 1985, whereas neighboring New Jersey had prohibited it since 1867. In 1873 a New York Board of Education meeting narrowly voted by 10–7 to reject a petition to do the same.[10] Therefore, in opposing the practice the YPA were not radical outliers.

School Curriculums

In addition to opposing corporal punishment, Pioneers also opposed teaching practices that they deemed anti-Communist. The content of lessons and the priorities of individual teachers were kept under close observation by the YPA with some Pioneers seeming to relish a role as the Communists' eyes and ears in the classrooms. The YPA recognized education as a system which had huge potential to shape children's lives. The classroom to them was a place of academic learning but also a place where they felt teachers as local government employees aimed to influence children's politics and pass on certain beliefs and cultures. New York Pioneer S. Eidelstein characterized public school curriculums as "patriotic bunk," an opinion many of their comrades likely shared.[11]

Some accounts of teaching recorded by the city's Pioneers would also have been concerning to a wider audience beyond their own Communist circles. For example, Jewish Italian American Pioneer Irving Gorbati complained in 1927 after his teacher had expressed enthusiastic support for the regime of Italian Fascist dictator Benito Mussolini. Similarly, Grace Zelnick, a daughter of Romanian immigrants, was outraged when her teacher praised Romania's Dowager Queen, "Bloody Queen Marie." Zelnick was not the only person to take exception. A Romanian boy in the class rose from his seat to shout in protestation, "But she's a murderer!"[12] These anecdotes show how classroom spaces in working-class areas were places where various ethnic, religious, and political backgrounds all met with the potential of significant disagreement. The YPA were likely not alone in finding teachers' praise of Mussolini and Queen Marie to be problematic.

American history caused an awful lot of friction between teachers and YPA-supporting students. Fifteen-year-old New York Pioneer Frank T. Valentine opined that "the schools and the churches are the best weapons for the capitalists to poison the minds of the workers." He said that one of the most potent tools in their arsenal was the history textbook, which "put lies in the workers' child's head." Valentine was wary of propagandistic, jingoistic, unrealistic portrayals of major historical figures and provided the use of popular legends or proverbs in his lessons as evidence this occurred. His first example was a teacher repeating the once popular legend that George Washington had never told a lie. Valentine explained that this was impossible for anybody but argued it to be even more impossible for Washington, a man he criticized as a "big slaveholder." He also took issue with his teacher's repetition of a proverb commonly attributed to Benjamin Franklin, the phrase "early to bed, early to rise, makes a man healthy and wise." In Valentine's opinion this was far from healthy and made people "worn out."[13] He insisted that it was certainly not healthy or wise for men to wake up at 5 a.m. to go to work in a steel mill. This proverb and romanticization of its attribution to Franklin constituted in Valentine's view an attempt to indoctrinate the working class into accepting their role in society, glorifying capitalistic abuse of workers, and its use in the classroom was anything but innocent.

Some Pioneers relished the opportunity to ask their teachers difficult questions or to completely dispute their characterization of historical figures or current events. One such student was Gussie Rosenfeld, a member of a New York YPA branch which had named itself the Karl Marx Pioneer troop. Rosenfeld became a regular contributor to *Young Comrade*'s school section in the mid-1920s. During a history lesson about Federalism,

Rosenfeld's teacher had told the class that the Federalists had "fallen away" due to their support of "alien and sedition laws," which went against the Constitution. Rosenfeld raised his hand and asked if there were similar laws in 1926. His teacher replied that no, "of course" there were not. Rosenfeld was likely anticipating that answer and seized the opportunity to state that he thought there were such laws in place, referencing the case of Benjamin Gitlow to make his point. The teacher quickly changed the subject, but Rosenfeld felt vindicated, explaining that he felt he had exposed his teacher's lies to his classmates. Mocking his teacher, he also felt that his being silenced in the classroom when raising the topic exposed capitalist authorities' hypocrisy regarding free speech and titled his letter "Yes we have freedom but arresting workers is different my dear."[14]

Rosenfeld's discussion of Gitlow in the classroom shows his awareness of current events. Gitlow had been convicted under New York's criminal anarchy law over publishing *Revolutionary Age*, a periodical deemed to have illegally encouraged a violent overthrow of the government. Freed after filing a writ of error, Gitlow had been the Communist candidate for vice president on William Z. Foster's ticket despite coming from the rival Charles Ruthenberg wing of the party. He was then returned to Sing Sing prison in 1925 after the Supreme Court deemed his conviction to be constitutional in *Gitlow v. New York*. Following pressure from the American Civil Liberties Union (ACLU), Governor Al Smith pardoned Gitlow, who then ran for the governorship in 1926, an election campaign which was ongoing when Rosenfeld made his classroom intervention.[15]

Rosenfeld had been able to identify a link between Gitlow's treatment and his history lesson about the Federalists. He likely hoped that as the Federalists had paid the price, the anti-Communist political forces of his day would eventually pay the price for what he viewed as their hypocritical relationship with their own Constitution. Rosenfeld was not alone in accusing teachers who spoke of America's freedoms but then strictly controlled students' speech in their classrooms. For example, in May 1931 Brooklyn's Joe Grossburg informed *New Pioneer* of an argument with his teacher. Grossburg was yelled at to "Sit down!" and threatened with being taken to the principal's office after telling classmates in his current events class that a "revolution led by the Communist party" was taking place in China where "workers and peasants" were "joining the Red Army of China." Grossburg interpreted the teacher's actions as an ironic act of censorship, adding "only the day before we learned about free speech in America."[16]

YPA children were encouraged to stage these classroom curriculum interventions by the print culture they consumed. In addition to reading of one another's latest antics in their periodical, something which could easily have fostered an element of one-upmanship, disruptive and defiant behavior was also glorified in the periodical's imagery. For example, *Young Pioneer* published a comic strip by well-known artist Ryan Walker where a YPA boy named "Little Billy Worker" irritates his teacher "Miss Snoop" on his first day at school. Little Billy Worker refused to learn to be patriotic and insisted on thinking for himself. Walker was a prolific cartoonist right up until his death in 1932 and was a veteran of the 1914 picketing of New York's Standard Oil building. In this strip for the Pioneers, he had given one of his most popular characters, Bill Worker, a son. Walker likely hoped to encourage Communistic youngsters to question the content and motives behind their school lessons and to refuse to learn how to be obedient to their bosses. The last of the series of six images shows an exasperated principal exclaiming, "I should have known it," as Little Billy Worker stands proud as punch, declaring "I'm Little Billy Worker, and a member of the Young Pioneers."[17] Youngsters like Gussie Rosenfeld and Joe Grossburg saw themselves as the real-life Little Billy Workers, much to the irritation of their teachers.

Chapter 7

School Lunch Revolts

PIONEERS IN NEW YORK CITY were particularly active on the issue of school lunch provision. In some respects, their campaign appears to have been slightly ahead of its time. The issue of food security came to a head during the Great Depression and resulted in agriculture secretary Henry Wallace overseeing the introduction of food stamps. After the Second World War, school lunches, as Susan Levine details in *Lunch Room Politics*, were embraced as a social benefit.[1] But in New York, the Young Pioneers of America's (YPA's) campaign for school lunches actually called for the return of a previously popular program which the city had abandoned in rather murky circumstances. The history of children's welfare provisions in New York is not a narrative of straightforward progress but of a series of local battles, resistance, and setbacks. YPA children's demands for hot lunch provision were met with a frosty reception much like their complaints about building safety. School officials were determined not to listen to them and to be seen as giving no quarter to Communism, not even in the lunchroom.

Even when Pioneers attempted to conduct themselves in a measured manner and go through official channels, they were punished. In November 1931 William Jansen, an executive at the New York Board of Education's office, called the police after hearing that YPA children had been collecting signatures and planned to deliver a petition demanding free hot lunches. The NYPD were happy to help. Jansen was guarded by a posse of ten police officers, and the frustrated students were unable to deliver their petition.² Once again, Jansen's tactics achieved what he wanted in the short term—keeping the kids away from his office—but handed an easy symbolic victory for the YPA who could tell all their peers about officials' refusal to engage with them over school lunch. It also gave the YPA very little incentive to use the proper channels going forward.

The School Lunch Committee

Working-class students' access to nutritious food was a long-term problem. Back in 1905 the Salvation Army had attempted to help by offering breakfast baskets to children across Manhattan. This proved much more challenging than was anticipated. Providing a single food basket that all children would eat was a difficult task. This was not about childish fussy palates but a reflection of the varied food cultures and religious food requirements of children from culturally diverse working-class neighborhoods. School lunch, therefore, was primarily a nutritional challenge, complicated by sociocultural factors. For Thanksgiving 1908 home economist Mabel Hyde Kittredge began providing free soup and bread to pupils at an elementary school in Hell's Kitchen. This was the humble beginning of a wider effort. Kittredge founded the School Lunch Committee (SLC), bringing together philanthropists, physicians, and home economists to try to improve school lunch across Manhattan. The SLC proved popular and quickly expanded beyond the borough, servicing schools on Long Island and in Brooklyn. The meals it served had to contain a minimum of 450 calories but were varied dependent on the individual demographics of each school. For example, when the SLC began serving food as PS 21 in the heart of Little Italy, it employed an Italian chef to cook dishes that the school's 2,100 pupils would be accustomed to. The benefits were clear. In 1909 143 children at PS 21 and another school, PS 53, were identified as suffering from acute malnutrition. The malnourished children at PS 21 who had access to the SLC's program gained weight at three times the rate of those at PS 53.³

The SLC program was championed by schoolteachers and principals who recognized its health benefits and noted an improvement in children's educational attainment, describing a sharp decline in bad behavior and lethargy, which they attributed to the children's being well-fed. In 1915 John J. Dempsey, the principal of PS 85, wrote to the *Times Union* newspaper to express his gratitude to all those who contributed to what he considered a "decided success." SLC meals were made freely available for qualifying children and available for purchase at the price of one penny for their classmates, earning the program a moniker of "the penny lunch." The press and various members of New York society got behind the program, particularly academics and the *Evening World* newspaper, which called for its expansion to every school in the city. The *World* considered it a "travesty" that some children still lacked access to "proper food."[4]

By the nature of the program the SLC was loss-making and relied on donations from benefactors. In December 1915 Columbia University's Dr. Thomas D. Wood and socialite Mary Wilkinson Grant hosted a fundraising ball at the Hotel Majestic to fund SLC expansion in Harlem. The *World* kept readers abreast of its fundraising campaign by recording donations large and small, which by that time had crossed the $5,000 threshold. In the same notice where it thanked the Federation of Women's Clubs, which had sold over 20,000 tickets for theatrical benefit performances, the paper also thanked the children of the Corona Class, Excelsior Sunday School, who had pooled two dollars of their pocket money for the cause.[5] School lunch was not a Communist fantasy but a thoroughly deliverable cause that a wide range of New Yorkers were willing to contribute toward.

Despite being practically universally well-regarded, the SLC first came under threat in 1915. It remained financially viable due to a budget apportionment from the powerful Board of Estimates, a body composed of the elected presidents of each of the city's boroughs. Many of those involved in carrying out the SLC's daily functions were employees of the public school system, and the Board of Estimates had until this point agreed to pay their salaries while they carried out SLC work. When the board first mooted that it might refuse to sanction this cost in the upcoming city budget, it provoked outrage from a cross-section of New Yorkers. A protest meeting at PS 3 was attended by over 3,000 people with even more being turned away at the door. Various local politicians and religious leaders spoke out in support of the SLC, including Rabi Nissam Behar, municipal court justice Aaron J. Levey, and New York Assembly members Adolph Stern and Harry S. Shirwell. Prior to a 1915 meeting between the Board of Estimates and Republican Mayor John P. Mitchell, the East Side Protective Association staged a march past City Hall that was attended by an estimated 5,000 parents and children.[6] The SLC was eventually funded, but this victory was a short-term win for the city's children, and the Board of Estimates did end its support in 1919, refusing an application for an appropriation $49,000 in the 1920 budget, claiming it had been received too late.[7]

Democratic Mayor John F. Hylan and *Evening World* journalist Sophie Irene Loeb, who had dedicated much of her journalistic career to advocating for the SLC through the paper, both blamed individuals at the

Board of Education for engineering a delay in the application of funds, implying they had possessed a corrupt motive for doing so. The SLC's secretary called for a loophole to be found, holding it to be "sheer stupidity" to allow administrative issues to end the program. The principal of PS 120, Olive M. Jones, described the conduct of city business as "worse than a crime" because it caused "the greatest injustice" to the city's schoolchildren. Carrie Wallace, principal of the New York School for the Deaf, described the end of the SLC as "a serious menace to the health and mental growth of the children." Wallace begged for a sense of humanity to prevail, pointing out that some of her pupils "have never spoken a word" and that many others were just learning to speak. With no lunch in school she commented, "They would be absolutely lost if they had to go out upon the street and obtain a little lunch."[8]

Nobody in the city administration came out in favor of ending the program, but many did remarkably little to prevent its closure. City comptroller Charles Lacey Craig pointed out that passing a piece of legislation was one way to circumnavigate the technical obstruction to funding the scheme beyond administrative deadlines. No legislative effort was made, however, and SLC provision across forty-eight schools ceased in 1920, and tens of thousands of surplus dollars remained in the city treasury.

There was little talk of the SLC returning even from teachers and principals who had once eulogized it. Sophie Loeb's suspicions that something else had been going on behind the scenes appeared to be confirmed when the Board of Estimates quickly began offering concessionaire's contracts to private enterprises. There were very lucrative terms with half of some profits going to the Board of Estimates. Affordable penny lunches were no more, and profit became king in school canteens. There were no hygiene safety inspections or minimum nutritional standards as there had been in the SLC days. Private contractors' offerings catered only for the "typical American diet" and the SLC's individualized offerings to match the demographic profiles of its schools were quickly phased out. Where no profit could be made, concessionaires simply abandoned their contracts, and by 1925 lunch was available for purchase in twenty fewer schools than it had been in 1919. A dismayed Mabel Hyde Kittredge attempted to reenter the fray, forming the School Lunch Inquiry Committee (SLIC), but she was unable to prevent New York's falling behind other major American cities, many of whom began introducing their own penny lunch schemes just as New York had abandoned its in favor of profiteering.[9]

In the background, as historian A. R. Ruis points out, there was an ongoing politically charged "negotiation of responsibility" where officials in health, education, labor, and law departments of local government all believed that school lunches should be funded by each other's budgets. For Ruis this is proof enough that the SLC's closure was not another example of indifference to poor children where a series of public health interventions and non-interventions discriminated against immigrant communities.[10] Ruis does not convince, however, that no callous disregard or corruption ultimately shaped the departure from a carefully planned and executed public health initiative to provide nutritious food to the neediest children in favor of an exclusionary system motivated by profit. To the children of the YPA the decline in the availability of lunch in schools and expensive prices in schools where it remained embodied what they saw as the callous indifference of city governance to the welfare of working-class children. Their efforts to do something about it were met with institutional resistance. This later resistance, and the fact that no member of city administration was willing to concede any ground in that "negotiation of responsibility," weakens Ruis's argument. People in power did not care enough to ensure children were fed.

The YPA's School Lunch Protests

Two members of the Brownsville YPA, fifteen-year-old Sam Kessler and fourteen-year-old Joe Grossman, attempted to raise a protest at PS 109. In one respect they were lucky, as their school was one of a minority in New York which had a cafeteria. They objected to the school's rules being changed to prevent children from leaving during the lunch break, something which many did to either eat lunch at home or buy lunch in the surrounding area. The children became a captive market for the private contractor who promptly took advantage by raising prices across the board. With their principal unwilling to hear their complaints that they could not afford to eat lunch, Kessler and Grossman collected signatures for a petition and attempted to organize a meeting by distributing flyers on Liberty and Rockaway Avenues during the morning as children made their way to school. The school principal called the police who, despite there being no suspicion that Kessler or Grossman had broken the law in any way, were more than willing to act as intimidatory agents of the school. The NYPD confiscated the pair's remaining leaflets and arrested them. They were held at the police station long enough to ensure they missed the after-school meeting before being released with no further action to be taken. Other children still attended the meeting that was held at Krieger's Hall on Power and Blake Avenues. In Kessler's and Grossman's absence it was hosted by their friend, fourteen-year-old George Cohen, who managed to persuade over seventy-five children to sign the petition. All three were all suspended from school as a punishment, something the YPA criticized as having "no legal ground whatsoever." The trio joked in their correspondence with *Young Comrade* that they would at least now be able to afford lunch.[11]

These types of school lunch disputes in schools appear to have been semi-regular events. They were not always led by the YPA, but this did not stop school administrators from accusing any student involved of being a Communist. In 1934 the *Brooklyn Daily Eagle* provided extensive coverage of a spat between principal Dr. Harry A. Potter and students at New Utrecht High School, at 79th Street and Seventh Avenue in Brooklyn. In this "lunchroom war" Potter suspended seventeen-year-old Morris O'Shatz pending a Board of Education hearing to face allegations of repeatedly distributing circulars and being a Communist. Interviewed at his home, O'Shatz insisted he was not a Communist and that all his actions in the school were as part of the Students' Rights Committee, which advocated for the rights of all students of all political persuasions. As for the question of Communist involvement, O'Shatz said it was impossible for him to know the minds of 1,300 fellow students. O'Shatz claimed to have collected 1,300 signatures to protest "food prices in the lunchroom," which were "too high." School rules banned students from leaving the building to buy lunch, so they were "compelled to patronize" it. Example prices include five cents each for the following items—a glass of milk, ice cream, cakes, pies, spaghetti—and eight cents for a sandwich. O'Shatz told the paper that Potter was "very sinister" and had told him, "Don't tell us what to do with the profits"; he also denied students their "academic freedom."[12]

After Potter had ignored O'Shatz's petition the boy arranged for a protest meeting to take place directly outside of the principal's office. The demonstration was then promptly broken up by the police and the school's Reserve Officers' Training Corps. Upon insisting on an answer to the students' demands, O'Shatz claimed he was threatened with arrest and complained to the *Daily Eagle* that students had been "shoved, pushed, and terrified." Potter insisted to the paper that he had not acted "tyrannically" as the boy and his mother claimed. He said he did not permit students to leave during the day to "protect morals," claiming that allowing them to do so would result in a "back door club" where girls and boys could gamble or act with "immorality." As for the claim that he had threatened to raise prices to quell the lunchroom rebellion as students threatened to boycott it, he insisted he had only warned students that as prices in the supply chain had risen, that cost would have to be proportionately passed on to students when the next supplies were bought. He suspected that Communism was somehow to blame, claiming to have identified two Communists in the school, and stating he was "monitoring" suspicious persons he had observed loitering nearby.[13] Potter's reaction to student complaints over the price of spaghetti in a school cafeteria appears symptomatic of a Red Scare–like heightened suspicion and fear of Communism in New York schools' administration in the mid-1930s.[14]

Chapter 8

The Lenin Unit at PS 61

The Lenin Unit

THE YOUNG PIONEERS of America's (YPA's) activity in New York schools went beyond expressing dissatisfaction with unsafe conditions, corporal punishment, and lesson contents. The "school struggle" included a wider mission in which members used the school environment as a potential recruitment center. The YPA managed to develop a stronger presence in some schools than others. It managed to gain a particularly strong foothold in PS 61, a Bronx junior high school at 1550 Crotona Park East, which served a predominantly Jewish, Eastern European immigrant community. By the early 1930s the guidance the YPA offered on operating within schools stated, "It is not necessary to have Pioneers carry on this in the name of the YPA." Instead, it suggested that "Pioneers attending the same school get together with the leader, decide on the issue, on the type of activity, slogans, and proceed to mobilize the children for a struggle on this issue." Single-issue organizations and school clubs provided one route into the school with the hope of forcing incremental change and drawing more children toward the YPA.[1] Prior to this, the chosen methods of some Pioneers were much less subtle and caused significant headaches for school officials.

Harry Eisman was one of the main student leaders of the YPA's presence at PS 61. Eisman was born in December 1913 in the modern-day Moldovan capital Chișinău, which at that time was disputed territory between

Tsarist Russia and Romania. His life changed dramatically at the age of seven when his parents were killed in a pogrom. Traumatic childhood experiences of antisemitic and anti-Communist violence, what he recalled as the "Rumanian White Terror," undoubtedly shaped Eisman's worldview. He emigrated to New York as an orphaned nine-year-old to live with his older brother Alexander, who was in his mid-twenties, and their three sisters. This afforded Eisman the legal status of a bonded immigrant, sometimes known as a dependent alien. According to his sister Eda, Alexander paid his younger siblings very little attention, and the younger quartet were essentially housed, fed, and left to their own devices, though he did support Harry in school disciplinary and courtroom hearings.[2] Harry Eisman used his extensive freedoms to devote himself to revolutionary politics. In 1926 when he was twelve his name appeared in a list of prize draw entrants in the *Daily Worker* who had sold a large number of subscriptions. By 1928 he had become one of the New York YPA's most high-profile members. He wrote regular contributions for *Young Pioneer* and was a respected public speaker, so much so that he stumped for Rebecca Grecht during her state assembly campaign.[3] For Eisman, the YPA was not a hobby or something that he did in his spare time but something which he structured his whole life around, and he was therefore very keen to bring it to school with him.

The first evidence of a concerted YPA organizing effort in PS 61 appeared in December 1927's edition of *Young Comrade*. An anonymous article attributed to "XYZ" announced the presence of a "Lenin unit" at the school which distributed a pamphlet called *Young Spark* and hoped to stand candidates in the upcoming student council elections. In a follow-up note to *Young Comrade*, E. C. claimed that the Lenin unit had grown from its original core membership of twelve to twenty-five. They considered this to be particularly exciting because in addition to gaining members the Lenin unit believed they had managed to cultivate a greater number of "sympathizers" among the student body thanks to the literature they had distributed. Pioneers at PS 61 corresponded with the periodical not to boast of their success but to encourage children at other schools to do the same, telling them that "all Pioneer groups should carry out a lot of school work."[4]

Distributing a Communist school newspaper and looking to recruit other children made it very hard to operate in secret. By the summer of 1928 school authorities in the Bronx were boasting of how they had managed to uncover a clandestine network of young Reds, although they failed to identify the specific children involved. This smacks of either bungling incompetence or a period of indifference. Since May 1928 it was a matter of public record as reported in local newspapers that five of the school's students had been arrested at May Day demonstrations alongside Jessie Taft. It surely did not take much detective work to suspect that these students may have been involved in the appearance of the *Young Spark*, which vexed school leadership. There was an element of smug satisfaction to the Lenin unit's communications as they wrote of how increasingly "sore" principal Edward R. McGuire seemed every time they released the next version of their mimeographed publication. Although it seemed obvious who was involved with Eisman making campaign speeches for local Workers Party candidates on weekends, the school authorities did not identify the Lenin unit's leaders until November 1928.

By this time, based on their periodical correspondence, the YPA had been operating at PS 61 unchecked for almost a full calendar year. Students Harry Eisman, Bernard Kaplan, Lebe Kaplan, Jeanette Rubin, Nathan Singer, Daniel Metliz, and Louis Goldberg were all suspended. Demonstrating a fear of Communism betrayed by the school's sluggish investigation, their suspensions were reported in local newspapers in New York, New Jersey, and Maryland. Jonathan Hunt describes how a hysterical fear of Communism became a "central preoccupation" of the mid-twentieth century.[5] Rose Baron described in *Labor Defender* how the capitalist press had "snatched upon these cases as choice morsels," producing a raft of headlines about the "red menace" in schools.[6] The extent that children's Communism-related school disciplinary hearings occurred and were deemed newsworthy events in the mid-1920s suggests that this was not really an interlude between to two Red Scares in American history. An example page of the students' *Young Spark* (see Appendix C) was reproduced in the *Daily News*, and the *New York Times* expressed alarm at the content of "fiery Communistic literature:"[7]

Young Spark was rudimentary in its construction, wonkily mimeographed, and complemented with a childish sketch of a boxer delivering a knockout blow to a dollar sign imposed over the globe at the top left. Readers were asked to question if America's child laborers enjoyed the prosperity that Republicans and Democrats liked to "shout about." They were told that both those political parties worked for the bosses and against the workers. Only some of *Young Spark*'s messaging would have resonated with the student body. The allegation that a secret plot was being hatched to declare war on the Soviet Union would have gone over many heads. But these claims were surrounded by calls for improvements to the lives of working-class children, which would certainly have resonated in an area of the Bronx which seemed very far removed from the prosperity of the so-called roaring twenties. Not all children will have been sold on the idea of a revolution to achieve a workers' and farmers' government. But a great deal will have agreed with *Young Spark*'s calls for better schools in working-class neighborhoods and free clothes and food for workers' children.

It was hard for schools to clamp down on publications like *Young Spark* and the distribution of other pieces of YPA literature. Administrators did not want these materials in students' hands but were hampered by the fact that such pamphlets were perfectly legal. When schools called in the NYPD, officers quickly concluded it was not a police matter. A senior radical bureau officer, William van Walkenburgh, told the Congressional hearings into Communist propaganda that unless items were deemed obscene, there was little police could do. Van Walkenburgh gave the example of a 1928 case when a student at City College had contributed a poem to the *Daily Worker* that had compared the Statue of Liberty to a prostitute. It was the poetic description of prostitution in a daily newspaper that allowed police to take action, and both the poet and the editors responsible were convicted and fined under the Obscene Publications statute. Some of the Eisman-linked propaganda found in his and several other nearby schools was investigated by the police. Eisman's materials had found their way into circulation at another Bronx school, PS 89, much to the displeasure of its principal, Alfred Rado. Rado called the police, and the radical bureau's Louis Herman—one of the detectives who had arrested Leo Granoff back in 1923—investigated. He concluded after consulting with the Bronx district attorney's office and the US district attorney that the Pioneers involved had not committed any state or federal crimes.[8]

Rado testified to the congressional special committee to investigate Communist activities in the United States, which was chaired by New York Representative Hamilton Fish III and commonly known as the Fish Committee, that his school had between 150 and 200 Communists within its student population of 1,700. With the Lenin unit and their propaganda deemed not to not be a police matter, it was left to Principal McGuire at PS 61 to deal with the culprits. He punished Bernard Kaplan, Lebe Kaplan, and Jeanette Rubin by holding them back a grade. Harry Eisman was identified as the "head of the agitation" and remained suspended pending a disciplinary hearing before schools' superintendent Joseph H. Wade. McGuire accused Eisman of leading what he called an "insidious campaign . . . inflaming the minds of his classmates with Bolshevist propaganda." McGuire informed Wade that the boy had to be expelled "in order to save the school." Interestingly, McGuire's appraisal of Eisman as "fresh, stubborn and disrespectful" does not correlate with how he later testified under oath to the Fish committee.[9] According to the ILD (International Labor Defense), school authorities only began accusing Eisman and Kaplan partway through the disciplinary process of disruption and impudence. Rose Baron suggested that some liberal defenders of "free speech" had made it clear that they were uncomfortable punishing children for their membership in an organization and their writing their thoughts in pamphlets, so the administration engaged in a character assassination of the boys' wider conduct.[10]

McGuire's testimony to Congress could have been an act of self-preservation. He sought to justify his failure to identify and deal with Eisman as the chief YPA organizer in the school by claiming that he could not have done anything any sooner. McGuire told Congress that the children involved were generally well-behaved, had been careful not to break any of the formal school rules, and even described Eisman as "inoffensive." Two very different versions of Eisman were presented by his principal to the boy's disciplinary hearing and to Congress, where McGuire and Rado's testimonies were both full of blatant contradictions. They simultaneously claimed that the YPA was "very secretive" and complained about bold public tactics like "carrying banners" and interfering with other children on their way to school. They tried to have it both ways. The *Journal of Education* had already discussed the public performative activism of YPA children at Rado's school, citing student Louis Surfer, who was punished for loudly reciting the YPA's pledge to the Red Flag instead of the pledge of allegiance one morning.[11] The YPA was not a secretive organization. Its tactics had been shaped by the Granoff affair in late 1923, and members sought to be loud public nuisances to capitalist authority rather than operate in the shadows. It is impossible to avoid the conclusion that evidence stemming from school leaders about the YPA was at best inconsistent and at worst deliberately false. Either way, even if given under oath it is impossible to rely on.

Members of the congressional committee appeared not to pick up on these obvious contradictions in the testimony about the YPA. This is likely because the aim of the hearing was not a true, objective reflection of the evidence, but was to achieve an outcome which would advance Hamilton Fish III's policy agenda. Fish was an isolationist who wanted to reduce immigration to the United States. His strong opposition to Communism and his spreading of various antisemitic conspiracy theories meant that later in World War II Nazi Party officials identified him as a potential sympathizer in Congress. During McGuire's testimony the questioning was dominated by West Virginia Republican Carl G. Bachmann and Tennessee Democrat Edward E. Eslick. Mississippi Democrat Robert S. Hall and the committee's eventual dissenter, Maine Republican John E. Nelson, stayed silent. The committee's focus became sidetracked, considering not the true capabilities of the YPA but focusing on the nationality and ethnicity of its membership and their reported quoting of Karl Marx. The slant of this questioning indicated the predetermined position of some members that Communism was an alien non-American threat to the United States. All present, including the testifying McGuire, endorsed the idea of secretive Pioneer schools, something there is little evidence of. Some Communists did set up Communist Sunday schools, but this was not part of the YPA, which was fundamentally not a secretive organization, operating visibly at workers' halls and labor lyceums and putting a great deal of effort into public protest.[12]

At Eisman's disciplinary hearing he was expelled by superintendent Wade. He was given nominal credit for a good record of academic performance, including having previously won a $5 composition prize. Alexander Eisman stated that this prize had been put toward rent as the siblings were two months in arrears and had already been threatened with eviction. Wade concluded that Eisman was a "vociferous Communist" who remained intent on "proclaiming his politico-economic theories," so expulsion was the only solution. The YPA claimed that the hearing had been fundamentally unfair because Eisman had been forbidden to speak for himself and was denied the chance to call the character witnesses whom he had lined up. Wade had originally insisted that only education officials, legal counsel, and parents could speak but was then reminded that Eisman was an orphan so allowed the eldest sibling, Alexander, to speak. Wade claimed that the hearing was run that way to prevent a crowd of people wishing to "exploit the boy," referring to the presence of photographers and a crowd of supporters outside the Board of Education building.[13]

It is more probable that Wade wanted to ensure there was no chance of the hearing becoming a spectacle akin to YPA cases at the children's court. Eisman's punishment was likely agreed upon well in advance to the hearing, especially given the expressed views of other New York school administrators. Aaron I. Dotey, an assistant superintendent and chairman of the Teachers' Council's radical committee, publicly warned his colleagues that they should not give any Communists a second chance, declaring "children become fanatics. . . . Once infected with the virus of Communism, there is no hope for them."[14] Given that type of rhetoric, it is easy to see why Eisman's supporters suggested that the hearing was a predetermined sham.

Wade's conduct of Eisman's disciplinary hearing denied the YPA a chance to repeat one part of the Leo Granoff playbook, but the YPA still sought to emulate it in another way by turning Eisman into a similar cause célèbre. Immediately after the hearing a defiant and unrepentant Eisman addressed a crowd of supporters outside, perched upon a soapbox in what the *Daily News* described as "typical Communistic fashion." He also took to *Young Comrade* to tell other children to emulate his activity at PS 61. To rally support for his case he presented it as something bigger than himself. He told his comrades that "this is not the fight for one Pioneer" but instead a "fight for the right of the Pioneers to carry on their work in the schools in the interests of the workers' children," thus transforming his personal predicament into a crusade for the YPA's collective right to exist.[15] To protest the sanctions imposed on Eisman, the YPA organized a protest meeting at 1472 Boston Road with the backing of the United Council of Working Women (UCWW).

Figure 2. Harry Eisman, who was in school trouble over publishing a Communist school newspaper, telling crowd the results of the hearing in regular Communist soapbox style. (Photo by Vic Twyman/ NY Daily News Archive via Getty Images)

Fifty local children attended the meeting, most of whom were linked to PS 61. They were joined by members of the local Young Workers League (YWL) and several groups of women from the UCWW. The meeting was hosted by Jessie Taft and began in customary YPA fashion with a pledge of allegiance to the Red Flag. According to a local journalist who attended the meeting, Taft spoke "quite composedly." She roused the audience several times in a speech that lasted nearly an hour and only briefly faltered when two officers from the nearby Simpson Street station arrived to observe proceedings. Taft told the children of PS 61 to "stand firm" and offered them encouragement by telling them that their work at the school offered great inspiration to growing groups at PS 40, 55, 89, Monroe High school, the Morris School, and her own Walton High School. She estimated that across the Bronx and Brooklyn, the YPA numbered almost 1,200, citing recent growth in Williamsburg and Brownsville. Bernard Kaplan followed her at the rostrum, and he gave a defiant memorized speech. At one point he joked to the crowd that he would be back in kindergarten soon if Principal McGuire demoted him every time that he did something Communistic. Eisman was the last speaker, and after he had made his case, the meeting closed with the "singing of Communist songs."[16]

Eisman did not have immediate success in challenging his expulsion by Bronx school authorities, but they did eventually relent two months later. It seemed that several people with influence over the case who were not allies of Eisman by any stretch of the imagination formed the opinion that it was better to have him in school than out of it. His being free to do as he liked during the day rather than under the supervision of his teachers had only accelerated YPA activities in the Bronx. Authorities placed Eisman at PS 55, apparently unaware that the YPA had already cultivated a small presence in that school too. As for PS 61, if McGuire and Wade thought that removing Eisman would solve their YPA problem, they would be disappointed. The group had become established, and there were other students who were willing to step up and take the lead of the Lenin unit. If anything, they were emboldened and began posting notices addressed to the school's teachers on the hallway walls. One of these notices (Appendix D) criticized the school's treatment of Lebe Kaplan and accused staff of acting as willing agents of the capitalist class by suppressing working-class children and knowingly teaching propaganda. Few teachers were likely to be swayed by the Lenin unit's challenge to stand up for their own class, but the main target audience of these notices was likely other students in the school, even though they were addressed to the teachers.

Overall, the defiantly confident Lenin unit at PS 61 was more of an exception than the norm, representing the most significant YPA organization within a New York City public school. YPA presence in each school was subtly different and depended on the whims and characteristics of the individual Pioneers involved. The YPA's structural autonomy afforded children freedoms and independence, but it meant that their approach was at times fragmented or confused at a citywide or national level. YPA school newspapers were supposed to be published in English. But organizers at Brownsville's school 3 on Stone Avenue published their paper *The Young Fighters* in Yiddish, owing to that school's particular demographics. The first issue from March 1932 included sixteen pages of articles, drawings, and commentary from children. The lead essay, "Lindy's Baby," criticized the capitalist press for ignoring children who were exploited and mistreated, especially Black children, and writing only for the benefit of the rich.[17]

Many Pioneers tried to honor the resolution calling for work toward a so-called school struggle passed under Morris Spector's guidance at the 1925 convention, but they did this in their own way. Like the Lenin unit, some prioritized recruitment. Others, like Sam Kessler and Joe Grossman at PS 109, set their sights on advocating for improved school conditions. YPA children at PS 40 mounted a cultural campaign in which they tried to offer Communist alternatives to school-backed celebrations and cultural events. For example, in 1930 they issued leaflets condemning the school's planned Columbus Day celebrations. They offered children complimentary tickets to a rival event of their own at which they gave recitations, performed a short play, and provided live music for dancing. Two hundred local children attended what was in essence a free party. From a YPA perspective this was two hundred youngsters whom they had persuaded to attend their event rather than the school-sanctioned one they condemned as imperialistic. The fact that some of the attendees were persuaded to sign up for the YPA once they were there was a bonus.[18]

Fighting Fire with Fire and Americanization

As Harry Eisman found out at PS 61, authorities took a dim view of the YPA's attempts to gain influence in schools. After efforts to crack down on Pioneer activity the YPA alleged that capitalist school authorities were waging a witch-hunt. In March 1930 the *Brooklyn Daily Eagle* reported that college deans and school principals were embarking on a "drive to stamp out Communism," referring to two ongoing investigations. Max Weiss, a twenty-year-old Young Communist League (YCL) member who was a student at City College, had been arrested for distributing handbills near Union Square. Weiss spent five days on Welfare Island for his troubles and then returned to face a hearing as to whether he would be kicked out of college. At the same time Saul Wellman was facing removal from the Boys' High School. Wellman's principal, Dr. Eugene A. Colligan, insisted that he was merely "advising" Wellman's father that he discontinue his education due to low grades. The YPA insisted this was a *de facto* expulsion and claimed that Wellman's grades had never been a cause of concern until he had refused to sign a pledge of loyalty to the state and federal constitutions. These cases were argued by the Communist Party USA (CPUSA) to be part of a "wave of terror" alongside the plight of seventeen parents who were issued with court summonses after their children had skipped school to attend a labor demonstration.[19]

It is important to point out that the struggle between the YPA's efforts to organize in New York schools and the efforts of opponents to suppress them was not just a tussle between pupils and teachers. There were students who took a very dim view of the YPA. In November 1931, at James Madison High School in Brooklyn's New Utrecht neighborhood, a dispute between students engulfed the street one morning. Members of the school's "safety corps" had attempted to stop Pioneers from distributing handbills at the school gate and a nearby subway exit. As pupils made their way to school, they watched or in some cases joined in on one side or the other. Taxicab driver Nathan Shapiro gave a witness account to the *Times Union*. According to Shapiro the school's principal attempted to intervene but was rebuffed by the Communist faction with one boy telling him to "read the Constitution." Shapiro estimated two hundred or so pupils crowded around the skirmish, which only came to an end when police officers arrived from the nearby Bath Beach station. Students Joseph Cohen and Esther Asks were arrested and later admitted violating a local anti-handbill ordinance at the Coney Island magistrates' court.[20]

Some anti-Communists were weary of the kind of support Communist children like Harry Eisman and Saul Wellman were able to drum up to protest their school exclusions. Brooklyn Alderman James F. Kiernan proposed to the Board of Education in May 1931 that all those suspected of being Communists should be expelled from New York's public schools and colleges. The *Daily News* cautioned against his ultimately unsuccessful resolution, arguing that if it passed, it would provide "Russian Sovietism" a victory in the city by allowing them to "make martyrs of kids who are now nothing but pathetic little (or big) squirts." Keeping the public school truly public and available for everyone, the paper argued, was vital as was allowing freedoms of speech where possible. It hoped that if some Communist children were allowed to continue in school, they might change their principles. The paper also argued that a resolution it admitted was understandable may accidentally set a dangerous precedent and pointed out that "any group could be next," from those with religious differences such as Catholics and Protestants to so-called drys and wets from either side of the Prohibition issue.[21] The serious consideration of Kiernan's proposals to summarily expel mere suspects points to an intense fear of Communist children's presence in public schools and a Red Scare state.

Alderman Kiernan's proposals were one of a series in New York City made in reaction to the YPA. In March 1930, the New York City Chamber of Commerce suggested "fighting fire with fire" with a program of strict "Americanization." This included asking employers to screen employees and report suspected Communists and forcing children to "study the deportation laws" to deter foreign-born youngsters from becoming involved with the YPA. Immigration inspectors were known to visit schools and interrogate children with foreign heritage that had alleged links to the YPA, hoping to intimidate them.[22] The Chamber of Commerce believed there was a "Red Menace" and that the "adolescent radicals" of YPA had to be "taken seriously." These proposals also attracted criticisms, even from anti-Communists, which were articulated at length in the *Ithaca Journal*. The *Journal* argued that opposition would only breed opposition and that the Chamber of Commerce risked "fanning the flames" of division. It conceded that there were "unquestionable abuses in the present social and industrial systems" in America and argued that anti-Communist patriots would do better by organizing to address these. Denying young Communists jobs and school opportunities would only further radicalize them, it warned.[23] The *Journal* recognized what some local politicians and civic organizations did not, that persecuting YPA children had the potential to inspire them rather than dampen their enthusiasm.

It is evident that the 1920s and 1930s were not blissful periods between the two Red Scares in American history where New York schools were not acutely concerned about the potential influence of Communism. The YPA sought to be very active in the "school struggle" by challenging the curriculum, advocating for better conditions, and seeking to use schools as places for networking and recruitment. Even where there was no suspicion of lawbreaking as in the Kessler and Grossman case, the NYPD were used as intimidating agents of school authorities. Any hints of YPA activity in New York schools were subject to sensationalized reporting across the state and beyond. Most times the YPA was unsuccessful in achieving what they demanded, be that an end to corporal punishment or for free hot school lunches. Authorities' hardline approach to combating YPA influence in schools provided them with ample propaganda opportunities and often made it very easy for Pioneers to present themselves as the good guys or as victims of persecution, ultimately helping them increase their presence in certain schools like PS 61 and PS 89.

Part IV

PIONEERS AND POLITICAL OPPONENTS

Chapter 9

Periodical Culture, the Fish Inquiry, and the US Post Office

The Fish Inquiry

THE STEADY GROWTH of the Young Pioneers of America (YPA) during the late 1920s and its bold public tactics meant that by the early 1930s many journalists, public officials, and members of the public became increasingly concerned. One figure who regarded the Pioneers as a problem that needed to be dealt with was the well-known *Daily News* journalist Lowell Limpus. In 1931 he warned that although he felt that the adult Communist Party was struggling for influence, he thought that the YPA was "getting results," particularly on the Lower East Side, following a concerted effort to "arouse the children." Limpus informed readers that some youths had become "thoroughly fanatic" and were "welcoming the chance to work among their schoolmates," deploying tactics like "Red picnics" to slowly draw them into the children's Communist movement. Contrary to Limpus's opinion, historians such as Harvey Klehr regard the 1930s to be a "heyday" for American Communism.[1] Limpus was categorically correct, however, that the YPA was gaining members and recreation was a vital part of their strategy.

Limpus was not alone in harboring Pioneer-specific concerns. In his regular *Brooklyn Daily Eagle* column, the social commentator Frederick Boyd Stevenson stated ahead of the 1928 presidential election that the winner must "see that the Reds are put out of business in the United States." He told readers that in New York City around a thousand children, "many of the boys in knickerbockers," attended a mass meeting "under the auspices of the Young Pioneers of America—the juvenile branch of the workers' Communist party." At the meeting he reported they had sung "revolutionary Red songs" and applauded one another for giving "traitorous" speeches. Stevenson argued that to stop the YPA the rights of all people would have to be restricted. Freedoms were so great, he contended, that they allowed groups like the Pioneers to meet and in turn undermine the freedoms of "God-fearing decent Americans."[2] Of course, to Stevenson and others like him the presence of Judaism and atheism in the YPA and the fact that many Pioneers were either immigrants or the children of immigrants disqualified Pioneers from being "God-fearing," "decent," or "American." Xenophobia, racism, and Christian supremacy were undeniably driving forces in American anti-Communism and motivations for many prominent anti-Communists.

Similarly, in 1930 the *Newark Courier* accused the YPA of "spreading poison." It also advocated for restricting rights and freedoms for all to impede the Pioneers. Even things that it considered the very "cornerstones of the republic"—freedom of speech, freedom of assembly, and freedom of the press—it argued needed to be constrained.[3] In 1931 the president of the Daughters of the American Revolution (DAR), Mrs. Lowell Fletcher Hobart, claimed that Pioneers and their literature were grooming children to attempt to "overthrow the government." She urged members of her organization to "mobilize" to "protect the children and youth from the forces of Communism."[4] It is evident from these various calls from journalists and self-proclaimed patriotic organizations that the fear of Communism associated with the Red Scare of 1917–1920 had not dissipated. They made demands for the country and politicians to suppress the Reds, and proposals to limit the freedoms of all Americans were openly touted by the press. There was still a Red Scare mentality that was partly fueled by the activities of the YPA, which was specifically cited by journalists and anti-Communist leaders.

During what is commonly regarded as the First Red Scare in American history, across 1918–1919 the Overman Committee chaired by North Carolina Democrat Lee Slater Overman operated as a Senate Judiciary Committee subcommittee investigating German and "Bolshevik elements" in the United States. The Overman Committee's hearings into Bolshevik propaganda helped construct an image of a radical insurgent threat to the United States.[5] The most famous congressional investigations are associated with Wisconsin Senator Joseph McCarthy and the House of Representative's Un-American Activities Committee, which was created in 1938 and made a standing (permanent) committee in 1945, representing the start of so-called second Red Scare after the Second World War. However, the intervening years were not free from anti-Communist efforts in Congress. Republican New York representative Hamilton Fish III introduced a resolution in May 1930 to create a committee to investigate Communist activities. The resolution passed, and the committee was informally known as the Fish Committee.

The Fish Committee's inquiries targeted such leading Communists as William Z. Foster and the American Civil Liberties Union (ACLU). However, it also heard significant testimony about the Pioneers. Documentation about the Leo Granoff Affair in 1923 was submitted to the committee, and Harry Eisman's school principal was called to testify about Communist influence in schools. The committee is regarded as a failure, and Fish became a pariah. As Walter Goodman noted in 1964, the committee heard from 225 witnesses in fourteen cities, produced a voluminous report, and ultimately failed to achieve anything significant. As Alex Goodall summarizes, none of the committee's recommendations, such as greater powers for the FBI, were implemented, no legislation followed, and Fish, who denied being an antisemite despite distributing the *Protocols of the Elders of Zion* from his office, was ultimately gerrymandered out of Congress by his own party as an outspoken proponent for Nazi appeasement.[6] Fish's committee was in many ways a vehicle for his own anti-immigrant, xenophobic politics. It would be unwise to treat the committee's investigative work on somebody like Eisman, a Communist immigrant Jew, as reliable.

Fish's long-term ineffectiveness does not mean that the short-term impact of his committee, which was enthusiastically embraced by many police forces, should be ignored. The ACLU reported 930 arrests in the first three months of 1930 concerning free speech, and the number of meetings shut down by police—the majority of which were Communist or trade union gatherings—was higher than the total for any complete year between 1921 and 1929.[7] Though he failed in the long term, Fish and his committee did provoke a fresh wave of police action against Communists. This coincided with specific examples of action taken against the YPA, which had featured heavily in the committee's investigations into Communism and public schools.

After the Fish Committee's hearings had begun, the US Post office instituted a *de facto* ban on the Pioneers' periodical *Young Pioneer*. Several YPA summer camps were either raided by law enforcement acting without a warrant or attacked by members of extremist organizations including the KKK. The police and the KKK faced no consequences for their premeditated violence toward children. Harry Eisman received a near-six-year sentence for parole violation. Quite clearly there was a concerted effort to crack down on the YPA, which included targeting its periodical, its best-known activist, and its most successful leisure program.

Young Comrade

The YPA's periodical first appeared in December 1923 during the Junior Section of the Young Workers League (JSYWL) era as *Young Comrade* and was under the editorial care of two Young Workers League (YWL) members, Nat Kaplan and Max Schachtman. That early experience prepared Kaplan and Schachtman for long influential lives on the American Left. The periodical appeared thereafter monthly with occasional exceptions caused by financial difficulties. *Young Comrade* and its successor titles served numerous roles. On a practical level it helped coordinate YPA activity by printing notices of events and other communications to readers. Second, it served as a venue for influential Communist adults to reach out to a broadly sympathetic community of youngsters, whom they hoped were adult Communist organizers of tomorrow. Throughout its history senior party figures, including Israel Amter, William Z. Foster, and Robert Minor, contributed to the Juniors' periodical. The YPA's periodical was also a source of income, though steps were taken to ensure that costs were kept under control. After all, there was little point in publishing the periodical unless it was obtainable for its target audience of working-class children. Individual copies were priced at five cents and annual subscriptions were set a fifty cents per year. In December 1924, rather than increase the price, the periodical switched to using a lower quality paper.

Young Comrade could not simply imitate the plethora of existing political periodicals alongside which it existed. It had to offer something different to convince children that it was worth buying and reading. This target demographic was difficult to cater for. Some YPA children were as young as seven or eight, and others had received very little formal education. For some, English was a second or third language. Others wanted their intellects to be stretched and did not take kindly to being talked down to or being babied. *Young Comrade* offered a variety of content to ensure that it was accessible and enticing. There were longer adult-authored theoretical pieces, essays about Communism or influential Communists, shorter pieces written by children, and a considerable amount of entertainment. Regular readers followed serialized adventures of Communist siblings Johnny and Rosie Red as they took on capitalist adversaries, including schoolteachers, grotesquely fat bankers, and a young nemesis in the shape of an overprivileged child of the rich named Reggie van Sucker. The periodical maintained a strong visual element too, relying on illustrations and comic strips as much as words to convey its messages.

Though the YPA's periodical was curated by adult editors, it was a venue for children's voices too. In this sense *Young Comrade* and its subsequent reincarnations were literary and cultural environments facilitated by adults but shaped to a large extent by child contributors. Children were encouraged to write and send in their own reports or articles for publication. Thus, the YPA's periodicals were part of a wider periodical culture that had emerged, particularly for boys, in the late nineteenth century. Papers like *Happy Days* (1875–1924) provided spaces for young writers to voice their questions and ideas while improving their literary skills. Albeit under adult control, they created an environment where boys interacted with the editors and with one another, allowing them to help direct and influence the print entertainment they consumed.[8] *Young Comrade* did that too but for Communist boys and girls.

Pioneers were further encouraged to participate by sending in their solutions to puzzles including word jumbles and entirely pictorial cut-and-paste puzzles. Success was rewarded by printing names in the following issue and on special occasions a physical prize such as a commemorative Lenin pin badge was awarded. The education section, "The School Struggle," was usually composed entirely of children's reports and complaints about their schools. As such, the YPA's periodicals offer a relatively unexplored collection of child's-eye testimonies of school conditions and other aspects of daily life. In *Young Comrade*, a YPA member from New York could read the thoughts and opinions of children from beyond their local YPA troop, not just from elsewhere in the city but from California, Texas, and frequently from other YPA strongholds in Illinois, Massachusetts, and Pennsylvania. The periodical facilitated a national-level discussion among Communist children who sought to express themselves beyond their local Communist community. Children were encouraged to be creative in how they did this. The periodical regularly reproduced children's drawings and published their short stories and poems. Through the periodical, therefore, a great number of child members' thoughts and opinions are accessible as are insights into the YPA's culture.

On the first page of the first issue of *Young Comrade*, Kaplan and Schachtman addressed their young readership and told them what to expect from their periodical. They insisted that the organ should emulate the battles of the children whom it served and would do its best to always stand up for workers' children, who were forced into early employment and made to live in "some tenement house where the air stinks."[9] They contrasted these experiences to wealthy children who lived in comparative luxury and would never be found working in a factory, down a mine, or on street corners selling newspapers or shining shoes. Immediate emphasis was placed on material conditions and wealth inequality as well as letting children engaged in these employments know that editors understood the realities of their lives. Children were reassured that it was justified to feel dissatisfied with their lot. Disgruntlement was not ungratefulness or bad behavior as they may have been told but entirely understandable reactions to capitalist oppression.

Kaplan and Schachtman promised they would never "have your heads filled with fairy tales about how good this country is because it's not a good country for workers' children." They insisted that the tough conditions that children experienced were a deliberate creation of "the bosses" who refused to pay their parents a living wage and implemented unjust laws "made for the rich people only." That was a very similar argument to the one that Leo Granoff had made at the children's court earlier in 1923. Seeming to follow Granoff's lead, Kaplan and Schachtman explained that the US Supreme Court was the highest and most important in the land and had repeatedly reversed congressional attempts to legislate against child labor. Readers were asked to consider the question, "Now, what kind of great and glorious Constitution have we that does not allow a law to pass that will save the lives and health of hundreds of thousands of children?" This was proof, *Young Comrade* suggested, that the law, the courts, and the capitalist bosses were against the welfare of the children. *Young Comrade* would do its best to stand up for them, proclaiming it stood for "a government where there is no rich and poor, only human beings."[10] The editors empathized with children's experiences and told them that Communism was the solution to their problems. They sought to assure working-class children that their frustrations were valid and that they were valued as human beings. It is easy to see how these messages resonated with the children who read them, validating any dissatisfaction they had with the material realities of their working-class lives.

A particularly important function of *Young Comrade* and then *Young Pioneer* was providing a venue for children to express and explore their own minds. This extended to creative formats, and most issues published numerous songs, drawings, or poems submitted by children. Poetry was a particularly popular format within the radical literary culture the YPA's periodical facilitated. The poems cannot be assumed to be in anyway autobiographical in nature and are not quotable in terms of distinct facts like more traditional written historical sources. But as Allan Pasco comments on the use of literature in history more broadly, YPA children's poems when handled judiciously can provide answers to certain historical questions.[11] Children's poems or songs do not serve as a mirror to the mind, although details of their content or construction can enlighten us about the opinions and experiences of individual poets. For example, thirteen-year-old R. L. sent *Young Comrade* a song titled "Gonna Strike Some More."[12] Numerous children provided only initials or used a pseudonym such as "an organizer" or "a Pioneer." They were likely aware that both the police and teachers would take a dim view of their engagement with the publication and sought to protect themselves from repercussions by obscuring their identity. "Gonna Strike Some More" adapted the lyrics and tune of Wendell Hall's 1923 hit "It Ain't Gonna Rain No Mo" to express support for striking workers. The lyrics provide insight into the music R. L. encountered and the writer's political support of workers' labor struggles. In submitting poems or songs to the periodical for publication children made a communicative act and wished to engage in the discourse of the publication, expressing themselves to the national membership.

YPA Poetic Juvenilia

Many of the poems that children submitted to *Young Comrade* make explicit criticisms of American society, and these poems offer insight as to why children chose to read the periodical and join the YPA. For example, thirteen-year-old Mary Wytovich-Cokeburg's poem was published in the May 1928 issue and criticized Clara Bryant Ford, the wife of the automobile magnate Henry Ford for maintaining an opulent rose garden. She explained, "I read about the beautiful flower garden Mrs. Henry Ford has. So, I started thinking about it and I wrote this poem":

Mrs. Henry Ford's Flower Garden
Ten thousand roses brilliant red
Bloom in your garden so rare
Ten thousand children cry for bread
But you don't have no heed or care

Ten thousand roses bloom red
Ten thousand children cry for bread
But, if we fight, Mrs. Ford
Things will be different.[13]

After reading about Mrs. Ford's splendid flower garden, Wytovich-Cokeburg's immediate thought was of the wealth and social status that it represented and how this contrasted with the lives of working-class children. She alludes to the problem of food insecurity through the twice-used line "Ten thousand children cry for bread." Wytovich-Cokeburg was also clear in her belief that things did not have to be that way. In her mind significant inequalities were a deliberate choice made by wealthy elites and a symptom of selfishness and greed. She lamented the fact that Mrs. Ford and presumably the wider class of people Mrs. Ford represented had "no heed or care" for the poor. It is notable too that Wytovich-Cokeburg ended with a possible hint of violent revolution with "if we fight, Mrs. Ford." And instead of suggesting that things may get better, she chose the declarative "Things will be different." In eight lines, Mary Wytovich-Cokeburg laid out her revolutionary politics, an insistence that things should change, and her criticisms of American capitalist society. She used her poem to express dissatisfaction with the perceived lack of care from the rich, highlighting wealth inequality and greed by contrasting an emotive image of hungry children crying out for food with Clara Bryant Ford's luxurious rose garden.

Food insecurity was a topic in the YPA's poetic juvenilia and focus of its action, particularly as the Depression continued to bite during the presidency of Herbert Hoover. Within District 2 the YPA held several "hunger marches" to protest "child misery" in New York and New Jersey. In June 1932, the *Brooklyn Daily Eagle* reported a march of "almost 500 children" who were "aged seven to thirteen" on the Lower East Side. The YPA-organized demonstration paraded from Rutgers Avenue to Avenue B and Pill Street prior to holding an open-air meeting. Later that year, sixty YPA children representing their comrades from Paterson, Camden, Toms River, Dover, Atlantic City, Bayonne, Newark, New Brunswick, and Elizabeth, as well as some "allies" from New York City, descended on the New Jersey State Capitol in Trenton. They demanded state funds to establish "feeding stations" in schools and the abolishment of child labor. State police prevented them from entering the legislature where they hoped to present their petition to Governor A. Harry Moore and urge him to take responsibility for the one million children in the Garden State who were "denied the necessities of life." Determined to get their point across, no fewer than thirty-five children who had attended the demonstration at the New Jersey Capitol, some sharing envelopes with friends to help pay for postage, wrote to Moore in the aftermath.[14]

The National Pioneer Bureau also orchestrated a "children's hunger march," which involved somewhere between several hundred and one thousand youths heading to Washington, DC, for Thanksgiving 1932. They took inspiration from a series of similar adult protests including the Veterans' Bonus March the previous January and the Communist-led hunger marches, which had taken place around the world, including at the Palace of Westminster in London. By choosing a public holiday for the date, organizers ensured that children could not be detained on truancy charges as they participated. Representatives from the north's major industrial cities, including New York, were present as were a smaller number from farther afield, including one boy sent from California. Prior to converging on the District of Columbia, several delegations met in Baltimore, where they caused something of a stir by loudly "singing Communist songs" in public. The *Baltimore Sun* expressed its shock, especially with "twenty white and negro children ranging from 8 to 15 years old, accompanied by seven adults" who arrived in a bus together from Philadelphia. The shock seems to have stemmed from the YPA's practicing and support of racial mixing as much as it did their vocal Communism. The Pennsylvanians were joined by thirty children from the Baltimore YPA, each of whom represented a squad from the city, and an "automobile van" full of New Yorkers. The plan to picket the White House and present their petition against hunger and misery to President Hoover was scuppered by Capitol Police who were determined not to let them anywhere near the so-called People's House. But it seems that those in attendance managed to enjoy their day anyway by vocally protesting "the hunger problem" and advocating for a Communist solution to it across several areas of Washington, DC.[15]

Child labor was the chosen topic of numerous young contributors to the YPA's periodical. That topic inspired evocative poems, including "The Factory Child" by ten-year-old Eli Clayman, in which he decries child labor and advocates for revolutionary action to bring the practice to an end:

The Factory Child
He hardly sees the light
Slaving with all his might
From morn till night
But sometime the unhappy day will come
When his life will fade away
Then too late to think it over
Of how wise he would have been
To let the strike come in.

So now, oh faithful comrades
Keep the struggle on

We'll be sure to win some day
And everybody will be happy and gay
That we a new freedom have won![16]

Clayman begins with a particularly grim depiction of the life of a factory child, using the metaphor of light. The child not seeing "the light" refers to the long hours during which they "slave" from morning to night. "The light" could also allude to an enlightenment by embracing revolutionary politics. This double meaning seems likely as Clayman then discusses the mortality of his factory child, pointing out that at the end of life it would be too late to become wise and support change through labor organizing: "how wise he would have been / To let the strike come in." Clayman's second verse juxtaposes with the misery of work and death that dominate the first, and here he urges his fellow comrades reading *Young Comrade* to "keep the struggle on," referring to a utopian post-revolution future where the factory child does not exist, freedom has been won, and people will be "happy and gay."

Young Comrade's child contributors possessed very different ideals of society and childhood to what they experienced. A natural question for them to ponder was of how to achieve change. That question was considered in eleven-year-old Jennie Tomaszuski's poem, "Always Ready!" that appeared in November 1924's issue:

Always Ready!
We are juniors ready to fight,
To fight the bosses with all our might;
They're big and fat but we'll make them thin,
We are "always ready" to begin.

Don't give up comrades, just fight,
We'll overcome them all right.
Don't think we're too small, we'll get them all,
For we're juniors bearing the Light.[17]

Tomaszuski refers to the greed of capitalist bosses through the imagery of fatness in the line "They're big and fat but we'll make them thin." She suggests revolutionary change in the second verse when urging comrades to "fight," telling them, "We'll overcome them all right," and providing the assurance, "we'll get them all." The image of forcing the fat to become thin works in multiple ways, and it is ultimately impossible to determine which way(s) the young poet intended. Her poem conveys the idea of a distribution of wealth, stripping away the greed and excess of American capitalism to force the "fat" bosses to become "thin," but it is also possible to interpret this in a more physical bodily sense of forced weight loss through starvation, a type of torturous violence that is not out of the question due to the poem's revolutionary message and the wider rhetoric of the periodical it was submitted to. Tomaszuski's chosen title "Always Ready!" and repetition of the phrase showed her to have been party to the YPA's community-specific language and culture. Lifted directly from the rules, the phrase became a signifier of YPA membership and commitment to the cause, also cropping up in various speeches given by YPA children. Tomaszuski did not have a position of influence of some of these higher profile speechmakers so instead attempted to rally her peers by poetic submission to *Young Comrade*.

Tomaszuski's poem was one of many submissions by children which sought to address, and sometimes glorify, a violent revolution through their poetry. Twelve-year-old Harold Kirschner's "We Are the Young Communists" discussed the blood and violence of a revolution, arguing them to be collateral damage which Kirchner felt was fully justified:

We Are the Young Communists.
We are the Young Communists;
The world we will own.
And when the capitalists hear our name
They quake in every bone.

And we will march to victory
With our banner over our head—
The banner belongs to the worker,
The banner of purest red.

And this banner symbolizes
The blood of our workers bold:
The blood they shed for freedom,
The blood that will never grow cold.

And this blood will not only flow,
In the bodies of those who died,
Not only in those whose work is done
Not only in those who tried.

For we of this generation,
We'll give with all our might,
To do what is best for the workers,
Always to do what is right![18]

Kirschner's poem begins by expressing confidence that a global Communist revolution will occur, declaring, "The world we will own." That might be dismissed as childish naïvety, but this was an optimism that he shared with many adults. Kirschner was not naïve enough to believe that a Communist revolution could occur without significant violence and casualties on both sides. Red dominates the poem, referring both to the Communists' banner of "purest red" but also blood of "workers bold." Kirschner's acceptance of the bodily cost of a Communist revolution shows that he viewed it as a price worth paying, indicating the strength of his faith in Communism. In the process, his poem glorifies dying for the cause, defining doing so as a martyrdom.

The children's poems considered here exemplify the YPA's strong periodical culture of dialogue where children could express themselves and engage with like-minded Communist youth. Through poetry, creative literary expression was combined with politics. *Young Comrade*'s poetic juvenilia are not necessarily testimonial but have intrinsic literary and historical value. As a collection, they provide insight into what children did, such as reading about Clara Bryant Ford's rose garden, but also insight into their thoughts and opinions. Numerous children framed their Communism as being in defense of children and childhood, expressing their criticisms of the *status quo* in the process. Their idea of what childhood should be was incompatible with the material realities, such as child labor and food insecurity, that working-class children faced in 1920s America. Within the huge international ideological debate between Communism and capitalism these young poets had come to their decision and used their poems to engage in an ideological discussion. The poems provide great historical insight into children's motivation in joining the YPA and what some ultimately hoped would happen: a Communist revolution that would end food insecurity, unequal wealth distribution, and allow children to experience childhoods characterized by play rather than employment.

Protest at the Post Office

When the US Post Office denied *Young Pioneer* second-class mail privileges in 1931, the dedicated readers of Communist children were far from happy, and those in New York were intent on making their dissatisfaction known. On January 31, 1931, YPA members congregated on 33rd Street in between Manhattan's Seventh and Eighth Avenues to mount a protest. A group estimated to number between 200 and 250 children aged between twelve and seventeen marched together toward the General Post Office

Building near Pennsylvania Station and Madison Square Garden. As they approached the imposing Corinthian colonnade exterior of New York's main post office, they were met by a waiting formation of mounted NYPD officers. This did not deter them. According to the *Times Union* the main instigator of trouble was "a small bespectacled boy" who "broke through police lines and with vivid profanity directed at the police told children to rush the post office." In waves the children took several charges at the police line resulting in a "melee." Patrolman John Groves was injured after been thrown from his horse after the Pioneers had begun "throwing missiles" and "stoned" the animal. After breaking through the police line Pioneers entered and occupied the post office, forcing its closure. When NYPD reinforcements arrived, it took them two hours to remove the children. The story of Communist children breaking through a formation of mounted police to storm and occupy New York's postal headquarters was reported as far west as Long Beach, California, and as far south as Miami.[19]

This incident was one of several run-ins between the YPA and the NYPD and demonstrates Pioneers' abilities to cause significant localized disruption in the city. At its core, this was a protest against a perceived broader censorship of Communist ideas and publications by the US government, but it was also specific to *Young Pioneer*. The YPA's periodical was one that some of the readers were quite willing to go into battle for, even putting themselves in front of mounted police and in harm's way to stand up for it. The post office ban was not the end of the YPA's periodical project, and American Communists launched *New Pioneer* in a glossier magazine format. That publication outlived the YPA itself, becoming the youth organ of the International Workers Order (IWO) and continuing through to 1939. These various reincarnations of the YPA's periodical represent one of the most voluminous historical sources of information about the YPA, but they have not been utilized to their full potential thus far. Content was of course written from a Communist point of view. This offers a useful antidote to the explicitly anti-Communist perspectives dominating mainstream newspapers and expressed by the YPA's opponents.

Chapter 10

The Van Etten Camp Controversy

The YPA Camp at Van Etten

DURING THE SUMMER of 1930 a Young Pioneers of America (YPA) and Workers International Relief (WIR) summer camp at Van Etten in rural Chemung County, New York, became a focus of anti-Communist hostility. Despite being around 220 miles away from Manhattan, most of the children who attended the camp had arrived by bus from New York City, Westchester County, and New Jersey, as well as Syracuse to the north. There they met up with some local children who were part of a local radical Finnish American community. Some children also attended from northern Pennsylvania because the second district's camp was more easily accessible than their own district's encampment near Philadelphia.

The camp was run by Ailene Holmes and Mabel Husa, who both lived in New York City and were in their early twenties. From the outset the establishment of a Communist summer camp in Van Etten was an unwelcome development, and the local *Elmira Star-Gazette* reflected the anger and suspicions of locals. It told its readers that of the hundred or so children on the site the majority were either Finnish or of Finnish descent, and all of them were atheists. This was incorrect. Only two children had been born outside the United States, and nobody had asked them about their spiritual inclinations. This was an encampment of American citizens, but locals were informed that it was an encampment of anti-Christian, anti-American foreigners. This journalism capitalized on existing anti-immigrant and anti-atheist sentiments. The *Star-Gazette* pushed unfounded rumors about the camp, including falsely alleging that it was the source of a chicken pox outbreak. Disease or accusations of disease very easily foster animosity to a group of others within any community. Even as the *Star-Gazette* reported that public health complaints had been lodged with the relevant authorities, it gave the game away. The paper suggested that the "presence of a Red propaganda camp in Chemung County" had proved deeply unpopular but that no "excuse" had yet been found to compel its closure. It expressed a hope that "disease may provide legal grounds to disperse the gathering."[1] Local health authorities investigated the chicken pox rumor, and upon their finding it to be entirely baseless the camp continued to operate.

At this point hostile members of the public opted to take matters into their own hands and displayed little regard for the safety of the children they professed they wished to "save" from the evils of Communism. Quite how local some of these people were remains a matter of debate with several examples of people traveling across state lines with the purpose of disrupting the camp. On July 6 shots were fired at the camp by persons unknown traveling in a passing automobile. A further attempt to intimidate the camp was made by a local chapter of the KKK, which conducted a cross-burning opposite the camp on the other side of the road. The Klan, of course, believed in the power of summer camps too and operated them for child members of their youth clubs including the JKKK and other so-called Ku Klux Kiddies. Given their ideology, they likely held many grievances with the camp and its campers, including political, racial, and religious ones. The cross-burning was followed by daytime disruption and protest carried by members of two other organizations, the Patriotic Order of America (POA) and the American Legion. A group of people affiliated with both arrived at the camp and attempted to give Ailene Holmes and Mabel Husa an American flag. The people involved knew that their so-called gift would not be accepted and were planning to make some kind of fuss or protest based on this refusal. Holmes and Husa indeed refused the gift of the flag, citing the fact that no law mandated they had to fly one, and promptly asked their uninvited visitors to leave the camp property. The POA and American Legion retreated beyond the camp's gate, where they raised their flag on an eight-foot pole.

The camp already had a flag or banner of its own, which had been made by the children. It was red with an embroidered hammer and sickle, also featuring its name and the YPA's slogan, "WIR Camp Van Etten, Always Ready." The children in attendance at the camp were keen to show their disapproval of their flag-bearing visitors. Camper Jack McKela responded by taking the camp's banner and scaling a nearby telegraph pole. There was a tit-for-tat raising of flags as both McKela and the "patriots" tried to ensure their flag flew the higher. McKela's fellow campers were not shy about showing their displeasure, and they allegedly booed, hissed, and spat in the direction of their visitors and their American flag. After this was reported to police the camp's directors, Holmes and Husa, were arrested and charged with the offense of desecrating the American flag. Victoria Kroons, a POA member, later testified in court that the children had thrown rocks, jeered, and chanted antagonistic songs in her direction, including shouting "To Hell with the American government" and "Down with the American flag." Kroons seems to have taken particular offense to children sticking their tongues out, remarking, "I saw more yards of tongue than ever before."[2]

The flag-based standoff and Holmes's and Husa's arrest was not the end of the camp's drama. Despite the arrests, the camp continued to operate with additional staff from the Young Communist League (YCL) being sent to look after the children. Children from New York City or Syracuse could not simply go home at a moment's notice. Holmes and Husa successfully argued for their trial at the Chemung County Court to be delayed owing to a need to have legal representation, which was being arranged by the ILD (International Labor Defense) in New York City. Local authorities were keen to avoid accusations of a rushed or unfair trial. so they supported the adjournment application. When news of the trial's delay became public it provoked further anger. That evening an angry mob formed at the camp. The mob consisted of locals and people from further afield, many of whom were members of either the KKK, POA, or the American Legion. Both the *Standard Union* and the *Evening News* blamed the formation of the mob on the ILD for delaying the trial rather than the actual mob themselves. The Communists at the camp appear to have been expecting visitors as the campers had made several banners bearing slogans such as "Down with Racial Discrimination," "Down with Imperial Wars," and "Demand the Release of Harry Eisman" (more on that last slogan later).[3] Groups of American Legion and KKK members tore down the camp's red banner, physically accosted children who attempted to stand between them and it, and burned a second fiery cross by the gate. Children were left "huddled together" and "terrified" after twenty-five men, all of whom wore the white of the Klan, stormed the camp's office and threatened YCL camp counselors, saying they had thirty minutes to evacuate all the children before they torched the building.[4]

A significant law enforcement response combined with local farmers and members of the Finnish American community protected the children from more serious harm. Estimates of the size of the mob varied in local newspaper accounts, ranging from five hundred to as high as two thousand. The hubbub around the camp grew due to the proximity of two local meetings. A chapter of the KKK was meeting nearby and joined the mob while members of the local Finnish American cooperative lined up to defend the camp. Several local farmers, pitchforks in hand, helped separate the mob from the young campers. The *Syracuse Herald* praised local sheriff Harry J. Tifft, his six local deputies, and ten state highway patrolmen who with revolvers drawn forced the mob back. The mob's leaders refused to disperse and reiterated their desire to burn the camp before the children left on the next Saturday. The standoff lasted well into the night before numbers began to dwindle. When it was over, Holmes and Husa still faced their trial. Local authorities did not pursue any action against members of the mob. A decade after the supposed end of the Red Scare it would seem that threats to kill, threats of arson, and physically assaulting children were accepted in Chemung County if the victims were Communists. A bus hired from the Colonial Bus Company transported children back to New York City and Syracuse. The children were intent on having the last word and the bus was adorned with red banners, and the Pioneers sang "The International" out of the windows when it passed the town hall on their way out of town. Two children, Jack McKela and Walter Warwick were required to stay behind and appear as witnesses at Holmes's and Husa's trial.[5]

The Trial of Ailene Holmes and Mabel Husa

When Ailene Holmes and Mabel Husa arrived for their trial, a witness described them to journalists as "two pleasant young ladies, barely past the high school age with blonde bobbed hair and the healthy tan of a Summer in the open." This un-named witness appears to have possessed a good sense of humor. Making a quip about the sensationalist press coverage of the camp, they added that the pair "didn't have any horns on their heads nor any bombs secreted on their person, even if they are Ailene Holmes and Mabel Husa." When a reporter asked Holmes why she did not appear more upset at the prospect of going to jail, she replied, "Well, we aren't exactly pleased about it, but we know it can't be helped. We know they will railroad us anyhow, every chance they get." Regarding potential insults to the flag, she told the same reporter that if there had been any it had been committed by "the American Legion and the Ku Klux Klan," who had used the flag "as a screen for their unlawful acts."[6]

The prosecution relied on witness testimony from Andrew Dennis, Daisy Felt, and three members of the Kroons family, Victoria and her adult sons George and Sam. Despite all having traveled to the camp from Athens, Pennsylvania, the three families denied any prior association to one another, claiming all to have known independently that the American Legion planned to present a flag at the camp. The flaw in that story is that the decision to present the flag was something Dennis had taken upon himself and was never officially sanctioned by any organization. This raises the obvious question of what else they were willing to be dishonest about while under oath. As well as Holmes and Husa, the defense called the camp's neighbor Mrs. Wendella and the two campers, Warwick and McKela. Both boys had attended the camp for six weeks, and although their ages were not mentioned in proceedings, they appear to have been in their early teens. Warwick hailed from Port Chester, Westchester County, and had been listed on the local high school's honor roll, published in the *Daily Item* a few months prior. McKela's age was given as fifteen the following February after he was arrested over a dispute with another youth over a snow sled and a stack of newspapers. A photograph of the duo alongside two other campers was published by Wilmington, Delaware's *Morning Post* during its coverage of the trial.[7]

On the stand Warwick and McKela both denied booing, hissing, or throwing rocks at the American flag. Warwick stated that the "booing was at the opponents of our camp." Mrs. Wendella supported this version of events and characterized the conversation she had witnessed between Daisy Felt and the defendants as "very polite." Jack McKela admitted that he had scaled the telegraph pole with the camp's banner but testified that he had done it due to violence perpetrated by Victoria Kroons and Daisy Felt. McKela stated that the campers had been moving as a group to their athletic field for afternoon games when the women cornered another younger boy who had originally been carrying the banner and began "shaking" him. McKela then took possession of the banner and claimed he scaled the pole to protect it and himself. The pole was over fifty feet away from where the "patriots" had raised their flag, so he did not agree that his climbing the pole amounted to deliberately raising a hammer and sickle above the American flag. McKela's allegations of violence by the American Legion is certainly in line with that organization at the time. In fact, it made public statements calling for violence against YPA children across the country. For example, after YPA students at Roosevelt High School in Los Angeles held a demonstration against the increasing cost of mandated school supplies, the American Legion passed a resolution advocating the use of "physical force" to combat striking school children. For their part, the YPA considered the American Legion to be a "real bosses' organization" to which capitalists delegated their "real dirty work."

The trial had been hyped by the *Star-Gazette*, leading to an overcrowded courtroom and many people being denied entry and left to stand outside. Proceedings consisted of a series of remarkably petty allegations, most of which pertained to the behavior of the children rather than the actual defendants, Holmes and Husa. The flimsy nature of the charges was best seen in Daisy Felt's testimony in which she twice implicated young Walter Warwick in leading chants hostile to the American flag and government. Warwick was not on trial. Felt belatedly attempted to implicate the defendants by saying that they must have taught and encouraged him to do it. Holmes and Husa suspected that the trial was fixed and that they were to be "railroaded" irrespective of the unconvincing prosecution witnesses. The actions of the presiding justice of the peace, William Westbrook, did little to alleviate concerns about the validity of the trial. At the closing of arguments Westbrook took no time to deliberate whatsoever and immediately pronounced both of the accused guilty. He sentenced the pair on the spot to $50 fines apiece and to three months imprisonment at the Monroe County penitentiary. He jailed Holmes and Husa even though the prosecuting counsel had said in his closing statement that he did not wish to see them jailed.[8]

Westbrook's justification for his speedily delivered sentence did not pertain to the facts of the case at all but instead referenced the local community dynamics. He stated that he felt a jail sentence was necessary because since the camp had opened there had been "strife in the village." He admitted to jailing Holmes and Husa because local people who did not like them demanded it. Westbrook claimed that he had a duty to "protect" the local citizenry. Of course, neither Westbrook nor any other local official felt it necessary to expand this duty of protection to the children at the camp who had been assaulted by a violent mob. Those young American citizens were not entitled to justice. Protection from the law and the court was on offer only to the "right" type of white, anti-Communist citizen and certainly not a Communist child who had been faced down by the KKK.

Although the majority of the local press refused to condemn the actions of the mob who stormed the camp, some people did raise objections. Even though it had previously raised concerns that the camp was being used to "train youths to fight capitalism," the Ogdensburg, New York, *Republican Journal* was less than impressed. It adjudged the patriotism on display to have been "the poorest sort" which "the country would most definitely be better without." It argued that this behavior going unpunished set a dangerous precedent. Regardless of politics, it considered the camp to have been a "peacefully operating ... private business" on private land. This "mob" had no "exceptional virtues" or "right" to dictate to any private enterprise, it argued. It worried that allowing this sort of behavior against Communists could mean that private businesses may be subjected to intimidation. It concluded that "no medals for bravery need be awarded for the mobbing of two women and a group of children."[9]

Newspapers based further afield and away from the intense local atmosphere that surrounded the camp offered much harsher criticism, even condemnation. The *Emporia Weekly Gazette* of Kansas concluded that "the mob has no brains." It added that any person with a "thimble full of brains" would have recognized that "forming a mob and storming a camp where a few Communist children are spending the summer" would do very little to "convert" the Communist youths present or other young Communists further afield. Rather than attack Communism, the paper was concerned that all the mob achieved was strengthening the convictions of young Reds. "If they should be frightened or hurt by the violence of the raging beast that is man when he forms a mob, the Communist doctrine of these children might be encouraged." The *Weekly Gazette* concluded that far from being patriots or good citizens, "the mob which charged the children in the New York camp was doing the devil's own work," justifying this by referring to the KKK's presence: "they burned the fiery cross."[10] Opposition to the YPA was split as to the best tactics. Some, like the *Republican Journal*, the *Emporia Weekly Gazette*, or judge Franklin Hoyt, hoped its children could be converted. More extreme anti-Communists who belonged to the American Legion and the KKK, and certain NYPD officers felt they had to be crushed with force.

Ailene Holmes and Mabel Husa appealed against the judgment and sentence passed by William Westbrook thanks to assistance from the ILD and the American Civil Liberties Union (ACLU). Both were ultimately upheld on appeal by County Judge Bertram L. Newman. As part of its work to aid Holmes's and Husa's appeals, the ACLU obtained further witness testimonies via affidavits of the "riotous mob" that had targeted the camp. Through this the ACLU claimed to have identified two of the leading Klansmen who participated from Athens, Pennsylvania, and Waverly, New York, respectively. The ACLU and ILD passed this evidence on to police, but neither of the two men was questioned or arrested. Police refused to investigate the allegations of assault by the pair on children at the camp even after being handed a dossier of evidence.[11] Violence by adults against YPA children was thus supported at an institutional level by law enforcement in New York. Consider the summary offered by the *Poughkeepsie Eagle-News*: "70 children cowered in terror" as their camp was "stormed by a mob, many of whom were Klansmen" who had "burned a fiery cross" prior to their violent trespass.[12] The only people prosecuted were two of the victims. The events in Chemung County, the role of the press, the actions of law enforcement, the conduct of Holmes's and Husa's trial, all add up to create a picture of a Red Scare state in New York during the summer of 1930. There was a profound fear of Communism and its impacts on society, which had been exacerbated by hyperbolic and downright false local newspaper stories. These fears were acted upon with violence targeting children, and there was never any indication of repercussions for those involved in that obvious criminality simply because the child victims were Communists.

Other Camp Controversies

The mob's attack on the YPA camp at Van Etten in New York was one of a series of actions taken against YPA summer camps during 1930 and 1931, following the beginning of Hamilton Fish's congressional inquiries. Together these present an intriguing picture of a widespread scare specific to Communist summer camps. Each incident was different, but there were common themes. The same 1930 summer as the Chemung County case also saw a raid on a YPA summer camp near Pontiac, Michigan. An undersheriff and deputies raided the camp, arrested six of the adults present, and confiscated Communistic literature. As the raid took place, the camp's complement of seventy children "followed officers" in a group, shouted at them, and sang "Communist songs."[13]

In 1929 five YCL camp leaders had been arrested on flag-based charges, similar to those against Holmes and Husa, but were ultimately acquitted in Yucaipa, California. That camp's director Yetta Stromberg, a University of California graduate, and four teenage women had been convicted after flying a Red Flag at their YPA summer camp on private land near San Bernardino. Similar to the way that the YPA camp in Elmira was purposefully targeted by the American Legion and POA, the Yucaipa camp had been the focus of attentions from the Better America Foundation (BAF), a group that aimed to clear the Golden State of what it deemed dangerous unpatriotic dissent. The BAF had surveilled the camp and urged the local sheriff to investigate. Stromberg was originally sentenced to six months to ten years imprisonment at the notorious San Quentin state prison. Appeals within California were unsuccessful, but in *Stromberg v. California* (1931) the US Supreme Court ruled 7–2 that California's 1919 law was an unconstitutional repression of symbolic speech. Even political opponents of Stromberg contended that she should have the right to criticize the government and to express that sentiment by flying a flag.[14] The fact that California had used a 1919 Red Scare law to attempt to repress YPA summer camping in 1929 inextricably links the repression of the YPA to Red Scare sentiments.[15]

The BAF was founded in Los Angeles in May 1920 by a group of businessmen including the railway developer Eli Clark and Harry Haldeman. It performed anti-Communist surveillance, lobbied law enforcement and the state Assembly, and attempted to influence local school board elections and curriculum decisions. Arguably, the tactics employed by the BAF have been replicated by so-called MAGA Republicans in the 2020s. BAF opposed any type of constitutional amendment, compulsory secondary education, trade unions, and any regulation of private business. Among its claimed successes were having *The Nation* and *The New Republic* banned from California schools.[16] BAF's continued existence and influence during the 1920s demonstrates a continued state of nervous hypervigilance against Communism, radicalism, and in this particular case anything to the left of a strict textualist reading of the Constitution and completely unregulated capitalism. Given the extremity of some of its own positions, BAF is the type of organization that could only hold sway during a Red Scare period.

In 1932 a remarkably similar series of events to those that had transpired in Van Etten occurred at a YPA summer camp in Conneaut, Ohio, where twenty-year-old camp director Irene Dixon was arrested and accused of violating Ohio's criminal syndicalism law. The local sheriff, C. H. Blanche, admitted to not having a search warrant but had proceeded owing to his desire to "rid the county of the camp." Blanche was accompanied by four of his deputies and fifteen other men who were members of the American Legion. In this case, rather than simply refuse to prosecute camp trespassers, the local law enforcement had joined in. The camp hosted around sixty children who were all wearing red bandannas or neckerchiefs when lawmen and Legionnaires arrived. Not all of the children were local, with some attending from cities including Cleveland, Boston, and New York City. The "star exhibits" picked up during the raid of the camp were a series of pamphlets. One was about the Paris Commune, another opposed lynching, another opposed child labor, and one encouraged YPA membership by selling the organization as one for "workers' children," which was committed to fighting improvements to their lives.[17]

Sheriff Blanche admitted that he did not know if there was a law that explicitly forbade Communism but stated he did know of the criminal syndicalism law. Dixon's lawyer, Yetta Land, described the sheriff's actions as an "outrage" and a "disgrace to the community" in that his warrantless raid targeted "the children of the unemployed" who were there hoping to "enjoy a vacation." Carl Rautio, the president of the Finnish Workers' Educational Association which owned the land where the camp took place, filed an injunction, which was subsequently denied, to prevent the sheriff from "interfering" with their land. Rautio stated, "I thought people were allowed to meet on private land," adding that it "seems the officers don't understand democracy." Rather than not understanding what was and what was not permitted, it appears that various local authorities in this case colluded in order to allow each other to act outside of the law. The probation officer Howard Warner threatened Rautio: "If you re-open the camp, we'll put the children in the Detention Home." The law was of no concern to Warner as he threatened to summarily detain without cause or essentially kidnap a large number of children. He stated, "I don't know if there's a law against what they're preaching, but we'll arrest them anyhow." His justification was that "most of us here date back to the Revolution and won't stand for that type of talk." Blanche and Warner felt emboldened to act as they pleased as they enjoyed the support of Ashtabula County Prosecutor Howard Nazor, who told the *Dayton Herald* that he was happy to join in what he called "the sheriff's fight against Communists," expressing a hope that they could "drive the Reds out of Ashtabula County." Acting within the law was of secondary importance to these officials compared to their desire to combat Communism. Dixon and Land accused Blanche of enabling a violent attack by the American Legion, which they said had "clubbed" some of the children, leaving them "bruised by swishes." They further alleged that deputies had "menaced" youngsters by pointing a "machine gun" in their direction.[18]

The machine gun allegation was denied, but Blanche admitted using tear gas during the raid. This tactic had been decided upon in advance as Blanche said he wished to "check the resistance" of the campers.[19] Although the Ohio press reported Dixon's arrest, her indictment by a jury, and her bail being set at a monstrous $3,000, they never reported an outcome of the case. There is no evidence of a trial date being set, never mind the case actually coming to trial, although Dixon did take advantage of her arrest, giving speeches at various Communist events. It is possible that local officials' public boasting about their being so committed to "drive" out the Reds that they had no heed to the law or protocols could have cost them a conviction they could likely have otherwise achieved.

It is very easy to see why the YPA's adoption of popular American activities and trusted tools of youth development caused unease among their opponents. That being said, the reaction to some YPA recreational activities can only be described as extreme. In the late 1920s and early 1930s YPA summer camps on private land faced significant threats of violence from organizations of adults, including the KKK, POA, and the American Legion. The mobbing and storming of YPA summer camps was supported by local newspapers and law enforcement in two notable disturbances, one in Chemung County, New York, and another in Ohio. The only prosecutions arising from those events were of camp directors on somewhat spurious charges relating to alleged insults to the American flag by proxy of children sticking their tongues out. Law enforcement who conducted warrantless raids and deployed tear gas on children in the process faced no consequences for their actions. Nor did members of the public who threatened arson, burned crosses as part of KKK intimidation tactics, or who assaulted children, leaving them with painful bruises.

The reactions of some local officials to what were relatively small gatherings of children were at times unhinged, with some being much more focused on eradicating "the Reds" than what the law permitted them to do. Matters such as search warrants and needing a legal reason to threaten children with the detention home mattered not in localities which hosted rabid, extrajudicial, and occasionally violent, crusades to rid areas of Communists. The extremity of these approaches is best demonstrated by the fact that some opponents of Communism derided them and questioned the quality of patriotism on display. A fear, and a very legitimate one given events, was that by going so far, the anti-Communists would cede the moral high ground to the Communists. These voices of dissent on the anti-Communist side demonstrate both disagreement but also a shared view that the YPA and Communism were a capable threat which necessitated well-planned, tactically astute opposition. The furor surrounding the YPA's summer camps demonstrates that in New York State and beyond a significant fear of and opposition to Communism, so severe that violence toward children went unpunished, demonstrated continuity of elements of a Red Scare through the 1920s and into the 1930s.

These concerted attacks on YPA summer camps by law enforcement, local officials, and members of various so-called patriotic organizations did not deter the YPA from holding summer camps. In New York they made the wise decision not to return to Van Etten but continued holding camps at other campgrounds. Two boys wrote to the *Daily Worker* in July 1934 to tell of their experiences at Camp Wo-Chi-Cha in Dutchess County, New York. Eleven-year-old Harold Young described camp as "our little soviet." Young wrote that he enjoyed the free period where he could talk in his tent with fellow campers and read copies of the *Daily Worker*, which were provided every day. Similar to Helen Weiss's recollection of the camp "Kremlin," Young described how the dining hall had been christened "Lenin Hall" and the main thoroughfare was named "Marx Road." Speaking of the harsh realities of working-class young lives during the Great Depression, Young added that one of the best parts of summer camp was receiving the "warm supper" that was served every evening. A campmate of Young's, Louis Javitz, who gave his age as eleven and a half, also mentioned supper in his letter as well as how much he enjoyed using the sports field. Javitz wrote that his YPA summer camp experience had made him pledge to fight even harder for playgrounds, free clothing, and free milk for workers' children, having experienced the benefits of all three firsthand during his time in Wingdale.[20]

Chapter 11

Bashing the Boy Scouts and the Campaigns to Free Harry Eisman

Bashing the Boy Scouts

THE YOUNG PIONEERS of America (YPA) and its members were suspicious of potential schemes to promote militarism or imperialism in any child-targeted popular culture. They felt that capitalists wanted to glorify war to working-class children to ensure they would willingly participate in future conflicts. Children wrote to *Young Comrade* to warn others about "militaristic" books that they should avoid and tell their friends to steer clear of. In 1923 ten-year-old Martin Miroff expressed his disapproval of Arthur Winfield's *Rover Boys* book series. Miroff derided the books as "lying and untruthful" and believed that their true purpose was to teach young readers to "be soldiers and cannon fodder for the bosses." He urged, "Tell your friends about these rotten books." Similarly, ten-year-old Edward Shatz wrote to the periodical to complain about motion pictures. Though he considered the movies to be a "great American institution," he believed that many encouraged boys to go to war even though "the horrors of war are indescribable." Shatz thought that the film industry was being used by "American capitalists to spread propaganda and patriotism." He felt that too many movies made heroes out of "Wall Street fat bellies" and featured "a president" plus "Old Glory waving proudly overhead."[1]

Young Pioneers were alive to any youth organizations that promoted similar ideals to these frowned-upon books and films. Any military-linked youth or cadet groups and any groups perceived as being imperialist in nature like the Boy Scouts were the enemies of the YPA. Again, evidence of this opposition and suspicion is abundant in children's correspondence with the YPA's periodicals. The April 1928 issue of *Young Comrade* included two letters from young New Yorkers who expressed concerns about rival youth organizations. The first letter complained that the Guggenheim Foundation for Aviation, which in the view of the author wished to "crush the Soviet Union," had begun providing funding for "military training" in high schools. The second letter complained about a new group of US Junior Naval Guards, a cadet-style organization that was apparently being pushed to children at schools. Some children were apparently attracted by the stylish blue uniforms, but the Pioneers worried that it had been formed to foster "militarism and patriotism" in the minds of working-class children.[2]

To Pioneers such groups were not simply other children's organizations but were examples of the capitalist class attempting to indoctrinate, influence, and entice working-class children into being willing participants in future military conflicts or accept a position in life as a small cog in the capitalist money-making machine. New York Pioneer Thelma Kahn summarized this point of view in *Young Comrade*. Kahn complained that capitalism not only taught a boy how to shoot a rifle for his own interest but to "shoot down his own father and brothers when there is a strike."[3] Chief among these capitalist youth organizations was the Boy Scouts, which the YPA considered to be in the hands of the bosses. As Mischa Honeck describes, to child Communists the scouts represented the old world while the YPA represented the goodness and newness of Communism, which promised them a more self-determined and fulfilling childhood.[4]

During its existence the YPA became known for opposing the Boy Scouts of America (BSA) and seeking to protest and disrupt their activities. New York Pioneer Irving Shavelson demonstrated the strength of anti-Scout opinion in the YPA's ranks in his *Young Comrade* article by labeling them as "one of the greatest dangers to the working class." Shavelson believed that the Scouts were building "future strikebreakers" and were "one of the most effective weapons by which the capitalists turn children to their own purposes."[5]

According to the *New York Herald Tribune* this anti-Scout sentiment saw youthful Communists "falling upon the Scouts when the latter are alone, tearing their uniforms and committing other acts of violence." Likewise, the Fish Committee heard testimony that the YPA were not only encouraged to interfere with the Scouts but even practiced their "street fighting expertise" to prepare for attacking them.[6] The leadership of the

Boy Scouts was reluctant to engage with YPA and decided on a strategy of "paying little attention to the efforts of intimidation." The leaders acknowledged that the YPA was "firmly entrenched" in its opinion that the "Boy Scouts are a militaristic and capitalistic organization." They concluded that it would do little good for the Scouts to oppose or complain about the YPA, wary of giving them a "cheap martyrdom."[7] In that sense scouting leaders seemed more clued in on what the YPA wanted and their tactics than the NYPD or other city authorities who gifted them many a cheap martyrdom. That strategy of non-engagement did not completely deter the YPA from attempts to antagonize or disrupt the Scouts. The June 1929 issue of *Young Pioneer* called on readers to "smash the Boy Scouts," declaring them to be the "scouts of the US imperialist government."[8]

The YPA held a conference in New York City on June 23, 1929, chaired by Jessie Taft, who by this point had risen even higher up the Pioneer organization. The former District 2 leader was now the national organizer on the national Pioneer Bureau executive committee. The convention opened with typical festivities, including the recitation of the pledge to the Red Flag and singing "The International." The Soviet film *Breaking the Chains* was screened. Various grievances with the BSA were raised at the meeting, likely due to large groups of Scouts planning to depart from New York to travel to an international jamboree in Birkenhead, England, the next month. Several resolutions were passed to condemn the BSA not only as capitalist but also for its continued racial segregation. The main purpose of the convention was to select the YPA's delegates to attend the planned first International Children's Congress in Moscow. Three New Yorkers were chosen. These were Harry Eisman, "an orphan"; Jessie Taft, "a daughter of needle workers"; and Herbert Halpern, "a shoe worker's son." Also selected were Delia Morelli, a fourteen-year-old miner's daughter of Pittsburgh; Marion Semchyschen, a twelve-year-old auto worker's son from Detroit; and Shelley Strickland, a twelve-year-old African American former Boy Scout whose father worked as a miller in Philadelphia. The delegation was to be joined by the smaller Canadian Pioneer organization's chosen representative, Albert Soren of Toronto, and escorted by the YCL's Joe Shiffman. In light of the recent high-profile labor struggles in Gastonia, North Carolina, one place was given to the local YPA group there, which was represented at the conference by the eleven-year-old textile worker Binny Green. The Gastonia Pioneers ultimately selected another eleven-year-old, Elmer McDonald, whose father was one of the sixteen striking workers who had been arrested on a murder charge during the struggle.[9]

After the anti-Scout article in *Young Pioneer* and the anti-Scout resolutions passed at the YPA conference in June a good number of New York Pioneers turned out to show their disapproval of the Boy Scouts when they arrived in the city in July 1929. One of these demonstrators was the now fifteen-year-old Harry Eisman, fresh from his May Day arrest and the probation he had received following the disturbance at the dressmakers' strike. Newspaper and witness accounts vary as to what exactly happened next. But Mischa Honeck rightly summarizes that the YPA's "send-off" targeting the Scouts quickly descended into a "fully-fledged brawl."[10] The YPA's protest began with a march down West Street before they arrived at Pier 14 on the North River where they demonstrated and sang "The Solidarity." What began as verbal demonstrations turned violent as the parents of the departing 239 Scouts who were mostly on board their ship by this point took offense at the YPA's presence. The first police on the scene requested backup, and the disorder on the docks was severe enough to delay the departure of the ship, Cunard Line's 20,000 gross ton *RMS Samaria*.[11] The YPA did not target another departing ship also carrying Boy Scouts. Pioneers appear to have been aware that it carried a troop of Native American scouts, a demographic that the YPA routinely made dispensation for when planning its activities, as it considered Native Americans to be victims of the imperialism which it opposed.

The *Tarrytown Daily News* lambasted the actions of the "Cack-brained Communists" for "booing and hissing" at parents who were on the pier to wish their children *bon voyage*. The *Brooklyn Daily Eagle* reported that the YPA shouted protest slogans, including, "The bosses are sending the Boy Scouts to War" and "Fight the Boy Scouts." In these press reports the PAPD officers who were first on the scene were said to have been "reluctant" to use their clubs on "mere boys and girls," who "kicked, scratched, and clawed" at officers attempting to disperse them from the quayside. The YPA wholeheartedly disputed this characterization of the police response, alleging several instances of police brutality. The *Daily Worker* reported that "police seized Eva Resnikoff, a Pioneer, and began to choke her" and that "Charles Cohn, another Pioneer" was "so badly . . . manhandled by police that he was sent to a doctor for treatment." Order was eventually restored after the arrival of mounted NYPD officers. Several Pioneers were arrested, including Harry Eisman, who faced a charge of disorderly conduct. Some newspapers alleged that Eisman had been apprehended after attacking a police horse via "branding," "striking," "kicking," or "hitting" the animal with "a slab of concrete." Others alleged his crime was committed against a human rather than an equine member of the NYPD. One account accused him of biting an officer while attempting to take possession of his nightstick. Either way this resulted in Eisman's fifth appearance at the Manhattan Children's Court in the space of twelve months. There he was adjudged a delinquent and sentenced to six months at a reformatory.[12]

Some newspapers called for foreign-born Eisman's deportation, but that idea seemed to be dead on arrival due to his protective legal status as a dependent alien. The YPA claimed that Eisman had been arrested "simply because he dared to demonstrate" but undermined that line somewhat when coverage of the incident in *Young Pioneer* was headlined "Pioneers Fight Boy Scouts." Eisman won praise in the *Daily Worker* where he was described as an inspiration not only to other juniors but to Communist adults too. Using Leo Granoff–style tactics, Eisman ensured that his court appearance was dramatic. The *Daily Worker* considered him to be "most militant and courageous" in standing up to the magistrate who "threatened him" by telling him that he had better "learn how to behave" in the reformatory, otherwise he would face more severe consequences. Eisman scoffed, raised a clenched fist, and defiantly exclaimed, "I stand always ready!"[13]

The First Free Harry Campaign and the Moscow Children's Conference

Eisman had obviously been expecting a custodial sentence, as the day he was sentenced to six months at the Hawthorne Institute, the reformatory school for Jews, a letter by him to his supporters was published in the *Daily Worker*. Eisman instructed YPA children not to worry about him and assured them that his spirit remained "at its highest." In addition, he promised that as soon as he was released, he would "lose no time" in rejoining the ranks of the Pioneers. Eisman was determined that his punishment would not dampen his revolutionary spirit and insisted that it had only made him more determined than ever before to "fight for working class children," for the "improvement of their conditions" and to "defend the Soviet Union," "fight against the Boy Scouts," and stop "the bosses' wars."[14]

That Eisman had been sent to the reformatory was not a bad thing for the YPA. It was a prime opportunity for them to make a martyr for their movement, doing the exact thing the leadership of the Scouts had been keen to avoid. Like Leo Granoff six years earlier, Eisman became a *cause célèbre*. This was enhanced by the profile Eisman already enjoyed as a dedicated, popular member of the movement. He was already widely respected within his own circles for his work "in the school struggle" and frequent participation in labor demonstrations. The YPA launched a "Free Harry" campaign, which no doubt was partly motivated by concern for him but also sought to capitalize on the opportunity his plight presented to rally the wider movement. Eisman and the ILD (International Labor Defense) legal team pursued an appeal at the state Supreme Court's Appellate division, but this effort was stymied by procedural delays. He was granted leave to appeal, but with arguments set for a December date only a matter of weeks before his scheduled release, pursuing the appeal and associated costs made little sense.[15]

The first Free Harry campaign took a similar format to appeals that had been made on behalf of Rose Plotkin when she was being held at the Society for the Prevention of Cruelty to Children (SPCC) and the campaign in support of John Potter, a Young Communist League (YCL) member who had been jailed due to his role in the New Bedford textiles strike. *Young Pioneer* readers were encouraged to "inundate" Hawthorne's superintendent Mr. Klein with letters and to otherwise put up a "strong protest" to "get Harry out of this Hell hole." Authorities wanted to ensure that Eisman was unable to continue to influence the YPA while inside Hawthorne and restricted his mail access. Eisman saw this as an opportunity, embarking on a hunger strike, and Klein backed down after less than forty-eight hours.[16]

Due to the activities of the YPA and the significant newspaper coverage of his case, Eisman was a high-profile inmate whom it was impossible to let starve. Reformatory school conditions in New York were also facing scrutiny from certain Progressives. They were under pressure to appear to the public as institutions that served the best interests of the young people sent there by meeting a dual obligation of punishing them and seeking to rehabilitate and educate them. This does not mean that conditions were good or that abuses did not happen. They certainly did. But with an inmate like Eisman youth authorities had to be mindful of perceptions and had little choice but to submit to his hunger strike. Eisman took advantage of several factors, including a celebrity-like status in the YPA and a degree of public name recognition, which combined in his favor. He got access to his post in exchange for a weekend's worth of meals. Eisman seemed to derive a certain amount of pleasure from the way he achieved his goals inside Hawthorne, writing boastfully in his 1933 youth-targeted booklet *An American Boy in the Soviet Union* of how he "carried on Red propaganda" even on the inside. He was a known nuisance to the guards, insisting that he was a "political prisoner" and that he be treated accordingly.[17]

Ultimately, this six-month stint at Hawthorne achieved very little for all concerned, or at least it appeared to have achieved little. It was not long enough for a Free Harry campaign to build significant momentum. There were some protests in Harlem, particularly around Lexington Avenue, the site of Leo Granoff's 1923 arrest, which had been something of a YPA stronghold ever since. Twenty-six were detained by police at one protest there made up of YCL members and twelve YPA members. The Pioneers in question ultimately had their charges of "disturbing the public peace" dismissed by the magistrate, though he did warn them to "act like children" going forward and commented that in his view "children should not take part in politics."[18] By this point nobody could have expected Pioneers to suddenly subscribe to this notion of a meek apolitical childhood. As far as they were concerned, they were acting like children: angry, working-class children discontent with their lot. The main reason why there were no further disturbances was that the stakes appeared to be relatively low. Eisman's sentence would be a personal inconvenience to him, but it was also a hazard that he and other YPA members presumably willingly risked. He would be released within a matter of months. Being sent to Hawthorne did disrupt Eisman's planned attendance at the children's congress in Moscow. The delegates' travel had been organized by the Pioneer movement in the Soviet Union, which was, of course, an official Soviet state entity and the Communist Party USA (CPUSA). None of Eisman's or the YPA's limited resources were at risk. Yet his non-attendance at the children's congress transpired to be very significant indeed.

The YPA delegation departed from New York for Moscow on July 25, 1929, with the congress scheduled to take place August 23–24. Some members of the YPA attempted to hold a parade to mark their departure, but the police were ready and waiting after the incident at the Boy Scouts' sailing. The delegation sailed on the *RMS Mauretania*, which departed without issue. The passenger manifest also included the banker J. P. Morgan, who was traveling to Scotland for his annual grouse-hunting trip and was of course the owner of the Wall Street building Rose Plotkin had vandalized. Rather than replace Eisman in their delegation, the YPA sailed for the Soviet Union one light, a conscious decision that they planned to make the most of.

The Soviet press fairly frequently reported on the activities of Pioneers abroad, especially those in Germany and the United States. Readers of youth-targeted publications would already have been familiar with the YPA to an extent, and by time of the First International Children's Congress *Pionerskaya pravda* had already highlighted Harry Eisman's plight.[19] The

Figure 3. Members of the Young Pioneers of America as they appeared on the RMS Mauretania when they sailed for Russia in July 1929. They were scheduled to attend the conference of the central organization in Moscow, Russia. (Bettman Archive/Getty Images)

YPA's delegation were able to take advantage of attendees' prior knowledge in order to promote Eisman's and their own causes.

Events at the congress were described in detail within correspondence by Sir Ronald Lindsey, the British Ambassador to the United States. Lindsey had become interested in the YPA and Harry Eisman, as he believed Eisman was playing a role in circulating to American Jews what he considered "anti-British propaganda." Several influential Soviet politicians attended the congress including the keynote speaker, education minister and Lenin's widow Nadezhda Krupskaya. She was joined by other notable guests, including the writer Maxim Gorky, the Hungarian Communist revolutionary Béla Kun, and the prominent German Communist Max Hoelz. Speaking in front of this type of audience and the young representatives of Communist children's organizations from around the world was a major honor for the American Pioneers. Thanks to their actions, Harry Eisman's missing out on this opportunity wound up raising his profile much more than attending ever would have. Shelley Strickland, the Black former Boy

Scout from Philadelphia, and Taft made a dramatic "show" of Eisman's empty chair in the convention hall. They presented him as an abused oppressed Communist child who had been imprisoned by American capitalists. Instead of being one of many delegates at the congress, Eisman was transformed into a symbolic cause among the Communist youth movement. His plight as presented by Taft and Strickland apparently struck a chord with Gorky and Krupskaya in particular, his case naturally aligning with some of their interests and work focusing on the development of Soviet children's literature.[20] The children present were enamored too and elected Harry Eisman as the honorary president of the International Children's Congress.

After the YPA delegation's return from Moscow they were met with a significant amount of suspicion. Gastonia's Elmer McDonald received a threat to "lynch" him. When a journalist asked him if he was afraid, he responded with a defiant, "Hell, no! I ain't never been afraid of them."[21] Shelley Strickland made the point of contrasting the diverse attendance of the international Pioneers' gathering in Moscow with the Scout gathering near Liverpool where he said there had been "not one Negro boy" among the 1,500 Scouts. American newspapers were convinced that these children were being "used extensively" by the Soviet government who had funded their travel to "spread Communist propaganda." Their actions on their return did little to alleviate these concerns. The delegation stopped off in London on their way home to address a Communist gathering at Tower Hill. Once back on American soil the delegates embarked on significant speaking programs, traveling around to local Pioneer troops to speak about their time in the Soviet Union.

An account of one of these events featuring Jessie Taft, Herbert Halpern, Sammy Sussman, and Ruth Yonkelson appeared in the *Journal of Education* and was subsequently considered as evidence by the Fish Committee. The original author seems to have focused on commenting on Taft, and particularly her mannerisms and body, twice describing her as "chubby":

> Wearing the Red bandannas of the Young Pioneers of America, 125 children in knee trousers and short dresses cheered at the Labor Temple yesterday when their leaders told them to spread the gospel of Soviet Russia in the city's public schools. The principal speakers of the occasion were Herbert Halpern, 14 years old, and Jessie Taft, a chubby miss of 14, who is a pupil in the Walton High School, in

Figure 4. A delegation of Young Pioneers of America who had been attending the first international all union pioneer rally in Moscow and were now in London for a visit to address a mass meeting of communists on Tower Hill, London, before returning to the United States. England, August 1929. (Photo by The Montifraulo Collection/Getty Images)

the Bronx. Jessie's parents, despite her name, which is a recent acquisition of the family, were born in Russia, and she and Halpern reported to their associates in the Soviet's equivalent to the Boy Scouts and Girl Scouts of their recent trip to Russia as guests of the Soviet Union. . . . Jessie was a favorite of the children. She was more emotional in her denunciation of American democracy and her praise of the proletariat dictatorship of Russia than Halpern, Sammy Sussman, or Ruth Yonkelson. . . . "Get up in your classrooms, comrades, and expose the Kellogg pact and carry to the Children [what] you have heard here," exclaimed Jessie, who is left-handed and swung a chubby left fist like Lew Tendler in his prime. . . . [She] pushed back a wisp of dark hazel hair which persisted in concealing her right eye. "And remember, comrades, we children of to-day will be the leaders of the revolutionary movement of a few years hence, when we will make this country another Russia."[22]

After the delegation's return Harry Eisman was released and put on probation at a court hearing on January 29, 1930. The children's court imposed stringent conditions on him which were designed to restrict his ability to re-involve himself with the YPA. This included prohibiting him from taking part in any "political activities." If placed on an adult, these conditions would likely have been seen as unconstitutional restrictions on the rights of speech and assembly, but Eisman was a minor who appeared at juvenile court. It was not until the 1960s when the Supreme Court ruled that children were entitled to the same constitutional protections regarding due process as adults. The major issue with these conditions in 1930 was that Harry Eisman had no intention whatsoever of paying them any notice at all.

When Eisman descended the steps of the children's court in Manhattan, he was met by a crowd of jubilant supporters. His release was notable enough that it was covered by various out-of-state newspapers including the *Baltimore Sun* and Pennsylvania's *Reading Times*. These papers told how the "infant branch" of the Communist Party staged a celebratory "riot" to mark the release of their favorite "martyr." The crowd of around two hundred children, whom journalists estimated to have an average age of twelve, cheered, holding aloft various placards. Some were dedicated to Harry, some denounced child labor, and one or two "vulgar" ones were aimed at Police Commissioner Grover Whalen. One group hoisted Eisman aloft and carried him on their shoulders "like a football player" as they marched down Fourth Avenue to Communist headquarters in Union Square. Once there, Eisman stepped up to the plate and delivered a characteristically incendiary speech from an open window to children in the square below. He whipped them up into a frenzy by discussing his own case and the death of Steve Katovis. Katovis had been an active member of the Building Maintenance Workers' Union and the CPUSA. He was shot in the back and killed by NYPD patrolman Harry Kiritz at a protest meeting called to express solidarity with the Food Clerks' Union, which had been striking against Miller's Market in the Bronx. A grand jury ultimately cleared the officer, but this meant nothing to Communists who were of the view that Katovis had been murdered in cold blood.[23]

Two passing NYPD patrolmen were attracted to the raucous hubbub on the street and moved in to disperse what they categorized as an unpermitted gathering. This did not go down well with the YPA. Pioneers "bared their fingernails and clamored upon the policemen," refusing to disperse, and a riot call went out. It took an additional thirty-eight officers to bring the situation back under control. The press saw a funny side in this situation, unlike other instances of YPA-NYPD disorder; the press mocked the police for their struggles to contain children "weighing between 50 and 100 pounds," some of whom were even "chewing lollipops" as they aimed a kick or a slap. The press may have capitalized on these events as a chance to increase the pressure on Police Commissioner Whalen, whose position at the top of the NYPD was coming under scrutiny. Journalists eschewed their usual hyperbolic descriptions of the dangers posed by the YPA to describe them as candy-eating children. One eleven-year-old girl attracted particular attention after expressing great pride in herself for having "given 'em hell," as she proudly brandished a police officer's button as her "souvenir" of the day. Two NYPD officers were injured in the scuffles, and while chaos reigned on the square below, Harry Eisman sensibly disappeared away from the window, out of sight.[24]

Eisman did not manage to stay out of trouble for very long. The Communist International declared March 6, 1930, as International Unemployment Day, which followed another Communist protest at New York's City Hall on Saturday, March 1. At that first protest five hundred women and child demonstrators arrived at City Hall to protest Mayor Jimmy Walker's refusal to accommodate Communist protests and to demand unemployment support for women and children. A committee of six YPA children, six CPUSA women, and representatives from numerous trade unions attempted to submit their petition but were rushed by around 100 NYPD officers, some on horseback. The police admitted that two boys suffered "minor injuries," suggesting they "fell down" as officers "shooed" them away. Though it attempted to dismiss the incident as a "fracas," the *Brooklyn Daily Eagle* admitted that some youngsters had faced the "full force of a wedge of policemen." The *Daily Worker* accused them of "mercilessly clubbing down the young children" of the Pioneers. Perry Blumkins, thirteen, was "attacked by three police," and despite several other children attempting to defend him, Blumkins was "badly beaten" and rushed to St. Mark's Hospital for treatment. Frank Pogano, fifteen years old and mocked by the press for being "without a hat or haircut," was held down by two officers; he accused a third of attempting to gouge his eye out. Two YPA girls, Fay Caller, sixteen, and Rosella Scheck, fourteen, were arrested and charged with "disorderly conduct."[25]

On March 6 Communists around the world held demonstrations to protest the economic hardships of the Great Depression. These were mostly peaceful in London and Sydney, but more violent protests took place in cities including Bilbao, Berlin, and Vienna. In the United States thirty cities from the East Coast to the West Coast hosted protest marches, with large-scale disorder reported in Detroit and New York City after police had used batons to attack protesters. According to Harvey Klehr, the turnout in New York vastly exceeded CPUSA expectations. The trouble at City Hall a few days earlier likely helped boost attendance because New York Communists were incensed by the police's tactics against young demonstrators a few days prior. Communists claimed that 110,000 had turned out while the *New York Times* insisted the crowd was "only" 35,000 strong. When the crowd assembled in Union Square to hear from the event's organizer, Sam Darcy, Police Commissioner Whalen, and Communist leader William Z. Foster were holding hasty negotiations. Whalen refused to allow a march to City Hall as no parade permit had been granted. When Foster took to the rostrum, he asked the gathered crowd if they were willing to take that for an answer. The consensus, as Foster had likely banked on, was that they were not.[26]

Foster began leading a march toward City Hall, and the NYPD responded. Over a thousand officers were dispatched into the heart of the demonstration. The police were undeniably the aggressors. The *New York Times* described how officers rushed forward "swinging nightsticks, blackjacks, and bare fists." A period of bitter street fighting followed. The *Times* added that the "screams of women and the cries of men" came from the "battle scene" as people emerged with "bloody heads and faces." The *Times* did not admit that children were there too and subjected to this violence. But we know some were there. The YPA was not inclined to miss such a big day. Firemen were also dispatched to the scene and used their hoses on the crowd. NYPD reinforcements arrived with tear gas, some brandishing machine guns. Foster and fellow party leaders Israel Amter and Robert Minor were arrested on the steps of City Hall and eventually sentenced to six months in jail apiece for their role in orchestrating and participating in the protest. To American Communists all of this stunk to high heaven. As detailed in *The Militant*'s editorial, they alleged that the riot had been "precipitated by the police." The conduct of the trial did little to alleviate suspicions of a plan to ensnare leading Communists. The trio were convicted in a special session by a panel of three judges rather than by a jury of their peers. Communists derided this as a "premeditated sham," complaining that they were not allowed to present footage in their defense which showed police officers initiating the violence. *The Militant* alleged that "bosses and their government agents were bent on railroading the workers to prison" and stated that capitalist repression of workers had become particularly "virulent" in New York.[27]

The Second Free Harry Campaign

Foster, Minor, and Amter were not the only Communists jailed after the March 1930 unemployment demonstration. They did not receive the longest sentences, either. Harry Eisman was also arrested and the consequences for the high-profile Pioneer were much more severe than those faced by the adult party grandees. Eisman's mere presence at the event violated the terms of his release. For breaching the court order, he was sentenced to five-and-a-half years in juvenile custody. Eisman was scheduled to be released on his twenty-first birthday, the day he would lose the protective status of being a "dependent alien" and become eligible for deportation.[28] Eisman's previous brief spell at the reformatory had caused a certain amount of commotion, so it was no surprise that after this lengthy sentence was handed down that the YPA relaunched their Free Harry campaign with vigor. New York's Communist children rallied around the cause of a popular orphan who had attained a celebrity status and cult-like following of his own within the YPA. This time the stakes were higher. *Young Pioneer* readers were told that "Harry was arrested for his political opinions" and this showed that the bosses were attempting to "smash" the Pioneers. An attack on Harry was an attack on all of them, such was his status. Eisman had proven that he was always ready to fight for the cause of the working class, and it was now the turn of readers to do likewise for him: "YOU MUST FIGHT FOR HIS FREEDOM. Organize demonstrations, protest meetings! FIGHT FOR THE FREEDOM OF HARRY EISMAN!"[29]

Eisman's eldest brother, Alexander, continued to provide support, as he had done with his younger brother's previous school disciplinary hearings. However, another brother, Herbert, was clearly less impressed. Harry wrote to him, "The last time I saw Alex in court, on March 20, he told me that you and Jack were sore at me for breaking my probation. I don't blame you in the least." Even among family there was a perception that the youngest Eisman brother's inability to stay out of trouble was a problem of his own making. He went on to explain that his trial had been fundamentally unfair. Given his and the YPA's history of turning the courtroom into a performance stage, authorities may have not wanted to give him an opportunity to repeat previous outbursts. "Neither Alex, my lawyer, nor I were permitted to say anything. The trial lasted seven and a half minutes."[30] It is evident that the outcome was predetermined. Juvenile proceedings at the time were not bound by due process, hence the judge's ability to deny Eisman the chance to give any evidence in his defense.

Eisman's return to the reformatory had the potential to be a catalyst for further YPA action. The logic of the approach authorities took to dealing with Eisman was questioned by those who actually knew him. When assistant school superintendent Aaron Dotey testified before the Fish Committee, he disputed Carl Bachman's attempts to characterize Eisman as an unintelligent delinquent, stating, "On the contrary, he is a very bright boy." The committee's eventual dissenter, John Nelson, questioned why Eisman was being jailed. If the United States was going to start jailing vociferous Communists, why start with a schoolboy, he queried. Nelson asked Dotey if he felt the reformatory would be any good for Eisman, and he responded in the negative, quoting a conversation he'd had with the boy. "No. He said, 'Don't they realize when they send me to jail that they will make me a more ardent fighter?'"[31]

An early success for the YPA's relaunched Free Harry campaign came with their securing support from larger, sympathetic adult organizations and periodicals. George Clarke, who would go on to serve on the Socialist Workers' Party national committee, urged readers of *The Militant* to support Eisman. Clarke argued that his case was not an individual matter of a boy's liberty but instead one of huge symbolic importance to the wider American Left. Clarke cited this "ridiculous farce" as part of a wider worrying pattern of the persecution of working-class youths who sought to be active on the Left, pointing to the ongoing school and college disciplinary cases concerning Max Weiss and Saul Wellman.[32] The *Daily Worker* called on "all workers and workers' organizations to pass resolutions against the savage sentence of Harry Eisman." Judge Young was castigated as a "capitalist lacky" after he had expressed "regret that the law did not permit" him to initiate deportation proceedings against Eisman. Communists further alleged that Eisman was being mistreated and persecuted at Hawthorne. Eisman had smuggled in forbidden reading materials on topics such as "historical materialism" and after being caught was subject to punishment. One of these punishments was known as being made to "stand on the line," where the child was made to stand to attention with their arms raised for up to three hours.[33] This was a standard reformatory punishment, not a tactic solely employed against Eisman, but nevertheless in retrospect it is child abuse, plain and simple.

A protest march was advertised in the *Daily Worker* for March 22, 1930. A crowd, described as "mostly children led by a handful of elders," was estimated to number up to 500. The protesters met on East 110th Street, Manhattan. They marched as a group toward the Heckscher Foundation for Children on Fifth Avenue. They "tied up traffic," and their signs included ones reading "Down with Whalen's Cossacks," "Prepare for May Day Celebrations," and "Defend Harry Eisman." The police were ready for the demonstration and a battalion of fifty NYPD officers were secreted in a nearby basement. When the "singing Communists straggled into view," the police rushed from their hiding spot toward the YPA. Some fled immediately, bolting across the street and leapfrogging the railings into Central Park. Others attempted to stand their ground. The *Times* of Shreveport, Louisiana, reported that "rioting sprawled across the neighborhood," and the police "swung their fists freely," as the operation to disperse the youngsters descended into chaos. A score of people were "beaten and bruised" when the police attempted to hem protesters in small clusters against the walls of buildings and the park railings. The "chief troublemakers wormed their way to freedom," slipping "like eels" from police clutches. Five men and a woman, YCL stewards at the protest, were arrested. They refused to pay $50 fines and ultimately each served ten days in jail. Thirteen-year-old Pioneer Perry Blumkins, who had been injured by police at a previous protest, was arrested for punching patrolman Richard Collins in the face. Collins testified that the boy had given him a "powerful wallop" that had left him in pain for four days. In typical YPA fashion Blumkins told the court that Collins was making "a fuss over a sore beak" and that he was a "political prisoner." Magistrate Samuel Levey was unimpressed and sentenced Blumkins to six months' probation for juvenile delinquency.[34]

Discontent at Harry Eisman's treatment spread beyond New York. The YPA in Chicago staged a protest at the Board of Education building. When the police arrived, they found almost three hundred youths wearing red neckerchiefs staging a sit-in. Four boys and twelve girls were arrested as they resisted removal.[35] When the national conference of the children of the unemployed met in Chicago during the summer, their two slogans were "Free food and clothing for the children and the unemployed" and "Campaign for the immediate and unconditional release of Harry Eisman." *Young Pioneer* published children's letters from local YPA groups expressing support for Eisman and calling for his release. Pioneer troops across the country soon adopted the ACLU's description of Eisman, describing him as "America's youngest political prisoner."[36] The ILD's Washington, DC, branch adopted a resolution demanding Eisman's release. Andrew Overgaard, the national secretary of the Metal Workers Union, wrote to Mayor Jimmy Walker to complain about city authorities' relentless pursuit of Eisman, also demanding his release. The Ukrainian Working Women's Association in New York raised $25 to contribute to Eisman's legal costs and condemned his incarceration as a "threat against all working-class children who celebrate May Day."[37]

Immigration officials investigated the possibility of deporting Eisman as a minor irrespective of his status as a bonded immigrant, holding him to be an exceptional case. One significant barrier to this was Eisman's place of birth in December 1913 in Chişinău. That was disputed territory at the time between Romania and Tsarist Russia. Eisman claimed Russian nationality and by extension a right to Soviet citizenship. Immigration officials preferred to consider him Romanian. The possibility of Eisman being sent to Romania helped invigorate his supporters in their campaign. The YPA's campaign changed from being one to free America's youngest political prisoner to one to save his life. Although Romania's 1923 constitution prohibited the death penalty during peacetime, the 1924 Mârzescu Law banned Communism and made Communist agitation punishable by death. The *Daily Worker* reported that if sent to Romania, Eisman would be subjected to "white terror" and almost certainly be jailed or murdered.[38]

Officials who wished to see Eisman deported ran into several obstacles. The first of these was a writ of *habeas corpus* filed by the ILD, which also called for a judge to rule on Eisman's nationality. In the end this was much ado about nothing. The children's court was more than annoyed by maneuvers to circumnavigate the protections afforded to juvenile dependents. Officials eventually accepted that Eisman had a right to claim Soviet nationality, halting deportation proceedings as the United States did not have diplomatic relations with the USSR.[39] As good as this news was for Eisman, it did look like he would be stuck at the Hawthorne Institute until he was twenty-one.

This is where the YPA's Russian relations and Eisman's profile as the honorary president of the children's congress would come into play. Up until this point the YPA had made clear their disapproval of Eisman's treatment with several disruptive protests in several American cities. Although ensuring that Eisman was not deported to Romania was certainly some kind of win, it did not appear that they would get what they asked for—a free Harry. Pioneer youth groups around the world were informed that Eisman had once again been locked up by authorities in New York. At one point it looked as though the next children's congress in Berlin would be a very poorly attended affair. The YPA and numerous other international Communist youth groups, including the influential Leningrad Pioneers, symbolically nominated Harry Eisman as their delegate. The Leningrad

Pioneers wrote to Eisman, telling him, "Harry, we elected you as our representative from Leningrad district to the next international flock together." They promised, "We will demand that you are let out."[40]

Although the Pioneer movement in the Soviet Union certainly could exert grassroots pressure, they were not able to dictate to the regime. Any conduct deemed too dissenting by officials would have led to a crackdown on those involved. This pressure was likely carried out with the blessing of party officials. Eisman's case was recognized as an easy opportunity to please the youth groups and to annoy American authorities. Eisman's nationality status gave Soviet officials legitimate ammunition to intercede. Despite the lack of formally open diplomatic channels between the two countries Soviet officials made an offer for the Soviet Pioneers to "host" Eisman. This was agreed to on the condition that Eisman could not return to the United States for at least two years. Although the YPA's propagandistic claim that Eisman's treatment prompted protests around the globe was perhaps hyperbolic, the Pioneer movement across Europe and North America did attempt to take up his cause. His triumphant journey to the Soviet Union came about after what Catriona Kelly describes as a "campaign at the international level."[41]

Eisman in the Soviet Union

American Communists young and old celebrated Eisman's release to the Soviet Union. He set sail from New York on November 17, 1930. During a week of freedom prior to his departure he maintained a packed schedule. As part of this victory tour he attended events and gave speeches in New York, New Jersey, and Pennsylvania before a final farewell party at the Manhattan Labor Lyceum. There Eisman spoke to a crowd of around 2,500. Jessie Taft, who by this point had been expelled from her school, also spoke. William Z. Foster and Israel Amter, also March 6 arrestees, gave speeches as well. Given the party atmosphere at some of these events, press observers and anti-Communists were far from happy, questioning why the Communists were being allowed to send their "prize bad-boy" for a "post-graduate course in Revolution." The *Orlando Evening Star* argued that Eisman's veneration by the YPA showed that Communists had a "low standard of heroism," remarking that he had a "good batting average at annoyance" and excelled in the art of "making himself disagreeable," adding "one of his most daring adventures was kicking a policeman's horse." The *Brooklyn Daily Eagle* had enjoyed a strangely mutually beneficial relationship with Eisman and told its readers that "there is something steely about this young Red," alluding to his "keen brown eyes," "faintly flushed cheeks," and "olive-skinned" complexion. He had generated a good deal of stories for the paper over the years and was willing to speak to journalists, while their sensationalized coverage of his antics boosted his profile and that of the YPA. Eisman spoke with a *Daily Eagle* journalist when he was packing his possessions in preparation to sail to the Soviet Union via Germany; he could not resist the temptation to give them a final incendiary quote. Eisman stated that his aim was to "overthrow the capitalist yoke," and although he hoped to do this peacefully, he quipped, "If not, dead men tell no tales." To coincide with his departure Eisman arranged for a letter to be printed in the *New Pioneer*, thanking all his supporters in the YPA who had advocated for his release (Appendix E).[42]

In *An American Boy in the Soviet Union* Eisman describes having been "wildly excited" as his ship steamed through the Gulf of Finland toward the Soviet Union. Through that booklet it is possible to understand in detail how Eisman spent the next few years, but this is an account brimming of bravado and is Eisman's own propaganda effort targeted at American youths from his new Soviet home. Soviet state security services boarded at Kronstadt on Kotlin Island to inspect passengers' papers. One spoke a smattering of English, German, and "Jewish," three languages Eisman was competent in, and held a conversation with the young traveler. This talk with "that first representative of Soviet power" was the topic of his first letter to his friends back in New York. The ship docked in the port of Leningrad where "Red Flags were fluttering in the cold December dusk." The telegram announcing Eisman's departure from Berlin had gone astray so no one was there to greet him. He had fourteen rubles in his pocket to try to get to Moscow. He approached a GPU guard, who pointed him in the direction of an Intourist representative, who arranged for a taxi to take him to Hotel Europe in the center of Leningrad. At the hotel he produced a letter he had received in New York from the editors of *Leninskaya Iskra* as provenance. The editors were surprised, as they were under the impression Eisman had not yet left Berlin but vouched for him and instructed that he be given a room and something to eat before they arrived at the hotel to meet him. Eisman felt "a little embarrassed" at receiving a luxurious hotel room and expensive food.[43]

Eisman's hotel was located opposite the Leningrad Philharmonic, which happened to be hosting a concert for 2,000 local Leningrad Young Pioneers that night. When Eisman's arrival was announced to the crowd, they "burst into cheers" and with the help of a translator Eisman answered questions for over an hour. He spent four more days in Leningrad, visiting plants and factories, including the famous Electrosila and Karl Marx plants. He wrote of the "energy and enthusiasm" of the workforce that he credited as the "driving force of Socialist construction," concluding that the "cheerful and healthy looking, simply but warmly clad" workers were "living proof" of the "slander" of the American capitalist press. The extent that his tour may have been carefully choreographed seems to have been lost on him. The night of his departure from Leningrad, December 12, 1930, he spoke at the Leningrad Children's House of Culture, which was full of children "eager to greet the Pioneer from America."

From Leningrad Eisman traveled to Moscow, a journey he described as "swell." When his train arrived at October Station, the platform was lined with Pioneers who displayed banners and played drums and bugles to welcome him. When he detrained, they "broke ranks" and ran toward him shouting their greetings. On the platform Eisman's "big German trunk" served as a makeshift speakers' stand for himself and a man he identified only as "Smirnov," then head of the International Children's Bureau of the Young Communist International. With Ivan Smirnov and Vladimir Smirnov already out of favor this appears to have been Lev Nikolaevich Smirnov, who was then a student at the Leningrad State University and who went on to be a prosecutor at the Tokyo Trial in 1946, and chair of the Soviet Supreme Court, 1972–1984. Eisman spoke, pledging not to forget the "heroic struggles of the American workers and the American Pioneers" and promising he would equip himself "for a place on the revolutionary battlefront." One thing Eisman noticed about the "young and eager" crowd that greeted him on the platform was their diversity. He described them to be of "many nationalities," including "Russian, Jewish, Eastern." He reflected in *An American Boy in the Soviet Union* on the contrast between that image and the Scottsboro case, Georgia chain-gangs, and American lynchings. He characterized the US as home to "White Chauvinism, anti-semitism," and "race prejudice."

Eisman's account fails to contend with any problems people faced in the Soviet Union, but his criticisms of race politics the United States were fundamentally correct observations. Some may accuse Eisman of political point scoring and using the Scottsboro case purely for his own ends, but this charge would be unfair in light of his and the YPA's reaction to the 1929 murder of Henry Clarke in New York. Even once in the Soviet Union, Eisman continued to try to encourage activists fighting against segregation and racism. Scottsboro was a useful talking point for Eisman in the Soviet Union, but his interest was sincere. He entered into correspondence with Ella Lucille Wright, a younger sister of two of the Scottsboro boys, Andy and Roy. He assured her "we will always answer you," commended her "militancy in your defense of your two brothers and the other boys," and expressed optimism for the campaign on the boys' behalf by concluding that "the Alabama Ku Kluxers will never dare roast our boys in the chair if we raise a mighty protest that will swing open their prison door."[44]

While Eisman was doing what he could from thousands of miles away to stay engaged with the YPA in New York, it managed to remain very active in his absence. On some days it staged multiple public demonstrations. For example, on November 3, 1934, the YPA started the day with a protest at the German Consulate at 17 Battery Place at 10:30 am. This anti-Nazi picket had been prompted by a desire to express anger at the imprisonment of Ernst Thälmann, a former leader of the German Communist Party. Ultimately, Thälmann was executed on Adolf Hitler's orders at the Buchenwald concentration camp in 1944. After picketing the German Consulate Pioneers descended on Harlem to meet up on Lenox Avenue at 2:30 pm where they held a parade in protest of the Scottsboro case, and as Eisman called it, American white chauvinism.[45] Alabama Governor Benjamin Miller received protest letters from local YPA troops. One of the thirty signatories of Chicago's Karl Marx YPA troop demanded the "immediate release of the Scottsboro Boys," declaring, "They are innocent." That letter was particularly striking, as inked over the main body was the outline of clenched fist bearing the bold letters "Y.P.A."[46]

In Moscow Harry Eisman lived at the First Pioneer Commune, a home for homeless children and orphans that had opened in 1926. With the "dread memory" of the Hawthorne reformatory still fresh in his mind he admitted that arriving at an institution "unnerved" him. Likely reflecting on his time at the SPCC in New York, he wrote that "under capitalism" a children's home was "always something of a jail." After getting over these reservations the home would grow on Eisman, who wrote fondly of the cook he nicknamed "Auntie Jean" and other young residents including an American boy named Dick, a Korean orphan named Sagi, and Mati Baechinski, the daughter of an imprisoned Polish Communist parliamentarian. It was there that Eisman learned his first words of Russian. "The children would sit me down and teach me. When I made a mistake, they would burst into gay laughter and correct me." Moscow's First Pioneer Commune was even visited by the Bengali Nobel Laureate Rabindranath Tagore, who remarked, "I shall always remember the delightful evening that I spent with these Pioneers." This anecdote of Eisman's correlates with a visit Tagore is known to have made to Moscow.[47]

Eisman also provided an update for *New Pioneer* from the children's commune where he detailed a visit from John Louis Engdahl, who was the secretary of the ILD, which had, of course, advocated for Eisman in many New York courtrooms. Although he hinted at challenging conditions when the commune first opened, Eisman described it as an exemplary place by his time there.[48] When Engdahl died in Moscow in late 1932, Eisman was chosen as one of the eulogists at his funeral, which has been described as an "imposing revolutionary mass," demonstrating the esteem Eisman was held in. The other eulogists included Sen Katayama, a co-founder of both the American and Japanese Communist Parties who had lived predominantly outside of Japan after being released from a sentence of imprisonment over his role in the 1912 Tokyo subway strike, future East German President Wilhelm Pieck, and leading French Communist André Marty. Eisman took his place among this lineup of internationalists as their equal and the "deported militant leader of the working youth of New York."[49]

As for Eisman's descriptions of the commune, he should be considered a willing propagandist by this point. Given his profile, it is safe to assume that care was taken to accommodate him in reasonable enough conditions. His account certainly does not reflect the reality faced by many Soviet children. The so-called *besprizornye*, a mass of homeless children, was one of the greatest social problems the Soviet Union faced, many of them forming gangs and engaging in theft to ensure their survival. Children in orphanages generally suffered from chronically poor conditions. Of course, American observers of this problem often refused to acknowledge the obvious comparison between the *besprizornye* and the estimated quarter of a million young Americans left "riding the rails" during the Great Depression. Eisman's account differs from other accounts of Soviet children's communes. In 1937 fifteen-year-old Vladimir Moroz was sent to one after his Jewish Bolshevist-party-member parents were arrested as enemies of the state. In letters to his older brother Moroz described the home as a "place of banishment" and accused staff of attempting to silence him. In his diary Moroz described new party leadership figures as corrupt hypocrites and lamented that the people he regarded as the best specialists had been arrested. Despite the fact that children under the age of sixteen were theoretically not allowed to face trial for political opposition, Moroz was arrested and sentenced to three years at a labor camp, which he was *en route* to when he died of tuberculosis.[50] Though Eisman's spell at the children's commune came years before the Great Purges that Moroz and his parents were victims of, it underlines how his account of the commune should be treated with caution.

After a time in Moscow Eisman was then taken on a tour of the Soviet

Union, and his first destination was Kharkiv, Ukraine, which included attending the Ukrainian Pioneers' eighth convention at the Opera House. Eisman reflected that the "real" Ukraine of the "great Dnieprostroi dam" was very different from the one he had read about in American newspapers, which had led him to "imagine every Ukrainian with a sword, or at any rate a whip in hand, dressed in black, with top boots and sporting a fierce moustache." After visiting the Voroshilov Jewish Children's home Eisman reflected emotionally on his own Jewishness and some of the horrors of history. Referring to the White Terror of the Russian Civil War (1917–1923), which had orphaned some of the residents he met there, he wrote, "There was an angry national hatred and antisemitism. To be known as a Jew at that period was to be strung upon a tree, to be shot and mutilated."[51]

The next stop was Horlivka, a coal-mining town, which was followed by Dnepropetrovsk, where Eisman visited schools, Pioneer groups, the Palace of Culture, and an artillery regiment, which gave him a Red Army uniform, which made him "very proud." By train he then traveled to the Soviet-Romanian border, which proved particularly emotional, especially seeing the heavily guarded frozen Dniester River:

> To me the plight of Bessarabia is a personal affliction. For Bessarabia was my birthplace. My parents are buried in the Kishinev Jewish cemetery. I have many relatives struggling for a living under the iron heel of Rumanian white terror. Yes, and as I stood on that border all my thoughts went back to my early childhood, to the vague picture that remained in my mind—the Kishinev pogroms and the marching of troops. That's all I could remember. I wanted to go back to Kishinev to find my relations. . . . But there was that soldier with the shining bayonet on the other side.[52]

The largest pogroms in Kishinev (modern-day Chişinău) took place in 1903 and 1906 before Eisman's birth in 1913, but his memories of antisemitic violence and the deaths of his parents seem an accurate appraisal of their times. It is evident that his earlier childhood experiences had a profound impact on his behavior in New York and the formation of his political views.

Eisman spent four more days near the border. In his writings he dismissed the atrocities he had heard of, recalling a Hawthorne guard showing him reports in the *Sun*, demonstrating how much he was invested in his Soviet Communist dream. He met with "President Voronovich of the

Autonomous Moldavian Soviet Republic," likely receiving a very one-sided appraisal of events from the man he termed "undoubtedly the most popular person in Moldavia." A tour of a Red Army base followed where Eisman spoke with the commanders and at the end of his visit was made an honorary member of the division and tossed three times into the air in celebratory fashion by the men. Next Eisman travelled to Odessa, the sight of the famous steps already familiar to him having watched the 1926 film *Battleship Potemkin* four times during his youth in New York. From there he traveled by steamer through the Black Sea and along the Crimean coast, stopping at Yalta, Novorossiysk, and Rostov before arriving at Stalingrad, a place where "old and new ways of life stood in sharp contrast." In Stalingrad he visited the English-language school for foreigners where old habits seemed to die hard and he became involved in an altercation with a teacher originally from Detroit, holding the teacher to be not critical enough of the United States.

While in Stalingrad Eisman fell ill. He blamed this on his life being "too much" for him following over a year and a half in the "strict jail regime" in New York. He spent almost two months at a sanatorium, where the daily regime included two hours of lessons and plenty of recreational activities, including skiing, skating, and watching movies. The robust diet there meant he "gained several pounds in weight" while he also continued to work on his Russian—a doctor gave him lessons. He recovered sufficiently to make the 1931 May Day celebrations in Leningrad where he spoke at the Philharmonic, centering his speech on racial discrimination in the United States and the Scottsboro case. There he met the writer, Maxim Gorky, with whom he discussed America, Scottsboro, and the importance of children's literature. Summer was spent at a Pioneer summer camp in Artek by the Black Sea.[53]

After nine months of traveling and resting it was "time to work" as Eisman put it, and he enrolled in a factory school in Moscow in September 1931. Now aged over seventeen he did not return to the Children's Commune where he had first stayed but instead moved into a Comsomol Commune on the outskirts of the city. Here he came in for criticism even in Pioneer circles, accused of being too much of an individualist and not fully embracing "true collectivism." His insistence that he *was* a special case and should be treated as such by the instructors as he tried to get out of mandatory Russian literature classes was a prime example. Being paraded around the land and celebrated everywhere he went for nine months can only have grown Eisman's ego and he admitted in *An American Boy in the*

Soviet Union that "the publicity I received as a kid had somewhat spoiled me and I took too much personal credit."⁵⁴

For a young man who had spent so much of his life perfecting the art of being as big a thorn as possible in the sides of school authorities, adapting to the factory school environment in his chosen country was not easy. He made friends with Boris "Bobska" Korobashkin and was very much more interested in the social side of life there than the work and study. He admitted that it was difficult for the institution to "function because of students like myself who fooled around." He remembered being sat "red as a tomato" after being scolded by the secretary, but it still took a formal disciplinary warning for him to knuckle down before graduating with his diploma in June 1933. Despite focusing on heavy industry during this education, Eisman ended up working as a journalist. Writing was a skill he had practiced since those childhood articles for *Young Comrade*, *Young Pioneer*, and the *Daily Worker*. It is probably fair to adjudge his strengths to have been as a wordsmith. His skills as an orator and writer certainly outweighed his appetite for manual labor. He worked as a Pioneer leader at a Moscow school in the early 1930s while employed as a journalist with the Comintern (Communist International). He authored a book, *Khausorn*, in Yiddish for middle-grade children about the United States in 1933, which included memoirs of the Hawthorne reformatory and generally criticized American capitalism.⁵⁵

The next year Eisman published *An American Boy in the Soviet Union*, a booklet that chronicled his first couple of years in the Soviet Union. It is undeniably a propagandistic effort to reach working-class American children; it was promoted and reviewed in the *Daily Worker*.⁵⁶ Eisman did not fade away entirely into his professional life and was remembered in the Pioneer movement; he helped run a local troop. The "Internationalist quiz" section of one Soviet youth magazine included in its puzzle section the question, "Who is Harry Eisman, and where does he live now?"⁵⁷

The Second World War saw Eisman join the Red Army on November 25, 1941. He served as a junior officer, roughly equivalent to a lieutenant, in various regiments, including the 973rd Rifle Regiment and the 620th Infantry. Some of his wartime experiences are described in a 1963 Russian magazine article that focuses on the "Battles of the Rivers Don and Volga"—Voronezh and Stalingrad. After a close call in a minefield more comfortable administrative service beckoned for Eisman as senior officers often required the service of "the one who knows all the languages." For his Red Army service, he received the medal for Military Merit in June 1944, and in April 1945 he was awarded the Order of the Red Star.⁵⁸

Despite those accolades things were not plain sailing for Eisman and his Russian wife, Faina, after the war. In the 1950s he was exiled to Siberia. Some sources even suggest he spent time in a Gulag, having fallen out with influential figures in the Stalin regime. In Mary Leder's memoir *My Life in Stalinist Russia*, this is attributed to Eisman's association with the American writer Anna Louise Strong, a Communist who while defending the Soviet Union from anti-Communists adopted an increasingly pro-Chinese position during the prelude to the Sino-Soviet split.[59] This did not shake Eisman's faith in Communism, though he did not return to Moscow until after Stalin's death. It was Marx and Lenin, not Stalin, who had been revered during his youth in the New York YPA. Although Eisman did not enjoy the same celebrity-like status that he did as a young rebel in New York or during his first year in the Soviet Union, he remained a known entity and kept up correspondence with William Z. Foster until Foster's death.

Eisman was not forgotten by American authorities either. Congressional reports into Communism, propaganda, and un-American activities authored during the height of McCarthyism conveniently forget that it was American authorities who had permitted Eisman to travel to the Soviet Union and describe him as a "fugitive from American justice."[60] The FBI continued to monitor Eisman to the mid-1960s using undercover agents who were part of its long-running Operation Solo. Those FBI records are flawed. They mistook basic information such as his age but recorded Eisman to be living happily with his wife and their daughter and again working as a journalist. That journalistic work also brought him to the attention of the CIA through the Foreign Broadcast Information Service. The daily report for November 15, 1962, detailed his stance on several issues. He often wrote of "two Americas," one which had advanced technology, had magnificent structures, and had given the world Thomas Edison and Abraham Lincoln. "But there is another America," he would always say before going on to talk about "children in despair," "a multimillion unemployed army," and a "system and discrimination" that condemned millions of African Americans to second-class citizenship. The cost of rent and medical care in "the richest capitalist country" condemned many of its ordinary working people to poverty, and Eisman argued this alone should be a "death sentence" for capitalism.[61]

Eisman was older, but his rhetoric had changed very little since his teenage years in the Bronx and still troubled American authorities. He published again, writing *Red Ties in the Country of the Dollar* in 1972. American authorities' attitudes softened toward Eisman to the extent that he was allowed to travel back to New York in 1974, meeting relatives, and visiting sites of his childhood, including what had been PS 61. He died in May 1979 in Moscow, and the *Daily World* published a memorial notice from his sisters. The Young Pioneers of the Soviet Union placed a memorial on his grave in Moscow, reading "Harry Eisman, Americansky Pioneer."[62]

CONCLUSION

THE HISTORY OF the Young Pioneers of America (YPA) is of greater importance to the wider history of the American Left than it has previously been given credit for. The alumni of the New York YPA constitute a strong case for that alone. Consider the three Pioneers arrested together on May Day 1929 in Manhattan: Jessie Taft, Saul Wellman, and Harry Eisman. The YPA was just the very start of their Communistic activities. Their stars shone brightly within the YPA, and they are examples of what Communists hoped the YPA could be, a kind of training ground for youths who would then graduate into prominence in the adult party. Eisman worked for the Comintern before joining the Red Army and was awarded the Order of the Red Star. Taft remained in New York and grew from organizing fellow YPA children to organizing working-class women in the laundry and garment industries. Wellman organized Long Island truckers before he fought against fascism twice, in the Spanish Civil War and in the Second World War. He went on to chair the Michigan Communist Party and helped lead the national party's activism in the auto industry. Others, like the novelist William Herrick, had quiet but dedicated YPA careers and emerged as notable figures on the Left in adulthood.

Characterizing the YPA as an organization is challenging because both the YPA and its opponents made it out to be much bigger and scarier than it actually was. In terms of its size in New York City the most reliable indications are the attendances at events during the late 1920s and early 1930s, which if estimates are to be believed seemed to have been capped at 1,200 children. In addition to overstating the YPA's size, anti-Communist opponents made all members out to be hardline atheist anti-Christians who hated anything American; opponents saw the YPA as part of a wider alien-led insurgency in the United States. These criticisms reveal more about the YPA's opponents. The YPA in some respects valued Americanness and attempted to make use of its appeal as part of its mission to be a group for the children of an American proletariat. It embraced quintessentially American activities like baseball, basketball, and summer camp as part of its offering to American youths, albeit radically repurposed to reflect its ideals, including staunch opposition to American racial politics and gender norms. Many Pioneers were either naturalized American citizens or born to immigrant parents in the United States—not American as far as their opponents were concerned but unequivocally American, nonetheless. Some were religious, and religion was accepted in the organization as long as the individual did not see it as clashing with Communism. This type of faith was the wrong kind of religion to their opponents but was religious. Historians need to refrain from repeating prior partisan judgments and generalizations of Pioneers' spiritual convictions.

The YPA developed its own organizational culture, language, and methods, which enabled Pioneers to feel like they were a part of a community. The phrase "Always Ready," for example, was lifted from the rules set out for Pioneers by adults and became a rallying call, a slogan, and a phrase that signified knowledge and participation within the community. It was deployed in various ways by children in their poetry, in public speeches, and even in defiance to punishment at the children's court. YPA children's tactics in New York at times baffled those outside the organization. These tactics included outlandish press-seeking behavior; predetermined explosive courtroom displays; and an acceptance of or even preference for punishment from school authorities, police, and the courts, which came from a desire to create mini martyrdoms for the movement. Such tactics can be traced back to Leo Granoff's Harlem arrest in November 1923 and remained evident through to the YPA's official end in 1934. A desire to create martyrdom-like causes around punished Pioneers meant a culture of celebrity or almost cult-like hero worship of some prominent YPA children was observed. Granoff was the first case, and Harry Eisman the most high-profile. Eisman, Granoff, Rose Plotkin, Jessie Taft, Morris Spector, and other YPA children showed impressive organizational or speechmaking abilities that positioned them to act as political actors in their own right. These were not children passively subjected to a Communist cultural environment by adults but young activists who sought to shape and challenge elements of American Communist discourse, often advocating for greater attention to be paid to children's issues.

There is no easy answer to the question as to quite how radical the YPA was. Much of the YPA's rhetoric was that of revolution, and it consistently advocated for a workers' and farmers' Communist government in a manner that made it easy for opponents to accuse them of sedition. At times YPA members were violent and disruptive, leaving their adult opponents with at the very least painful bruises. Examples include the storming of the main New York post office in January 1931, the May Day assault of school official John Esposito in Coney Island, and the skirmishes with police following Harry Eisman's first release from Hawthorne reformatory. Overzealous recruitment and urgings to strike from school turned into the bullying and intimidation of other children. Pioneers were implicated in rumored violent attacks on Boy Scouts, though actual accounts of this happening seem somewhere between rare and nonexistent. Overall, YPA members showed a great deal of tenacity on the streets of New York and proved themselves very capable of choreographing public disorder, including achieving the relatively significant feats of forcing the closure of a major post office and delaying an ocean liner's departure.

Radicalism is also contextual. Nearly a century after YPA campaigns against child labor, against corporal punishment, against racial segregation, and for playgrounds and affordable school meals, its demands may not seem particularly radical. But at the time these were bold demonstrations against the *status quo* that brought Pioneers punishment and condemnation. The fact that these stances were condemned as radical says rather a lot about the society that the YPA existed in. These causes show a distinct focus on incremental change and attention to the material conditions which affected the welfare of working-class children. The majority of the YPA's campaigns though energetic appear to have been unsuccessful, the exception being the campaign for Harry Eisman's liberty, and that campaign was ultimately swayed by the intervention of influential Soviets with whom YPA children had cultivated impressive networks.

The YPA's critics frequently indulged in two temptations. On one hand, the Pioneers were a golden opportunity to write of a sensationalized Communist threat to America, Americans, and Americanness. As the *Philadelphia Inquirer* wrote of New York's Morris Spector in 1925, these youths were often accused of issuing a "battle cry" or said to have been "mobilized in the fight of the Reds."[1] On the other hand, it often proved irresistible for detractors to seize an opportunity to mock the YPA for their youthfulness or accuse them of youthful naïvety and dysfunction. The *Chicago Tribune* dismissed the importance of one well-attended school strike by pointing out that "many of the strikers came on roller skates."[2] The implication was that these children were incapable of proper organizing and were something to be laughed at. Of course, a strike is still a strike even if strikers are wearing roller skates. A protest is still a protest even if protesters are, as Pioneers were observed in New York, chewing on lollipops. These things were the trimmings of youth but were not barriers to political thinking or participation. Striking schoolchildren risked consequences including corporal punishment and accepted that risk—this was more than a laugh or a chance to truant but a choice to demand changes for the collective at potential individual detriment. These two different lines of attack were inconsistent and failed to mesh well, and the YPA's opponents were caught in a middle ground where anti-Communists were never fully convinced that the Pioneers were a threat to the American way of life nor that they were so incapable that they need only be laughed at.

Pioneers believed it to be good to be a politically active child and to advocate for other working-class children. Their opponents contended that good children did not engage in politics but instead played in the park and held beliefs shaped by fantasies like a belief in Santa Claus rather than political doctrines. They made exceptions to this rule, of course, if a youth wished to challenge the YPA on the grounds of patriotism or the American flag. This embodied a type of hypocrisy the YPA observed in American capitalists, which is seen best in their discussions of free speech and American freedoms. Self-proclaimed free-speech advocates were often very keen to silence a Pioneer's Communist speech. The YPA believed that children should be able to challenge adults, including their own parents, and that it was their duty to do so in some instances. They railed against adult authority more widely, not just capitalist adult authority. The only thing that seems to have been agreed upon was that children should play, but the YPA was quick to point out that capitalists could not live up to this ideal despite their support of summer camping, due to the widespread use of child labor in a profit-driven economy.

The history of the YPA in New York is certainly eventful, and it is history that unfolded at a particularly noteworthy time. A dominant narrative in American history is that there were two distinct Red Scares, with one tightly confined to 1917–1920 and a second after the Second World War.[3] Yet the distinct American Communist children's organization rose to prominence and existed from 1923 to 1934. This narrative has evolved somewhat recently via discussions of miniature panics, or "little Red Scares."[4] But that characterization seems woefully inadequate in regard to the YPA in New York City and the surrounding area, never mind the wider radical community that the YPA was a part of. Some may contend that a Red Scare is a national or international event, but this argument ignores the significance of New York both politically and as a major population center.

The *Militant* argued in 1930 that there was a specific brand of American anti-Communism in the Empire State.[5] The children of the YPA were certainly not spared any scrutiny or attempted suppression owing to their age. New York Communists and the YPA believed they operated in a Red Scare environment, even making specific references to it after the arrest of Leo Granoff in late 1923. During the following years local politicians called for purges of suspected Communist children from public schools, and the city's Chamber of Commerce warned of a YPA-fueled "Red Menace" and demanded that a program of "Americanization" be implemented in immigrant communities.[6] All of this supported the YPA's perception that it was encountering a Red Scare environment.

The NYPD's frequent observation of and numerous physical altercations with the YPA, school authorities' hysteria surrounding and punishment of suspected YPA members, and commentary regarding the YPA in the mainstream press and from so-called patriotic organizations all support the notion of a Red Scare environment too. The fact that YPA children at a summer camp encountered drive-by shootings, KKK cross-burnings, and mob violence from the American Legion demonstrates that this Red Scare sentiment escalated beyond fear and at times led to orchestrated political violence targeting children. This occurred in an environment where perpetrators could be sure there would no consequences owing to law enforcement attitudes toward the YPA. The history of the YPA in New York City showcases historical children's capacity for political organizing and the politicization of children and childhood among both the American Left and Right. The actions taken against the YPA's existence between 1923 and 1934 show that the group operated within a fluctuating but ever-present Red Scare–type environment in New York.

In 1923 the founders of the YPA's forerunner, the Junior Section of the Young Workers League (JSYWL), put forward a new vision for Communist American childhoods, recasting the Communist child from being a student in a radical classroom to a foot soldier on the proletariat front line. Even within the American Left only a minority would even subscribe to the YPA's vision, primarily because it challenged the authority adults found very useful to hold over their children. In addition to holding up the Communist child as a political member of the movement the YPA vision also emphasized sports, play, and leisure as key rights of the childhood experience, disputing American capitalist child labor practices. The relatively small number of children who became part of the YPA in New York City and beyond in the 1920s and 1930s certainly found a radical community space. But with the exception of the Soviet-assisted campaign to free Harry Eisman, the YPA was relatively unsuccessful. Ultimately its history comes at a very important place in the history of American Communism and the history of the United States. It demonstrates that the idea of the 1920s as some return to an un-radical normalcy is a complete fallacy. Anti-Communist sentiment remained strong. Fear of Communism shaped public schools, laws, and society. The desire to defeat the Reds was so strong and such a well-regarded cause that just about anything done in its name was accepted, creating an environment where there were no consequences for adults orchestrating a violent attack on a children's summer camp. There was no interregnum between the two Red Scares.

ACKNOWLEDGMENTS

WRITING A BOOK can be a lonely and difficult endeavor which relies on the support and goodwill of countless people around you. I am sure that there are people to whom I owe considerable thanks that, due to unfortunate aberration, I forget to mention here. Like all historians, I am indebted to archivists and librarians, with particular thanks to the archival staff at Portland City Archives, New York University, and the University of Wisconsin.

I must acknowledge the editorial support and enthusiasm from the dedicated people at Fordham University Press and thank Fredric Nachbaur for believing in the project. Thanks also to Teresa Jesionowski. The sage advice and valuable feedback from the anonymous manuscript readers proved invaluable. One reader is now known to me as Paul Mishler. Paul published *Raising Reds* when I was three years old, and it has stood the test of time to be one of the most important pieces of scholarship for my work. Additionally, I am grateful to Vincent DiGirolamo and David Huyssen—two scholars whose work I look up to and who were generous with their time to discuss my work on youth, radicalism, and New York history.

Academically, I must acknowledge Ultan Gillen, my undergraduate advisor at Teesside University, who was instrumental in my early development as a scholar and encouraged me to pursue postgraduate studies. The history of the Young Pioneers in New York became an addictive and welcome distraction to my California-centered PhD thesis. My PhD supervisors at Northumbria University, Tony Badger and Joe Street, tolerated this with remarkable good grace and even active encouragement. The wider department including Patrick Andelic, Elsa Devienne, and Brian Ward were also hugely supportive during my time there and have remained so afterward.

In more recent times I have characteristically attempted to do several ambitious and difficult things simultaneously. Many people have helped me keep all the plates spinning. Thanks to Oliver Harness and Lindsey Tennant-Williams at Teesside University. Thanks to my teaching mentors Matthew Thompson and James Cowan. Thanks to my colleagues at the University of Roehampton, including but not limited to Andrew Wareham, Caroline Sharples, and Ian Kinane. I also thank my students at Roehampton, who took my "Student Activism and Making Change in America" module and who have engaged with my ideas both good and bad as we explored the history of youth activism together.

My family have managed to put up with my various ramblings about the history of New York Communism, summer camps, and youth activism. They have supported and encouraged me to pursue my goals. Thanks to Teresa, Christopher, Peter, Tracy, Ellissa, Joyce, and Anne. I must also remember Eileen, Ron, Geoff, Madge, and David, who each meant so much to me. Lastly, I need to thank Conor, my flatmate from my postgraduate days and Covid lockdowns, who may as well be family to me at this point. Conor is one of the many great people I met working at YMCA Camp Mason in New Jersey. I extend this thanks to the whole camp community.

APPENDICES

Appendix A: The Rules and Regulations of the Young Pioneers of America (1932)

1) A Pioneer is always faithful to the cause of the working class.
2) A Pioneer is a comrade of all Pioneers and all of the workers' and farmers' children the world over.
3) A Pioneer is always honest and faithful to his comrades and to his class, the working class.
4) A Pioneer is always trying to learn. Knowledge is power in the struggle of the working class.
5) A Pioneer organizes the children around him. He takes part in the life and interest of these children and draws them into the Young Pioneers. He is the model for all workers' and farmers' children.
6) A Pioneer is a reader of the *New Pioneer* and all Pioneer Press. He distributes it to other children.
7) A Pioneer is disciplined. A Pioneer puts the interests of the workers and farmers above his own individual interests. He carries out all decisions of the troop for this cause.
8) A Pioneer is brave. Whether in school, at work, or in the neighborhood, a Pioneer fearlessly fights for the interests of the working-class children, against race discrimination of Negro children, for free food and milk for children of the unemployed and all other interests of the workers' and farmers' children.

9) A Pioneer is alert. A Pioneer keeps his eyes open all the time; always observing how the workers and poor farmers are oppressed by the bosses and their servants—the government, the police, courts etc. A Pioneer is always on guard against these servants of the bosses and especially the police. He never gives any information to strangers or the police—either about his troop, troop leader, or the working class. A Pioneer knows the enemies of the working class and is always alert.

10) A Pioneer is clean. A Pioneer is careful of his own as well as other workers' health. He lives clean in body and thought, valuing his own time as well as the time of others. A Pioneer works with a collective spirit in his troop, carrying out all tasks quickly and punctually. A Pioneer does not curse, smoke or drink because these habits hurt the Pioneer's body and makes it hard for him to be always ready for the cause of the working class.

Appendix B: Transcript of YPA Poster Found at Thomas Jefferson High School, 1929, Instructing Children Not to Attend School on May Day

OUT OF SCHOOL ON MAY DAY.

Workers' children: We workers' children can indeed be proud of American workers. For they were the first, way back in 1886, to raise the cry, "Down tools on May Day" in protest against the long and bad conditions of the workers and against the increasing numbers and misery of the unemployed.

The very next year, at a meeting of trade-unions of the whole world, the workers saw that they all suffer alike under a system where the bosses, who do nothing, rule everything. And that year the workers of the whole world adopted the slogan "Down tools on May Day" to protest against this system of misery for the workers, who produce all but get nothing.

May Day is now the labor holiday the world over. On that day our parents put down their tools. We workers' children must stand with them. We must not scab on the workers. Out of school on May Day. Protest against:

The rotten school conditions.

The 3,500,000 child workers slaving away to make the bosses rich.

The increasing misery of the children of the unemployed.

Remember the brave fight of the miners and their children. Let us celebrate with all the workers at Madison Square Garden, Fiftieth Street and Eighth Avenue, on Tuesday, May 1, at 3pm. Come at noon to one of these places and we'll all go together:

Bronx: 1472 Boston Road, 2075 Clinton Avenue, 542 East One hundred and forty-fifth Street, 715 East One hundred and thirty-eighth Street. Harlem: 15 West One hundred and twenty-sixth Street, 143 East One hundred and third Street. Downtown: 60 St Mark's Place. Brownsville: 563 Stone Avenue, 1689 Pitkin Avenue. Williamsburg: 29 Graham Avenue. Borough Park: 1373 Forty-Third Street. Brighton Beach: 217 Brighton Beach Avenue. Bath Beach: 1940 Benson Avenue. Coney Island: 2901 Mermaid Avenue.

Appendix C: An Example Article from *Young Spark* That Was Distributed by the YPA's Lenin Unit at PS 61

SUPPORT THE COMMUNISTS!

The bosses shout about prosperity in America. But do the 3,500,000 child workers have prosperity? Do the miners and their starving families have prosperity? Do the striking Textile workers whose wages have been cut 10% have prosperity?

ONLY THE BOSSES HAVE PROSPERITY! They are the ones who are plotting a war against Soviet Russia, the only workers' and farmers' government in the world.

The bosses' parties, the Democrats and the Republicans are only for the bosses and against the workers. Only the WORKERS' (COMMUNIST) PARTY is for the workers. It is the only party that fights for a workers' and farmers' government and against bosses' wars.

The Workers' Party fights for the workers' children also. It fights for:

Right of workers' children to take part in labor struggles.

Against all child labor. The government must support all children now working.

Better and more schools in working-class neighborhoods.

Out with anti-labor propaganda in the schools. Out with military and religious teachings in the schools.

Free food and clothing for all children in the schools.

Rest homes for workers' children under workers' control.

WE MUST STAND BY THE WORKERS' COMMUNIST PARTY.[1]

Appendix D: Lenin Unit Notice to Teachers from PS 61

AN APPEAL TO THE TEACHERS OF 61 FROM
WORKERS' CHILDREN

During this period of increasing war preparations and propaganda, certain reactionary influences in our school are carrying on a campaign of terror and persecution directed against certain workers' children, members of a workers' children's organization, the Young Pioneers of America. In 61 we have had many such cases—Harry Eisman, who after two months suspended from school, was transferred to Public School 55; Bernard Kaplan, who was demoted; Jeanette Rubin, who was forced out of school; and Lebe Taft, who although she has completed her 9-A grade with high marks, is not permitted to the 9-B grade, where she belongs.

Mr McGuire is trying to wring a statement from Lebe Taft so that he can take away her right of belonging to a workers' children's organization, and expressing her right, as a worker's child, to labor opinion.

Teachers of 61, you are members of the working class placed in a position where you are the agents of the capitalist class. You are forced to teach jingoist and patriotic propaganda against the workers' and workers' children. Stand by your own class—the working class. Protest against these autocratic actions of the school authorities. Support these militant workers' children in their fight for freedom or labor opinion, for the right to belong to a workers' children's organization, and for the right of workers' children to fight for the interests of workers and workers' children.

YOUNG PIONEERS OF AMERICA—Lenin Group in 61.[2]

Appendix E: Open Letter from Harry Eisman on the Occasion of His Release, 1931

Dear Comrades:

I have received the invitation of the Pioneers of the Soviet Union to come to the USSR. I gladly accept this invitation from our Brother Pioneers.

The bosses thought they would split up out Pioneer groups by sending me to jail. They couldn't succeed. They thought that I would change my mind about being a Pioneer. In this case too, they failed. The authorities have talked to me, and have tried to convince me that the Pioneers was not a good organization. They wanted to make a real loyal patriot out of me.

But I told them I will tell all the workers' children that I am only loyal to the working class, and not the boss class.

While I am in the Soviet Union, I pledge to carry out all the work of the Pioneers there. The Russian Pioneers are working hard to help the Soviet Government build Socialism, to improve the conditions of their country, and I promise to do all I can to help them.

I also promise to write to the American workers' children, telling about the life of the children in the Soviet Union. I finally pledge, that when I will be in the Soviet Union, I will tell all the workers' children there about how the children in America live, and help them in their fight against the bosses of other countries.

I got out of this jail mainly because of the sentiment of the workers and their children who fought that I should be free. I am more determined to fight in the interests of the working class than ever before. I end this letter pledging to all the workers and their children, that IN THE CAUSE OF THE WORKING CLASS I STAND "ALWAYS READY!"

Your comrade,
Harry Eisman.[3]

NOTES

Introduction

1. Herbert Hoover, speech "Principles and Ideals of the United States' government," October 22, 1928, Madison Square Garden, New York City. Transcript: University of Virginia, Miller Center, Presidential speeches.

2. Theodore Draper, *The Roots of American Communism* (New York: Viking Press, 1957), 126; *Investigation of Communist Propaganda: Hearings before a Select Committee to Investigate Communist Activities in the United States* (hereafter *Investigation of Communist Propaganda*), part 3, vols. 1–5, H. Rep. 71st Cong., 2nd Sess., pursuant H.Res.220 (Washington, DC: US Government Printing Office, 1930), 110.

3. "Terrifying Facts about the Menace of Communism," *Knoxville Journal*, April 10, 1932, 4.

4. *Investigation of Communist Propaganda*, part 3, vols. 1–5, 110; "Pioneers to Present Children's Demands at Mass Rally, October 28," *Daily Worker*, October 23, 1928, 2.

5. Paul C. Mishler, *Raising Reds: The Young Pioneers, Radical Summer Camps, and Communist Political Culture in the United States* (New York: Columbia University Press, 1999), 1, 42.

6. Roger Keeran, "National Groups and the Popular Front: The Case of the International Workers Order," *Journal of American Ethnic History* 14, no. 3 (1995): 23–51.

7. "75 Child Communists Fail to See La Guardia," *Times Union*, May 12, 1935, 2.

8. "Hecklers Paid by Reds to Boo Landon," *San Bernardino County Sun*, October 25, 1936, 7; "Reds Get Blame for Razzberries," *Spokane Chronicle*, October 24, 1936, 2.

9. Bryan D. Palmer, "Rethinking the Historiography of United States Communism," *American Communist History* 2, no. 2 (2003): 139–173.

10. Michael J. Carley, Review of *The Secret World of American Communism*, ed. Harvey Klehr, John E. Haynes, and Fridrikh I. Firsov, H-Russia, H-Net Reviews, June 1995, http://www.h-net.org/reviews/showrev.php?id=91 (accessed 12/20/2022).

11. Mishler, *Raising Reds*, 2.

12. Mark Naison, *Communists in Harlem during the Depression* (Urbana: University of Illinois Press, 1983).

13. Britt Haas, *Fighting Authoritarianism, American Youth Activism in the 1930s* (New York: Fordham University Press, 2018), 12–13.

14. Brian Rouleau, "Children Are Hiding in Plain Sight in the History of US Foreign Relations," *Modern American History* 2, no. 3 (2019): 367–387.

15. Mischa Honeck, *Our Frontier Is the World: The Boy Scouts in the Age of American Ascendancy* (Ithaca, NY: Cornell University Press, 2018), 174–176.

16. Herbert Romerstein, *Communism and Your Child* (New York: Bookmailer, 1962), 28.

17. Ronald D. Cohen, "Review," *History of Education Quarterly* 40, no. 1 (2000): 103–104.

18. John C. Chalberg, "The Spirit of the 1920s," *OAH Magazine of History* 20, no. 1 (2006): 11.

19. William G. Carleton, "The Politics of the 1920s," *Current History* 47, no. 278 (1964): 210.

20. William H. Siener, "The Red Scare Revisited: Radicals and the Anti-Radical Movement in Buffalo, 1919–1920," *New York History* 79, no. 1 (1998): 23.

21. "Baby Reds Invade Council Chamber; Nine Are Nabbed," *Lincoln Star*, December 3, 1929, 6.

22. Robert K. Murray, *Red Scare: A Study in National Hysteria, 1919–1920* (Minneapolis: University of Minnesota Press, 1955); Larry Ceplair, "The Film Industry's Battle against Left-Wing Influences, from the Russian Revolution to the Blacklist," *Film History* 20, no. 4 (2008): 399–411; Julia M. Mickenberg, "Suffragettes and Soviets: American Feminists and the Specter of Revolutionary Russia," *Journal of American History* 100, no. 4, (2014): 1024; Kenyon Zimmer, *Immigrants against the State: Yiddish and Italian Anarchism in America* (Urbana: University of Illinois Press, 2015), 136; Jessie J. Norris, "Entrapment and Terrorism on the Left: an Analysis of Post-9/11 cases," *New Criminal Law Review* 19, no. 2 (2019): 241; Julie M. Powell, "Making 'The Case against the Reds': Racializing Communism, 1919–1920," in *Historicizing Fear, Ignorance, Vilification, and Othering*, ed. Travis D. Boyce and Winsome M. Chunnu (Boulder: University of Colorado Press, 2019): 101–121.

23. Robert Justin Goldstein, ed., *Little "Red Scares": Anti-Communism and Political Repression in the United States, 1921–1946* (Burlington, VT: Ashgate, 2014).

24. Murray B. Levin, *Political Hysteria in America: The Democratic Capacity for Repression* (New York: Basic Books, 1971), 29.

1. The JSYWL and YPA Regulations

1. Kenneth Thompson, "Operating a Socialist Sunday School," *Wilshire's Magazine* 14, no. 11 (1910): 12.

2. Kenneth Teitelbaum and William J. Reese, "American Socialist Pedagogy and Experimentation in the Progressive Era: The Socialist Sunday School," *History of Education Quarterly* 23, no. 4 (1983): 429–454.

3. "What, Then, Does Communist Action Mean?" *Daily Worker*, January 29, 1924, 6; Nat Kaplan, "Remarks to the Militant Parents," *Daily Worker*, May 23, 1925, New York Magazine Supplement, 8.

4. "Why We Organize the Junior Groups," *Young Comrade*, November 1923, 3; Ruth Miller, "My Friend Walter," *Young Comrade*, November 1923, 4.

5. Harry Eisman, "The Election Campaign and the Workers' Children," *Daily Worker*, August 22, 1930, 4.

6. David I. Macleod, Review, *Canadian Journal of History* 35, no. 3 (2000): 598–599.
7. "Follow in Lenin's Way" *Young Comrade*, January–February 1928, 1.
8. "Instructions for the General Pioneer Registration" and "Rules and Regulations of the YPA," Portland City Archives, Police Historical Archival Investigative Files, Communist Party—Young Pioneers of America, Record No. AF/160425.
9. "Instructions for the General Pioneer Registration" and "Rules and Regulations of the YPA."
10. Britt Haas, *Fighting Authoritarianism, American Youth Activism in the 1930s* (New York: Fordham University Press, 2018), 14.
11. Janet Biehly, *Ecology or Catastrophe, The Life of Murray Bookchin* (New York: Oxford University Press, 2015), 6–7.
12. Biehly, *Ecology or Catastrophe*, 8.
13. "Finds Young Reds Are Active in the U.S.," *The Tablet*, March 8, 1924, 10. Membership figures: *Young Comrade*, January 1924, 5. Estimated numbers in the Bronx and Brooklyn: "Student Reds Claim 1,000 Comrades in Brooklyn and the Bronx, Children Age 8 to 16, Salute Soviet Flag in Protest against Suspension of Leader," *Standard Union*, November 3, 1928.

2. Leo Granoff: Harlem's "Boy Trotsky" and YPA Tactics

1. Leo Granoff, "Why and How I Became a Member of the Junior Section," *Young Comrade* 1, no. 4 (February 1924): 4, and *Daily Worker*, February 20, 1924, 4.
2. "Eleven-Year-Old Youth is 'Boy Trotzky,'" *Shamokin News Dispatch*, December 6, 1923, 1.
3. *Investigation of Communist Propaganda: Hearings before a Select Committee to Investigate Activities in the United States*, H. Rep. 71st Cong., 2nd Sess., pursuant H.Res.220, (Washington, DC: US Government Printing Office, 1930), part 3, vols. 1–5 (hereafter: *Investigation of Communist Propaganda*), 324–325; "Red, a Leader at Eleven, Taken as Communist," *Standard Union*, November 28, 1923, 2.
4. "Boy Trotzky Leads Young NY Reds," *San Francisco Examiner*, November 23, 1923, 1; "Band of Juvenile Revolutionaries Discovered," *Kingsport Times*, November 27, 1923, 18; "Band of Juvenile 'Reds' Discovered, A Boy Trotzky Leads Regular Band of Revolutionaries Say the Police Bomb Squad," *Daily News* (Newport, Virginia), November 28, 1923, 1; "Arrest Boy Anarchist," *Los Angeles Times*, December 5, 1923, 11; "Free Love, Free Speech, Under Red Flag, Preached by Communist, Age Eleven," *Lincoln Journal Star*, December 4, 1923, 12; "Eleven-Year-Old Youth Is 'Boy Trotzky,'" *Orlando Evening Star*, December 7, 1923, 4; "Free 'Boy Trotzky,'" *Fort Worth Star-Telegram*, December 9, 1923, 34; "'Boy Trotzky' Arrested," *The Tennessean*, December 9, 1923, 10; Jessie Henderson, "Seven Days in Little Old New York," *Sunday News* (Lancaster, PA), December 9, 1923, 5.
5. *Investigation of Communist Propaganda*, part 3, vols. 1–5, 324–325; "Leo Granoff Freed," *Des Moines Tribune*, December 11, 1923, 10; J. O. Bentall, "New York Is Shellshocked," *Daily Worker*, February 7, 1924, 6.
6. Joseph Anthony, ed., *The Best News Stories of 1923* (Boston: Small Maynard, 1924), 389.
7. "Judge Hoyt on the Needs of the Children's Court," *New York Times*, December 17, 1911, 13; "A Very Human Judge Needed for Children," *New York Times*, December 18, 1911, 9; Franklin Chase Hoyt, *Quicksands of Youth* (New York: Charles Scribner's Sons, 1921); "I Charge School Boards Foster Juvenile Crime by Ignoring Laws to Aid Under-Nourished Pupils," *Johnson City Chronicle*, October 10, 1926, 27; "Bad Boy's Friend Now Turns to Alcohol Control," *The Courier-News*, October 2, 1935, 13; "Folks We Know," *The Eagle* (Texas), October 9, 1935, 5.

8. *Investigation of Communist Propaganda*, part 3, vols. 1–5, 320.

9. *Investigation of Communist Propaganda*, part 3, vols. 1–5, 320.

10. For Children's First Amendment Rights see *Tinker v. Des Moines Independent Community School District*, 393 US 503 (1969).

11. J. O. Bentall, *Daily Worker*, February 7, 1924, 6.

12. "Dangerous Leo," *Indianapolis Times*, December 4, 1923, 4.

13. "The Supreme Court and the Children," *Social Service Review*, 15, no. 1 (1941): 116–119.

14. *Investigation of Communist Propaganda*, part 3, vols. 1–5, 320.

15. "Free Love, Free Speech, Under Red Flag, Preached by Boy Communist, Age 11," *Buffalo Enquirer*, December 8, 1923, 3; "Boy Trotsky Here Bars Bourgeoisie: Not Even a Rockefeller Kid Could Get into His Soviet Club, Says Leo Granoff," *New York Times*, November 28, 1923, 10. "What a Boy Red Thinks: 'I Got to Be a Communist All by Myself Nobody Helped,' Says Granoff," *New York Times*, December 6, 1923, sec. XX, 2, https://www.nytimes.com/1923/12/16/archives/what-a-boy-red-thinks-i-got-to-be-a-commu-nist-all-by-myself-nobody.html. Note: Georgy Tchitcherin (also spelt Chicherin) was commissar for foreign affairs of the Soviet Union from July 1923 to July 1930.

16. Heywood Broun, "It Seems to Me," *Buffalo Courier*, December 4, 1923, 6.

17. *Standard Union*, December 1, 1923, 6.

18. "Declares Children Are Prey of Reds," *Hartford Courant*, November 30, 1923, 20.

19. Anonymous letter in the *Tablet*, December 15, 1923, 20.

20. "Against Child Labor!" Issued by the City Executive Committee of the JSYWL, New York City, c. 1924, 2–3.

21. *Shamokin News Dispatch*, December 6, 1923, 1; "Free Love, Speech Is Preached by Youth, 11," *San Bernardino County Sun*, December 8, 1923, 11.

22. *Kingsport Times*, November 27, 1923; "Seven Days in Old New York, Between the Theatre and Boy Trotsky the Town Is Going to the Bad Fast," *Des Moines Register*, December 9, 1923, 30; J. O. Bentall, "New York Is Shellshocked," 6.

23. "10,000 NY Workers Join in Big Paris Commune Celebration," *Daily Worker*, March 19, 1925, 2.

24. "Jefferson Seniors Pick Class Officers," *Brooklyn Daily Eagle*, October 13, 1931, 14.

25. "With the Juniors," *Young Comrade* 1, no. 4 (February 1924): 7.

3. Radical Recreations

1. William Gershonowitz, "The Workers' Children" *Young Comrade*, September 1924.

2. For John Reed Clubs see Eric Homberger, "Proletarian Literature and the John Reed Clubs, 1929–1935," *Journal of American Studies* 13, no. 2 (1979): 221–244.

3. "Do You Remember This Old Favorite?" *Young Comrade*, November 1927, 3.

4. "3,000 Children Parade, Brownsville Marchers Demonstrate for More Playgrounds," *Times Union*, June 13, 1935, 6.

5. Paul C. Mishler, *Raising Reds: The Young Pioneers, Radical Summer Camps, and Communist Political Culture in the United States* (New York: Columbia University Press, 1999), 45; "De Luca Scoffs at Reds' Charges," *Daily News*, October 29, 1932, 26.

6. "Students See Soviet Ship," *Times Union*, April 9, 1934, 9.

7. "Help Pioneers with Wood-Working Circle," *Daily Worker*, November 18, 1933.

8. Mishler, *Raising Reds*, 45.

9. "An Invitation to All Workers Kids," *Daily Worker*, December 23, 1933, 6; "Workers and Artists Pay Last Respects to Potamkin," *Daily Worker*, July 22, 1933, 1.

10. *Daily Worker*, December 23, 1933, 6.

11. Sally Banes, *Writing Dancing in the Age of Postmodernism* (Middletown, CT: Wesleyan University Press, 2011), 200.

12. H. A. Reinhold, "The Catholic Worker Movement in America" *Blackfriars* 19, no. 222 (September 1938): 635–650; Sheila Webb, "Dorothy Day and the Early Years of the 'Catholic Worker': Social Action through the Pages of the Press," *U.S. Catholic Historian* 21, no. 3 (2003): 71–88; Tom Cornell, "The Catholic Worker, Communism and the Communist Party," *American Catholic Studies* 125, no. 1 (2014): 87–101.

13. Jack Hodgson, "'The Santy Claus Myth': The Politicisation of Santa Claus during the Great Depression," *Comparative American Studies: An International Journal* 20, no. 2–3 (2023): 291–307.

14. Comic Strip, "Another Christmas Present," *Young Pioneer*, December 1930.

15. Hodgson, "'The Santy Claus Myth,'": 297–301; "Young Reds Boo Kringle, Upset Tree," *Middletown Times Herald*, December 26, 1930, 9.

16. Gene Fein, "For Christ and Country: The Anti-Semitic Anticommunism of Christian Front Street Meetings in New York City," *U.S. Catholic Historian* 22, no. 4 (2004): 37.

17. "On the Youth Movement," *Wisconsin State Journal*, September 8, 1934, 5; "House Warned of Anti-Religious Communist Acts," *The Tablet*, February 28, 1931, 1; "An Extreme Sacrilege," *Sheboygan Press*, March 27, 1933, 16; Gilbert H. Parkes, untitled column, *Auburn Journal*, September 30, 1934, 11; "Sovietism a Menace to This Country," *Indianapolis Star*, July 30, 1935, 6.

18. "Jewish Clubs Mark Ancient Purim Feast," *Press and Sun-Bulletin*, March 10, 1933, 8.

19. *Pioneer (New Pioneer)* 1, no. 1 (May 1931): 1. For Bishop William Montgomery Brown., see William Montgomery Brown, *Communism and Christianity* (Galion, Ohio: Bradford-Brown Educational Company, 1920); Bill Mayr, "The Red Bishop," *Kenyon College Alumni Bulletin* 34, no. 1 (2011). For Grace Hutchins, see Joseph Kip Kosek, *Acts of Conscience: Christian Nonviolence and Modern American Democracy* (New York: Columbia University Press, 2009), and Julia M. Allen, *Passionate Commitments: The Lives of Anna Rochester and Grace Hutchins* (Albany: SUNY Press, 2013).

20. Leo Granoff and Thelma Kahn, "Telling It to the World," *Young Comrade*, June 1926, 4.

21. R. Greenburg, "A Dandy Game," *Young Comrade*, February 1927, 3.

22. Gabe Logan, "C'mon, You Reds: The US Communist Party's Workers' Soccer Association, 1927–1935," *Journal of Sport History* 44, no. 3 (2017): 384–385.

23. Gabe Logan, "Playing for the People: Labor Sports Union Athletic Clubs in the Lake Superior/Iron Range, 1927–1936," *Upper Country: A Journal of the Lake Superior Region* 4 (2016): 43–47.

24. Herbert Righthand and Albert Schneider, "A Challenge," *Young Comrade*, April 1927, 1.

25. William J. Barker, "Muscular Marxism and the Chicago Counter-Olympics of 1932," in *The New American Sport History: Recent Approaches and Perspectives*, ed. S. W. Pope (Urbana: University of Illinois Press, 1997), 284–289.

26. "Basketball Team of New York," *Young Pioneer* 6, no. 1 (February 1929): 12.

27. "Basketball Conference," *Young Pioneer* 6, no. 5 (October–November 1929): 4; "Sports," *Young Pioneer* 7, no. 1 (March 1930): 3.

28. Logan, "Playing for the People," 47.

29. "New York Workers Will Protest Murder of Negro Boy Athlete," *Daily Worker*, April 20, 1929, 1; "Negro Boy's Murder to Be Protested at Mass Meet Tonight," *Daily Worker*, April 22, 1929, 1; "Housing Evil in Clarke Killing," *Daily Worker*, April 1929, 1, 5; "Boy Slain in Race Fight," *Daily News*, April 15, 1929, 2.

30. "New York on Edge for Big Picnic of Sunday, August 10," *Daily Worker*, August 7, 1924, 3.

31. "Workers' Children Play Baseball," *Young Pioneer*, August 1930, 5.

32. "Workers' Children Prepare for Big Meet," *Young Pioneer* 7, no. 3 (August 1930): 5.

33. "Our Street Racing Meet in Coney Island," *Young Pioneer* 7, no. 4 (September–October 1930): 5.

34. Joshua Prager, *The Echoing Green* (New York: Knopf Doomsday Publishing Group, 2008), 194; Harold Seymour, *Baseball: The People's Game* (New York: Oxford University Press, 1990), 18; Stephen Jay Gould, *Triumph and Tragedy in Mudville: A Lifelong Passion in Baseball* (London: W. W. Norton, 2004), 41–42, 258; Steven A. Reiss, *Sports and the American Jew* (Syracuse, NY: Syracuse University Press, 1998), 43; Michael W. Robbins and Wendy Palitz, *A Brooklyn State of Mind* (New York: Workman Publishing, 2001), 84; Matt Doeden, *Sandy Koufax* (Minneapolis: Twenty-First Century Books, 2006), 6–7; "Bernie Sanders Back in the Old Neighborhood to Make His Case," *New York Times*, April 8, 2016; Matt Levy (director) and Hector Elizondo, *New York Street Games* (Motion Picture, 2011).

35. "Junior Sport News," *New Pioneer* 1, no. 2 (June 1931): 12.

36. W. Barksdale Maynard, "An Ideal Life in the Woods for Boys: Architecture and Culture in the Earliest Summer Camps," *Winterthur Portfolio* 34, no. 1 (1999): 3–29; Abigail A. Van Slyck, "Kitchen Technologies and Mealtime Rituals: Interpreting the Food Axis at American Summer Camps, 1890–1950," *Technology and Culture* 43, no. 4 (2002): 668–692; Michael B. Smith, "'The Ego Ideal of the Good Camper' and the Nature of Summer Camp," *Environmental History* 11, no. 1 (2006): 70–101; Abigail A. Van Slyck, *Manufactured Wilderness: Summer Camps and the Shaping of American Youth, 1890–1960* (Minneapolis: University of Minnesota Press, 2006); Maurice Cohen Feris, "'God First, You Second, Me Third': An Exploration of 'Quiet Jewishness' at Camp Wah-Kon-Dah," *Southern Cultures* 18, no. 1 (2012): 58–70.

37. Kenny Cupers, "Governing through Nature: Camps and Youth Movements in Interwar Germany and the United States," *Cultural Geographies* 15, no. 2 (2008): 173–205.

38. Jack Hodgson, "A Summer without Camp Is More Than a Bummer," *Washington Post*, June 21, 2020.

39. Mishler, *Raising Reds*, 83.

40. "Communist Children's Column," *Daily Worker*, November 17, 1924, 3; "First Group of Juniors League for Nitgedayget Camp, Sunday July 12," *Daily Worker*, July 12, 1925, 3; "For a Leninist Youth Camp," *Daily Worker*, August 7, 1925, 4.

41. *American Labor Year Book* (New York: Rand School of Social Science, various dates), 1923–23: 166–168. 1925: 164–166. 1926: 254–256; 1927: 135–136; *Red Dawn: Commencement Annual of the Northwest Young Workers Summer School* (Astoria, OR: Pacific Development Society, 1927); *Red Student: Commencement Annual of the Pacific Coast Workers Summer School* (Astoria, OR: Pacific Development Society, 1928).

42. "A Guide for Work in the Pioneer Camp," YPA Central Bureau, 1932, 2, 14, 16.

43. A Guide for Work in the Pioneer Camp."

44. Leslie Boyd, "Negro Boy Joins the Young Pioneers," *Young Pioneer* 6, no. 4, July–August 1929, 2.

45. Mishler, *Raising Reds*, 45; "A Guide for Work in the Pioneer Camp," 1; Harold Bell, "In Our Pioneer Camp," *Young Comrade* 4, no. 11 (November 1927): 8.
46. "A Guide for Work in the Pioneer Camp," 5.
47. "A Guide for Work in the Pioneer Camp," 5.
48. "A Guide for Work in the Pioneer Camp," 5.
49. M. K., "Sports in the Young Pioneer Camp" *Young Pioneer* 6, no. 4, July–August 1929, 14.
50. Helen Weiss, "New York WIR Camp," *Young Pioneer* 7, no. 3 (1930): 3.
51. "Washington Editor Warns against Sinister Propaganda," *Pittsburgh Post-Gazette*, February 23, 1934, 16.
52. "Human Element in Business Vital, Woman's Rotary Told," *Indianapolis Star*, February 4, 1930, 5.
53. *Proceedings of the Annual Convention of the Daughters of Union Veterans of the Civil War*, 1929, 219.
54. "Communist Camps Train Baby Reds, Woman Testifies," *Daily News*, June 20, 1930, 36.

4. Pioneer Politicians and the CPUSA

1. "Working Class Women Have Jamaica Meeting," *Times Union*, March 1935, 4.
2. "Celebration of Russian Republic," *Morning Call*, November 9, 1923, 10; "Untermeyer Raps Saklatvala Ban as Intolerance," *Brooklyn Daily Eagle*, September 20, 1925, 4; "Launch Election Drive in Dist. 2," *Daily Worker*, July 6, 1928, 1; "Rebecca Grecht Held at Hearing on Wednesday," *Daily Notes*, March 8, 1928, 1; "Rebecca Grecht Is under Arrest on Sedition Charge," *Passaic Daily News*, March 8, 1928, 2; "Stop Strike Meeting, Police Disband Gathering of Alleged Radical Group," *Pittsburgh Press*, March 10, 1928, 9; "8 Choose Jail Rather Than Pay Fine for Demonstration in Wall Street," *Reading Times*, July 10, 1928, 1; "Girl Agitator Jailed after Radicals Riot," *Standard Union*, August 10, 1928, 26; *Investigation of Communist Propaganda: Hearings before a Select Committee to Investigate Communist Activities in the United States* (hereafter *Investigation of Communist Propaganda*), part 3, vols. 1–5, H. Rep. 71st Cong., 2nd Sess., pursuant H.Res.220 (Washington, DC: US Government Printing Office, 1930), 220.
3. "Capital Hotly Scoured in NY Lenin Meeting," *Monroe Star-News*, February 2, 1925, 1; "14-Year-Old Boy Communist Orator Seeks Soviet Here," *Standard Union*, February 3, 1925, 2; "Swayed 15,000," *Knoxville News Sentinel*, February 12, 1925, 5; "Young Reds," *Boonville Enquirer*, February 27, 1925, 7.
4. Anna Thompson, "Communist Children's Column," *Daily Worker*, February 7, 1925, 5.
5. Morris Spector, "Why Child Labor?" *Daily Worker*, July 9, 1927, 7.
6. "Answers Boy Who Extolled Lenin," *Daily Times*, March 10, 1925, 2; "Boy Bolshevik Is Answered by Youth in Patriotic Talk," *Des Moines Tribune*, February 24, 1925, 16.
7. "Erasmus Boy, 15, Picked to Combat 'Red' Doctrine Preached by Lad, 14," *Times Union*, March 15, 1925, 7.
8. *Standard Union*, February 3, 1925, 2.
9. *The Tablet*, February 21, 1925, 9.
10. *Times Herald*, February 7, 1925, 4; "From the Managing Editor's Desk"; "Communists, Capitalists, and Children," *Daily Worker*, February 14, 1925, 6.
11. *Daily Worker*, February 14, 1925, 6; "Young Workers Protest Arrest of Hawaiians," *Daily Worker*, April 17, 1925, 2; "Big NY Throng Fights Religion in the Schools," *Daily Worker*, April 24, 1925, 5; "Brownsville YWL," *Daily Worker*, August 31, 1928, 5.

12. William J. Alderman, *Haymarket Revisited,* 2nd ed. (Chicago: Labor History Society, 1986). Timothy Messer-Kruse, *The Trial of the Haymarket Anarchists: Terrorism and Justice in the Gilded Age* (New York: Palgrave Macmillan, 2011).

13. "Out of School on the First of May," *Young Pioneer* 6, no. 2 (May 1929): 16.

14. *Investigation of Communist Propaganda,* 219–220.

15. "American Brigade Has Taken Revenge," *Lincoln Star Journal,* August 1, 1938, 4; "Former Key Red on Long Island Wins Bail Cut on Subversive Rap," *Newsday,* October 3, 1952, 4; "Convict 6 Reds in Michigan," *Valley Times,* February 18, 1954, 32; Saul Wellman, "Jewish Vets of the Spanish Civil War: Personal Observations of the Spanish Civil War," *Jewish Currents* 27, no. 6 (June 1973): 8–15; *Journal of the Senate of the State of Michigan,* 1980, vol. 2, 1479; Vincent P. Franklin, *African Americans and Jews in the Twentieth Century, Studies in Convergence and Conflict* (Columbia: University of Missouri Press, 1998), 242; "Saul Wellman, 1913–2003," *The Volunteer: Journal of the Veterans of the Abraham Lincoln Brigade,* XXVI, no. 1 (2004): 20–21; John Barnard, *American Vanguard: The United Auto Workers During the Ruether Years, 1935–1970* (Detroit: Wayne State University Press, 2005), 64, 193; Gerben Zaagsma, *Jewish Volunteers, The International Brigades, and the Spanish Civil War* (London: Bloomsbury, 2017), 24, 126, 174.

16. Alan M. Wald, *Trinity of Passion: The Literary Left and the Antifascist Crusade* (Chapel Hill: University of North Carolina Press, 2007), 27–30.

17. Harry Eisman, "Pioneer Tells of Children's Society," *Daily Worker,* May 22, 1929, 6.

18. Eisman, 6.

19. Eisman, 6.

20. "Police On Guard against Red Riots," *Standard Union,* May 1, 1938, 8; "9 Young Reds Seized in May Day Disorders," *Brooklyn Daily Eagle,* May 1, 1931, 1, 15; "6 Arrested Here; Police in Drive on May Day Riots," *Times Union,* May 1, 1931, 1, 8.

5. Pioneers and Picket Lines

1. "Hands off Nicaragua," *Young Comrade* 3, no. 1 (January 1927): 1; "Nicaraguan Natives Slaughtered While Yank Tyrants Feast," *Young Comrade* 4, no. 2 (November 1927): 3.

2. M. A. Skromny, "'We Are Always Ready!' Is Slogan of Junior Communists at Chicago Convention," *Daily Worker,* September 5, 1924, 4; "Junior Member Is Persecuted by Her Teacher," *Daily Worker,* November 22, 1924, 1; "Junior Groups Back Anti-Red Week Fighters," *Daily Worker,* November 25, 1924, 2.

3. "Pioneers Take Part in Demonstration against Wall Street," *Young Comrade* 5, no. 4 (June–July 1928): 2; "Word from Rose Plotkin," *Young Comrade* 5, no. 5 (September 1928): 2.

4. "Rap New York Terror Police," *Daily Worker,* July 7 1928,1; "Frame-up Seen with Militant up for Hearing," *Daily Worker,* July 9, 1928, 1, 2; "Minor, 4 Other Workers, Held Incommunicado, Young Pioneer Sent to Indiana," *Daily Worker,* July 11, 1928, 1; "Youth Condemn Plotkin Arrest," *Daily Worker,* July 16, 1928, 1; "Red Rose Sent Home," *Daily News,* July 17, 1928, 26; "Mass Picketing by Cafeteria Strikers Today," *Daily Worker,* April 8, 1929, 1.

5. "Kid Communists Arrested after Demonstrations," *Burlington Daily News,* October 23, 1931,1.

6. "Klan Votes on Strike, Endorses Paterson Mayor's Demand for Deportation of Silk Workers," *New York Times,* October 22, 1924, 9; Joseph Alukonis, "The Paterson Strike," *Young Comrade* 2, no. 1 (November 1924): 5; Joseph Alukonis, "Still on Strike in Paterson," *Young Comrade* 2, no. 2 (December 1924): 2.

7. C. E. W., "Pioneers Active among Children of NY Strikers," *Young Comrade* 3, no. 7 (August–September 1927): 1.

8. Leo Granoff, "The Poor Traction Millionaires," *Young Comrade* 5, no. 2 (April 1928): 5.

9. Harry Eisman, "Pioneers Active in Fruit Clerks Strike," *Young Comrade* 5, no. 3 (May 1928): 5.

10. "Truant Officers Cannot Scare Pioneers Off the Picket Line," *Young Pioneer* 6, no. 2 (April 1929): 6.

11. "For the Cafeteria Strikers," *Young Pioneer* 6, no. 3 (June 1929): 6.

12. "Big Children's Relief Conference Held in New York," *Young Comrade* 5, no.1 (January–February 1928): 1; "Our Fight," *Young Comrade* 5, no. 2 (April 1928): 10. For more on the "Coal War" and miners' strikes see Thomas G. Andrews, *Killing for Coal: America's Deadliest Labor War* (Cambridge, MA: Harvard University Press, 2008); David Montgomery, "Thinking about American Workers in the 1920s," *International Labor and Working-Class History*, no. 32 (1987): 4–24; Charles J. Bayard, "The 1927–1928 Colorado Coal Strike," *Pacific Historical Review* 32, no. 3 (1963): 235–250.

13. P. Q. R., "Miners Relief in School," *Young Comrade* 5, no. 2 (April 1928): 14.

14. A. B., "How I Organized a Miners' Relief Scout Group," *Young Comrade* 5, no. 1 (January–February 1928): 2.

15. *Investigation of Communist Propaganda: Hearings before a Select Committee to Investigate Communist Activities in the United States* (hereafter *Investigation of Communist Propaganda*), part 3, vols. 1–5, H. Rep. 71st Cong., 2nd Sess., pursuant H.Res.220 (Washington, DC: US Government Printing Office, 1930), 219.

16. Sylvia Gudisman, "Work of the Pioneers in Passaic," *Young Comrade* 2, no. 12 (April 1926): 2.

17. Harry Eisman, "Pioneer Confab to Open Today," *Daily Worker*, May 17, 1929, 5.

18. Montgomery, "Thinking about American Workers in the 1920s."

19. "Workers Center Raided by Tammany Cops while Police March," *Daily Worker*, May 20, 1929, 1, 3; "Pioneers Meet Despite Police," *Daily Worker*, May 20, 1929, 5; "District Two Holds Third District Convention," *Young Pioneer* 6, no. 3 (June 1929): 10.

20. For Lemlich see, Annelise Orleck, *Common Sense and a Little Fire: Women and Working-Class Politics in the United States, 1900–1965* (Chapel Hill: University of North Carolina Press, 1995). For Shavelson (Velson) see "Short Biographies of Candidates Who Will Be Voted upon Here Tuesday" *New York Times*, November 5, 1938; Testimony of Charles I. Velson, 26 September 1951, Unauthorized Travel of Subversives behind the Iron Curtain on United States Passports, US Congress, Subcommittee to Investigate the Administration of the Internal Security Act, Senate Judiciary Committee, 207–217; Testimony of Charles I. Velson, 6 May 1953, *Investigation of Communist Activities in the New York City Area*, US House of Representatives Committee on Un-American Activities; "Union Bars Irving Velson; Witness, Silent in Red Inquiry, Ousted 'for Life' by Group," *New York Times*, May 8, 1953; "Irving Velson," State Department, Security—1963–65. Bureau of Security and Consular Affairs. Hearings before the Subcommittee to Investigate the Administration of the Security Laws of the Committee on the Judiciary, US Sen. 89th Cong., 2nd Sess. Part 3 (1966), 993; John Earl Haynes and Harvey Klehr, *Verona, Decoding Soviet Espionage in America* (New Haven, CT: Yale University Press, 1999), 185–186, 369, 466.

21. Carl D. P., "Ferry Bootblacks Slave," *Young Comrade* 5, no. 4 (June–July 1928): 8.

22. Moey, "Messenger Boys Slave for Little Pay," *Young Comrade* 5, no. 5 (September 1928): 6.

6. Countering Capitalist Curriculum and Corporal Punishment

1. "Instructions for the General Pioneer Registration" and "Rules and Regulations of the YPA," 3, Portland City Archives, Police Historical Archival Investigative Files, Communist Party—Young Pioneers of America, Record No. AF/160425.
2. "'Baby Reds' Want to Be Dictators in Public School," *Redwood Gazette*, December 17, 1924, 4.
3. "Why We Fight against Public Schools," *Young Comrade* 1, no. 3 (January 1924): 1.
4. Morris Spector and Esther Gross, "NY Juniors Hold Membership Meeting Discussing Past Work and Making Plans for the Future," *Daily Worker*, January 10, 1925, 4.
5. Mark D'Alessandro, "Free Lunch After All? An Historical Review of Implementation of School Meals in New York Public Schools," *Journal of Child Nutrition and Management* 43, no. 1 (2019).
6. "Demand Better Conditions in New York Schools," *Young Comrade* 3, no. 3 (March 1927): 4.
7. Anna Schlopak, "Why No Heat?" *Young Comrade* 3, no. 2 (February 1927): 4.
8. NY Pioneer, "Police Can't Scare Us," *Young Comrade* 5, no. 2 (April 1928): 13.
9. James Rosen, "Our Teacher," *Young Comrade* 3, no. 4 (April 1927): 4.
10. "Corporal Punishment in Public Schools," *New York Times*, December 3, 1873; "The Question of Corporal Punishment," *New York Times*, December 4, 1873.
11. S. Edelstein, "In Our School," *Young Comrade* 3, no. 2 (February 1927): 4.
12. Letter by Irving Gorbati, *Young Comrade* 3, no. 3 (March 1927): 4; "Teacher Defends Bloody Queen Marie," *Young Comrade* 3, no. 2 (February 1927): 4.
13. Frank T. Valentine, "The Capitalist Schools," *Young Comrade* 2, no. 2 (December 1924): 6.
14. Gussie Rosenfeld, "Yes We Have Freedom But Arresting Workers Is Different, My Dear," *Young Comrade* 2, no. 14 (June 1926): 4.
15. Gitlow chronicled his own involvement with American Communism as a "confession" after turning to conservatism, even becoming a major anti-Communist figure during McCarthyism. See Benjamin Gitlow, *I Confess: The Truth about American Communism* (New York: E. P. Dutton, 1940), and *The Whole of Their Lives: Communism in America: A Personal History and Intimate Portrayal of Its Leaders* (New York: Charles Scribner's Sons, 1948).
16. Joe Grossburg, "Pioneer Speaks up for Red China," *New Pioneer* 1, no. 2 (June 1931): 18.
17. Ryan Walker, Comic Strip, "The First Day in School," *Young Pioneer*, October 1930.

7. School Lunch Revolts

1. Rachel Louise Moran, "Consuming Relief: Food Stamps and the New Welfare of the New Deal," *Journal of American History* 97, no. 4 (2011): 1001–1022; Susan A. Levine, *School Lunch Politics: The Surprising History of America's Favorite Welfare Program* (Princeton, NJ: Princeton University Press, 2010); Christyna M. Serrano, "The Political Economy of School Lunch and the Welfare State: An Analysis of Federal School Food Policy and Its Implementation at a Local Level" (PhD diss., University of California, Berkeley, 2017).
2. "Young Reds Fail to Call on O'Shea," *Brooklyn Daily Eagle*, November 29, 1931, 1.
3. Mark D'Alessandro, "Free Lunch after All? An Historical Review of Implementation of School Meals in New York City Public Schools," *Journal of Child Nutrition & Management* 43, no. 1 (2019): n.p.

4. "Many More Schools Plead for Penny Lunch Service; Pupils Lack Proper Food," *Evening World*, January 3, 1915. 8.

5. "Federation of Women's Clubs Aid Penny Lunch Fund Plans," *Evening World*, January 2, 1915, 6.

6. "Plan for March of 10,000 Women and Children for Penny Lunch Plan," *Evening World*, February 1, 1915, 4.

7. D'Alessandro, "Free Lunch after All."

8. "Hylan Declares Nobody Is Opposed to School Lunches," *Evening World*, December 13, 1919, 7; "Ending of School Lunches is Called Serious Injustice," *New-York Tribune*, December 5, 1919, 8.

9. D'Alessandro, "Free Lunch after All." See also Hasia R. Diner, *Hungering for America: Italian, Irish, and Jewish Foodways in the Age of Migration* (Cambridge, MA: Harvard University Press, 2003).

10. A. R. Ruis, "'The Penny Lunch Has Spread Faster Than the Measles': Children's Health and the Debate over School Lunches in New York City, 1908–1930," *History of Education Quarterly* 55, no. 2 (2015): 190–217.

11. Ruis, 190–217.

12. "Police Arrest 2 Pioneer Members," *Daily Worker*, February 9, 1928, 1; "Pupils Suspended for Distributing Leaflets," *Daily Worker*, February 11, 1928, 1.

13. "School Lunch Revolt Linked to Outsiders," *Brooklyn Daily Eagle*, January 14, 1934, 1.

14. "School Lunch Revolt Linked to Outsiders," 1.

8. The Lenin Unit at PS 61

1. "Instructions for the General Pioneer Registration" and "Rules and Regulations of the YPA," Portland City Archives, Police Historical Archival Investigative Files, Communist Party—Young Pioneers of America, Record No. AF/160425. See "Work in the Schools" on numbered pages 4–5.

2. Harry Eisman, *An American Boy in the Soviet Union* (New York: Youth Publishers, 1934), 21.

3. "California and New York Voters," *Daily Worker*, August 27, 1926, 4.

4. X. Y. Z., "Our Work in PS 61, New York City," *Young Comrade* 4, no. 12 (December 1927): 3; An Organizer, "We Want Real Self-Government," *Young Comrade* 5, no. 2 (April 1928): 14; E.S., "What Happened in PS 61," *Young Comrade* 5, no. 3 (May 1928): 12.

5. Jonathan Hunt, "Communists and the Classroom: Radicals in U.S. Education, 1930–1960," *Composition Studies* 43, no. 2 (2015): 22.

6. Rose Baron, "School Children Rebel against Goosestep," *Labor Defender*, December 1928, 274.

7. "Boy, 14, Suspended by School as Red," *Daily News*, November 3, 1928, 4; "Student Suspended," *Courier-News* (New Jersey), November 2, 1928, 1; "Well?" *Baltimore Evening Sun*, November 2, 1928, 33.

8. *Investigation of Communist Propaganda: Hearings before a Select Committee to Investigate Communist Activities in the United States* (hereafter *Investigation of Communist Propaganda*), part 3, vols. 1–5, H. Rep. 71st Cong., 2nd Sess., pursuant H.Res.220 (Washington, DC: US Government Printing Office, 1930), 63.

9. "High School Boy Ousted as Communist," *Standard Union*, November 2, 1928, 5; 1; "Gives Details of Reds Plotting," *Tablet*, July 19, 1930, 18.

10. *Labor Defender*, December 1928, 274.
11. "Young Reds in New York City," *Journal of Education* 111, no. 3 (1930): 82.
12. *Investigation of Communist Propaganda*, part 3, vols. 1–5, 218–220.
13. *Investigation of Communist Propaganda*, part 3, vols. 1–5, 63.
14. "Gives Details of Reds' Plotting," *Tablet*, July 19, 1930: 18.
15. *Standard Union*, November 3, 1928, 1, 2.
16. "Student Reds Claim 1,000 'Comrades' in Brooklyn and Bronx," *Standard Union*, November 3, 1928, 1, 2.
17. *The Young Fighters* 1 (1932): 1–16, International Workers Order Records #5276, Kheel Center for Labor-Management Documentation and Archives.
18. R. N., "An Example," *Young Comrade* 2, no. 9 (November 1930): 4.
19. "College Student Suspended as Red to Have Hearing," *Brooklyn Daily Eagle*, March 13, 1930, 19.
20. "200 High School Students in Riot with Young Reds," *Times Union*, November 21, 1931, 1.
21. "Expel Red School Pupils," *Daily News*, May 14, 1931, 26.
22. "Kid Communists Arrested after Demonstrations," *Burlington Daily News*, October 23, 1931, 1.
23. "Fuel for the Flames," *Ithaca Journal*, March 12, 1930, 4.

9. Periodical Culture, the Fish Inquiry, and the US Post Office

1. Lowell M. Limpus, "Reds Win Children and Lose Adults," *Daily News*, November 18, 1931, 22; Harvey Klehr, *The Heyday of American Communism: The Depression Decade* (New York: Basic Books, 1984).
2. Frederick Boyd Stevenson, "The Top of the News," *Brooklyn Daily Eagle*, October 30, 1928, 23.
3. "Spreading Poison," *Newark Courier*, July 24, 1930, 2.
4. "D.A.R. Demands Country Act to Suppress Reds," *Brooklyn Citizen*, December 10, 1931, 2.
5. Regin Schmidt, *Red Scare: FBI and the Origins of Anticommunism in the United States, 1919–1943* (Copenhagen: Museum Tusculanum Press, University of Copenhagen, 2000), 136–145.
6. Walter Goodman, *The Committee: The Extraordinary Career of the House Committee on Un-American Activities* (London: Specker and Warburg, 1964), 12; Alex Goodall, "Red Herrings? The Fish Committee and Anticommunism in the Early Depression Years," in *Little "Red Scares," Anti-Communism and Political Repression in the United States, 1921–1946* (London: Routledge, 2014), 71–75.
7. Robert Justin Goldstein, *Political Repression in Modern America from 1870 to the Present* (Cambridge, MA: Schenkman, 1978), 202.
8. Sara Lindey, "Boys Write Back: Self-Education and Periodical Authorship in Late-Nineteenth-Century Story Papers," *American Periodicals* 21, no. 1 (2011): 72–88.
9. "A Letter to Our Young Reader," *Young Comrade* 1, no. 1 (November 1923): 1–2.
10. "A Letter to Our Young Reader," 1–2.
11. Allan H. Pasco, "Literature as Historical Archive," *New Literary History* 35, no. 3 (2004): 373–394; Julia Ribeiro, "'Knowing You Will Understand': The Usage of Poetry as a Historical Source about the Experience of the First World War," *Alicante Journal of English Studies* 31 (2018): 109–124.
12. R. L., "Gonna Strike Some More," *Young Comrade*, August 1926.

13. Mary Wytovich-Cokeburg, "Mrs. Henry Ford's Flower Garden," *Young Comrade*, May 1928.

14. "Child Communists in Hunger Parade," *Brooklyn Daily Eagle*, June 26, 1932, 1; "Children to Start Hunger March on Trenton Today," *Courier-News*, December 22, 1932, 1; "35 Child Marchers to Present Demands by Mail to Moore," *Central New Jersey Home News*, December 24, 1932, 9.

15. "Capital's Police Await Communist Child March," *Boston Globe*, November 24, 1932, 8; "Problem of Hunger Marches Worries Capital Authorities," *Daily News*, November 24, 1932, 16; "Children on Way to White House," *Baltimore Sun*, November 24, 1932, 6.

16. Eli Clayman, "The Factory Child," *Young Comrade*, November 1924.

17. Jennie Tomaszuski, "Always Ready," *Young Comrade*, November 1924.

18. Harold Kirschner, "We Are the Young Communists," *Young Comrade*, January 1925.

19. "200 Young Reds Jeer Cops as Elders Aim for Violence," *Daily News*, February 1, 1931, 4; "Children Storm New York Post Office in Red Protest," *Long Beach Sun*, February 1, 1931, 18; "250 Children Storm Post Office," *Times Union*, February 1, 1931; "Rioters Close Post Office in New York City," *Miami Herald*, February 1, 1931, 1.

10. The Van Etten Camp Controversy

1. "Chicken Pox at 'Red' Camp Causes Health Survey, With Quarantine Action Possible," *Elmira Star-Gazette*, July 28, 1930, 3; "Mabel Husa, Ailene Holmes, Must Finish Their Term in Prison, Court Decides," *Evening Times*, October 18, 1930, 6.

2. "Trial of Reds Opens at Van Etten; Alleged Insults to Flag Described," *Elmira-Star Gazette*, August 16, 1930, 4.

3. "Put Off Hearing for 'Red' Camp Teachers," *Schenectady Gazette*, August 15, 1930, 8; "State Police Disperse Mob Menacing Red Camp," *Evening News*, August 15, 1930, 1.

4. "Guards Check 1,500 Raiders at Red Camp," *Daily Item*, August 15, 1930, 10.

5. "Armed Guards Control Crowds When Girl Communist Leaders Are Arraigned," *Syracuse Herald*, August 16, 1930, 7; "Sheriff Posse Holds Up Mob at Red Camp," *Standard Union*, August 15, 1930, 2; "Sheriff Balks Effort to Burn Camp of Reds," *Brooklyn Daily Eagle*, August 15, 1930, 2; "Sheriff Thwarts Mob's Torch for Red Labor Camp," *Daily News*, August 16, 1930, 6.

6. "Silly Bunch of Lies, Girl Communists Say of Trial Allegations," *Star-Gazette*, August 18, 1930, 15.

7. "First Honor List Contains 14 Pupils, Sixty-Six Names on Merit Roll of School," *Daily Item*, March 22, 1930, 8; "15-Year-Old-Red Is Under Arrest at Saline City," *Star-Gazette*, February 3, 1931, 8; "Prosecution Rests in Trial of Two Girl Communists at Van Etten," *Press and Sun-Bulletin*, August 16, 1930, 3. "World's News Told in Pictures," *Morning News*, August 18, 1930, 14.

8. For trial transcripts and summary see *Investigation of Communist Propaganda: Hearings before a Select Committee to Investigate Communist Activities in the United States* (hereafter *Investigation of Communist Propaganda*), part 3, vols. 1–5, H. Rep. 71st Cong., 2nd Sess., pursuant H.Res.220 (Washington, DC: US Government Printing Office, 1930), 4: 233–242.

9. "Communist Junior Camp Trains Youth to Fight Capitalism," *Republican-Journal*, August 5, 1930, 3; "Patriotism? Where Is It?" *Republican-Journal*, August 30, 1930, 2.

10. "The Red Camp Mob," *Emporia Weekly Gazette*, August 21, 1930, 3.

11. "Flag Desecration Sentence Appealed," *Standard Union*, August 26, 1930, 14.

12. "Where Angry Mob Raided Communist Child Camp," *Poughkeepsie Eagle-News*, August 19, 1930, 2.

13. "6 Young Radicals Seized in Camp Raid," *Times Union*, August 30, 1930, 15.

14. *Yetta Stromberg v. People of the State of California*. 283 US 359 (1931). Under California's 1919 Penal Code, 403a, "Any person who displays a red flag, banner or badge or any flag, badge, banner, or device of any color or form whatever in any public place or in any meeting place or public assembly, or from or on any house, building or window as a sign, symbol or emblem of opposition to organized government or as an invitation or stimulus to anarchistic action or as an aid to propaganda that is of a seditious character is guilty of a felony."

15. The American Civil Liberties Union, *The Fight for Civil Liberty, 1930–31* (New York: American Civil Liberties Union, 1931), 10–16. "Sentenced to San Quentin for Flying Red Flag over Communist Children Camp," *Star-Gazette*, August 2, 1930, 2.

16. Edwin Layton, "The Better America Federation: A Case Study of Superpatriotism," *Pacific Historical Review* 30, no. 2 (1961): 137–147.

17. "Syndicalism Law to Be Tested in Trial of Girl Communist," *Yonkers Statesman*, July 23, 1931, 4; "Girl, 20, Held as Ohio Communistic Director," *Sandusky Register*, July 21, 1931, 1; "Allege Criminal Syndicalism," *Piqua Daily Call*, July 21, 1931, 1; "Girl Arrested in Communist Camp," *News-Messenger*, July 20, 1931, 3; "Ohio Communist Camp for Boys and Girls Disbanded," *Lancaster Eagle-Gazette*, July 17, 1931, 1.

18. "County to Wage War against 'Reds,'" *Dayton Herald*, July 21, 1931, 17; "Prosecutor to Aid in Fight against Reds," *Greenville Daily Advocate*, July 21, 1931, 7; "Ohio's Syndicalism Law to Be Tested Anew," *Hamilton Evening Journal*, July 27, 1931, 11; "Girl Red, 20, Is Indicted by Jury," *Evening Independent*, September 25, 1931, 22; "Girl Communist, 20, Talks Here Tonight," *Akron Beacon Journal*, August 12, 1931, 17; *Yonkers Statesman*, September 25, 1931, 22.

19. "Arrest Communist Child Camp Leader after Ohio Raid," *Ithaca Journal*, July 24, 1931, 13.

20. "The Pioneers Speak Up," *Daily Worker*, July 12, 1934, 4.

11. Bashing the Boy Scouts and the Campaigns to Free Harry Eisman

1. Martin Miroff, "The Rover Boys," *Young Comrade* 1, no. 2 (December 1923): 8; Edward Shatz, "The Movies," *Young Comrade* 2, no. 2 (December 1924): 2.

2. A. M., "More Military Training for Workers' Children," and "The US Junior Naval Guards," *Young Comrade* 5, no. 2 (April 1928): 2.

3. Thelma Kahn, "Why We Are against the Boy Scouts," *Young Comrade* 1, no. 5 (March 1924): 5.

4. Mischa Honeck, *Our Frontier Is the World: The Boy Scouts in the Age of American Ascendancy* (Ithaca, NY: Cornell University Press, 2018), 174–176.

5. Irving Shavelson, "Scouts—Danger to Workers," *Young Comrade* 2, no. 12 (April 1926): 3.

6. *Investigation of Communist Propaganda: Hearings Before a Special Committee to Investigate Communist Activities in the United States House of Representatives*, 71st Cong. 2nd Sess., Pursuant to H. Res. 220, part I, vols. 1–3 (Washington, DC: United States Government Printing Office, 1930), 20–21.

7. "Boy Scout Activities," *Journal-News*, March 5, 1930, 10

8. "Smash the Boy Scouts," *Young Pioneer* 6, no. 3 (June 1929): 1, 3.

9. "Pioneers Pick USSR Delegate," *Daily Worker*, June 24, 1929, 3; "Pioneers Hate to Return to Capitalist USA after USSR," *Daily Worker*, October 11, 1929, 1.

10. Honeck, *Our Frontier is the World*, 174–176.

11. "Red Din for Scouts," *Daily News*, July 21, 1929, 2.

12. "Boy Scout Sailing Delayed by Riot of Young Reds," *Brooklyn Daily Eagle*, July 21, 1929, 2; "Reds Raise Din as Boy Scouts Sail on Liner," *Daily News*, July 21, 1929, 2, 6; "Radical Youths Stage Pier Riot," *Times Union*, July 21, 1929, 3; "Threaten to Deport Pioneer," *Daily Worker*, July 22, 1929, 1, 5; "Boy Red Adjudged a Delinquent," *New York Times*, July 27, 1929, 8. "Cack-Brained Communists," *Tarrytown Daily News*, July 27, 1929. 4.

13. "Pioneers Fight Boy Scouts," *Young Pioneer* 6, no. 4 (July–August 1929): 2.

14. "Eisman, Militant Pioneer, Gets 6 Month Sentence in a 'Home,'" *Daily Worker*, August 3, 1929, 1, 5.

15. *Reports of the Cases Heard and Determined in the Appellate Division of the Supreme Court of the State of New York* 277 (1929), 780.

16. "Eisman, in Detention, Goes on Hunger Strike and Wins His Demands," *Daily Worker*, October 9, 1929, 1.

17. Harry Eisman, *An American Boy in the Soviet Union* (New York: Progress Publishers, 1933), 2.

18. "Pioneers Will Protest Harry Eisman Sentence in Harlem Tonight," *Daily Worker*, August 30, 1929, 5; "Police Break Up Pioneers Rally," *Daily Worker*, September 16, 1929, 1, 2; "Drop Charges against 12 Pioneers, Jailed in Protest Meeting, Saturday," *Daily Worker*, September 18, 1929, 3.

19. Catriona Kelly, "'The Little Citizens of a Big Country': Childhood and International Relations in the Soviet Union," *Trondheim Studies on Eastern European Cultures & Societies*, no. 8 (2008): 12.

20. Boris Raymond, "A Sword with Two Edges: The Role of Children's Literature in the Writings of N. K. Krupskaia," *Library Quarterly* 44, no. 3 (1974): 206; Joseph Zajda, "The Moral Curriculum in the Soviet School," *Comparative Education* 24, no. 3 (1988): 389–404; Richard S. Prawat, "Dewey Meets the 'Mozart of Psychology' in Moscow: The Untold Story," *American Education Research Journal* 37, no. 3 (2000): 663–693.

21. *Daily Worker*, October 11, 1929, 1.

22. "Young Reds in New York City," *Journal of Education* 111, no. 3 (1930): 82.

23. "Police Murder Steve Katovis," *The Militant*, February 1, 1930, 1; "Policeman Praised in Katovis DEATH; Grand Jury Finds Shooting of Bronx Striker by Kiritz Was Justified. SEES CREDIT TO THE FORCE. Killing of Clerk Resulted in Communist Protests at City Hall and Union Square. Shot at Strike Meeting. A Dozen Witnesses Heard," *New York Times*, February 1, 1930, 12; A. B. Masil and Joseph North, *Steve Katovis, Life and Death of a Worker* (New York: International Pamphlets, 1930).

24. "Infant Communists Riot with Martyr of Their Own," *Reading (PA) Times*, January 30, 1930, 1; "Policeman Loses Button as Young Radicals Riot," *Baltimore Sun*, January 30, 1930, 1; "Two New York Patrolmen Nurse Bruises after Clash with Communist Children," *Press and Sun-Bulletin*, January 30, 1930, 1, "Child Communists Clash with Police," *New York Times*, January 30, 1930, 14.

25. "Cops Blackjack Women, Children, at City Hall," *Daily Worker*, March 3, 1930, 1, 3; "Women and Children Scream in City Hall Red Drive," *Standard Union*, March 1, 1930, 1; "Children Used in Clawing Mob against Police," *Daily News*, March 2, 1930, 1; "Police Disperse Red Riot by Women and Youths at City Hall," *Brooklyn Citizen*, March 2, 1930, 1; "Girl Reds Flee as Police Use Fists on Men," *Brooklyn Daily Eagle*, March 2, 1930, 1.

26. "World Unemployment Day Advanced to March 6," *Daily Worker*, February 17, 1930, 1; E. H. Carr, *Twilight of the Comintern, 1930–1935* (New York: Pantheon Books, 1982), 9–11;

Harvey Klehr, *The Heyday of American Communism: The Depression Decade* (New York: Basic Books, 1984), 33–39; Roy Rosenzweig, "Organizing the Unemployed: The Early Years of the Great Depression," in *Workers' Struggles, Past and Present: A "Radical America" Reader*, ed. James Green (Philadelphia: Temple University Press, 1983), 171.

27. "Five Communists Framed, Unite Working Class Forces for May Day Demonstrations," *The Militant*, April 19, 1930, 1, 3.

28. "Eisman Given Five Years by Boss Court," *Daily Worker*, March 21, 1930, 1, 3.

29. "Jail Harry Eisman Six Years," *Young Pioneer* 7, no. 1 (March 1930): 1.

30. "Youngest Political Prisoner Defends Self," *Daily Worker*, June 11, 1930, 3.

31. *Investigation of Communist Propaganda*, part 3, vols. 1–5 (1930), 70.

32. George Clarke, "The Fight for Harry Eisman," *The Militant*, May 24, 1930, 6.

33. "Harry Eisman Is Persecuted," *Daily Worker*, July 21, 1930, 2.

34. "Eisman Protest March Set Today against Jailings," *Daily Worker*, March 22, 1930, 1; "Get Ten Days for Fight against Jailing Eisman," *Daily Worker*, March 25, 1930, 2; "Three Young Boro Reds Are Seized in Police Clash, Five Others Arrested in Demonstration for Union Sq. Rioter," *Times Union*, March 23, 1930, 2; "New York Police Disperse Crowd of Young People," *The (Shreveport, LA) Times*, March 23, 1930, 1; "NY Police Clash with Communists," *Baltimore Sun*, March 23, 1930: 1; "Demand Release of Harry Eisman," *Daily Worker*, March 24, 1930, 1.

35. *Investigation of Communist Propaganda: Hearings Held in Detroit and Chicago, Special Committee on Communist Activities in the United States*, 71st Cong. 2nd Sess., Pursuant to H. Res. 220 (Washington, DC: United States Government Printing Office, 1930), 473. "Cop's Sore Beak Convicts Red, 13, as Riot Ruffian," *Daily News*, April 1, 1930, Brooklyn sec: 6; "Boy 'Red' Convicted," *Times Union*, April 5, 1930, 3.

36. American Civil Liberties Union, *The Story of Civil Liberty, 1929–1930*, 10; American Civil Liberties Union, *Annual Report, 1930–31*, 14.

37. "Wave of Protests for N.Y. Committee," *Daily Worker*, April 16, 1930, 3; "Int'l Labor Defense Conference to Be Held Sun. April 20," *Daily Worker*, April 18, 1930, 2.

38. Stanislaw Frankowski, "Post-Communist Europe," in *Capital Punishment: Global Issues and Prospects*, ed. Peter Hodgkinson and Andrew Rutherford (Winchester: Waterside Press, 1996), 217; "Do You Want Harry Eisman to Go to the Soviet Union?" *Young Pioneer* 7, no. 5 (November 1930): 3.

39. "Attack Pioneers for Jobless Aid," *Daily Worker*, March 11, 1930, 1, 2; "Difficulties Arise in Deportation of Eisman, Getting Habeas Corpus," *Daily Worker*, March 12, 1930, 2.

40. "Leningrad Young Pioneers Send Greetings to Harry Eisman," *Daily Worker*, June 28, 1930, 4.

41. Kelly, "'The Little Citizens of a Big Country,'" 12.

42. "Harry Eisman Out Saturday; Welcome," *Daily Worker*, November 12, 1930, 2; "Harry Eisman Is Greeted Here, Will Speak at Passaic," *Daily Worker*, November 17, 1930, 1; "H. Eisman Sails for USSR Today," *Daily News*, November 19, 1930, 1; "Boy Red Off Tonight to Study Revolution," *Brooklyn Daily Eagle*, November 17, 1930, 9; "Young Communist Seeks Red Training," *Palm Beach Post*, November 17, 1930, 1; "Young Bronx Red Goes to Russia for Communism Course," *Hartford Courant*, November 17, 1930, 13; "Harry Earns a Voyage," *Orlando Evening Star*, November 25, 1930, 6; "Eisman Goes to Russia," *Montana Standard*, November 30, 1930, 33; "Young Communists Seem to be Flourishing," *Journal-News* (Ohio), December 30, 1930, 4.

43. Eisman, *An American Boy in the Soviet Union*, 19.

44. "Russian Pioneers Pledge Fight for Scottsboro Boys," *Daily Worker*, October 26, 1931, 2.
45. "Pioneers Will Picket Nazi Consulate in Thaelmann Protest," *Daily Worker*, November 3, 1934, 1.
46. "Letter from the Karl Marx Troop of the Young Pioneers of America in Chicago, Illinois, to Governor Miller in Montgomery, Alabama, December 5, 1933." Alabama Department of Archives and History, Scottsboro Case Appeals to Governor, SG004240.
47. Eisman, *An American Boy in the Soviet Union*, 14; Choi Chatterjee, "Imperial Subjects in the Soviet Union: M. N. Roy, Rabindranath Tagore, and Re-Thinking Freedom and Authoritarianism," *Journal of Contemporary History* 52, no. 4 (2017): 913–934.
48. Eisman, *An American Boy in the Soviet Union*, 11.
49. "Engdahl Funeral Held in Moscow," *Daily Worker*, November 24, 1932, 1.
50. Corinna Kuhr, "Children of 'Enemies of the People' as Victims of the Great Purges," *Cahiers du Monde russe* 39, no. 1 / 2 (1998): 209–220. See also Margaret K. Stolee, "Homeless Children in the USSR, 1917–1957," *Soviet Studies* 40, no. 1 (1988): 64–83; Alan Ball, "Survival in the Street World of Soviet Russia's 'Besprizornye,'" *Jahrbücher für Geschichte Osteuropas* 39, no. 1 (1991): 228–247; "State Children: Soviet Russia's Besprizornye and the New Socialist Generation," *Russian Review* 52, no. 2 (1993): 64–83.
51. Eisman, *An American Boy in the Soviet Union*, 16.
52. Eisman, 21.
53. Eisman, 27–28.
54. Eisman, 55–58.
55. Gennady Estraikh, Kerstin Hoge, and Krutikov Mikhail, *Children and Yiddish Literature: From Early Modernity to Post-Modernity* (Cambridge: Taylor & Francis, 2016), 183.
56. "The Soviet Factory Is a Cultural, 'Living Centre,'" *Daily Worker*, December 27, 1934, 6; "New Pamphlets," *Daily Worker*, December 15, 1934, 7.
57. Catriona Kelly, "Defending Children's Rights, 'In Defense of Peace': Children and Soviet Cultural Diplomacy," in *Imagining the West in Eastern Europe and the Soviet Union*, ed. György Péteri (Pittsburgh: University of Pittsburgh Press, 2010), 68.
58. I. Rotkin, "Harry," *Smena*, no. 877, December 1963. Eisman's military records can be viewed online: https://pamyat-naroda.ru/heroes/person-hero91546897/.
59. Tracy B. Strong and Helene Keyssar, *Right in Her Soul: The Life of Anna Louise Strong* (New York: Random House, 1983); Mary M. Leder, *My Life in Stalinist Russia: An American Woman Looks Back* (Bloomington: Indiana University Press, 2001), 51.
60. *Appendix to the Journal of the Senate*, vol. 2, Legislature of the State of California, "Senate Interim Committee on Un-American Activities" (Sacramento, 1949), 182.
61. Foreign Broadcast Information Service, *Foreign Radio Broadcasts: Daily Report*, Thursday 15 November 1962: BB25–26.
62. Harry Eisman, *Red Ties in the Country of the Dollar* (Moscow, 1972); Paul C. Mishler, *Raising Reds, The Young Pioneers, Radical Summer Camps, and Communist Political Culture in the United States* (New York: Columbia University Press, 1999), 146.

Conclusion

1. "Children Mobilized in Fight of Red," *Philadelphia Inquirer*, April 2, 1925, 2.
2. "Gregier Pupils Strike Despite Peace Effort," *Chicago Tribune*, April 8, 1924, 15.
3. Robert K. Murray, *Red Scare: A Study in National Hysteria, 1919–1920* (Minneapolis: University of Minnesota Press, 1955); Larry Ceplair, "The Film Industry's Battle against

Left-Wing Influences, from the Russian Revolution to the Blacklist," *Film History* 20, no. 4 (2008): 399–411; Julia M. Mickenberg, "Suffragettes and Soviets: American Feminists and the Specter of Revolutionary Russia," *Journal of American History* 100, no. 4 (2014): 1024; Kenyon Zimmer, *Immigrants against the State: Yiddish and Italian Anarchism in America* (Urbana: University of Illinois Press, 2015), 136; Jessie J. Norris, "Entrapment and Terrorism on the Left: an Analysis of Post-9/11 cases," *New Criminal Law Review* 19, no. 2 (2019): 241; Julie M. Powell, "Making 'The Case against the Reds': Racializing Communism, 1919–1920," in *Historicizing Fear, Ignorance, Vilification, and Othering*, ed. Travis D. Boyce and Winsome M. Chunnu (Boulder: University of Colorado Press, 2019), 101–121.

4. Robert J. Goldstein, ed., *Little Red Scares: Anti-Communism and Political Repression in the United States, 1921–1946* (Burlington, VT: Ashgate, 2014).

5. George Clarke, "The Fight for Harry Eisman," *The Militant*, May 24, 1930, 6.

6. "Expel Red School Pupils," *Daily News*, May 14, 1931, 26. "Fuel for the Flames," *Ithaca Journal*, March 12, 1930, 4.

Appendices

1. "Boy, 14, Suspended by School as Red." *Daily News*, November 3, 1928, 4.

2. *Investigation of Communist Propaganda: Hearings before a Select Committee to Investigate Communist Activities in the United States*, part 3, vols. 1–5, H. Rep. 71st Cong., 2nd Sess., pursuant H.Res.220 (Washington, DC: US Government Printing Office, 1930), 224.

3. "A Letter from Harry Eisman," *New Pioneer* 1, no. 2 (June 1931): 19.

BIBLIOGRAPHY

Manuscript Sources

American Pamphlets. The British Library at Boston Spa. United Kingdom.
Ganley-Wellman Papers. Wayne State University Archives. Detroit.
International Workers Order (IWO) Records, 1915–2002. Kheel Center for Labor-Management Documentation and Archives. Martin P. Catherwood Library. Cornell University.
Nat Ganley Papers. Wayne State University Archives. Detroit.
Records of the Communist Party—Junior Section of the Young Workers League. Tamiment Library and Robert F. Wagner Labor Archives. New York University.
Records of the Communist Party—Young Pioneers of America. Tamiment Library and Robert F. Wagner Labor Archives. New York University.
Saul Wellman Papers. Tamiment Library and Robert F. Wagner Labor Archives. New York University.
Scottsboro Case Appeals to Governor. Alabama Department of Archives and History.
Sir Ronald Lindsey papers. The National Archives. Kew, United Kingdom.
Will Lee papers. American Heritage Center. University of Wyoming.

Online Archives / Manuscript Sources

Military Records: "Eisman, Harry Eduardovic." Central Archives of the Russian Ministry of Defence, Moscow.
newspapers.com. Historic Newspapers.
Proceedings of *Investigation of Communist Propaganda, Hearings Before a Select Committee to Investigate Communist Activities in the United States*" Google Books.
US Library of Congress, Chronicling America, Historic American Newspapers.
vault.fbi.com. Operation SOLO.

Periodicals

Labor Defender. Published by the International Labor Defense. Collected online at marxists.org.

New Pioneer. The Wisconsin Historical Society. University of Wisconsin-Madison.

The Militant. Riazanov Library. Brooklyn, New York.

The Young Fighters. International Workers Order Records #5276. Kheel Center for Labor-Management Documentation and Archives.

Wilshere's Magazine.

Young Comrade. Riazanov Library. Brooklyn, New York; The Tamiment Library. New York University Archives; The Wisconsin Historical Society. University of Wisconsin-Madison. Collected online at marxists.org.

Young Pioneer. Riazanov Library. Brooklyn, New York; The Tamiment Library, New York University Archives; The Wisconsin Historical Society. University of Wisconsin-Madison. Collected online at marxists.org.

Published Primary Sources and Memoir

American Legion. *Isms: A Review of Alien Isms, Revolutionary Communism and Their Active Sympathizers in the United States.* New York, 1937.

Anthony, Joseph, ed. *The Best News Stories of 1923.* Boston: Small Maynard, 1924.

Brown, William Montgomery. *Communism and Christianity.* Galion, Ohio: Bradford-Brown Educational Company, 1920.

Campion, Martha. *Who Are the Young Pioneers.* New York: New Pioneer Publishing, 1934.

Eisman, Harry. *An American Boy in the Soviet Union.* New York: Youth Publishers, 1934.

Foreign Broadcast Information Service. *Foreign Radio Broadcasts*: Daily Report, Thursday, November 15, 1962.

Foster, William Z. *History of the Communist Party of the United States.* New York: International Publishers, 1952.

Gitlow, Benjamin. *I Confess: The Truth about American Communism.* New York: E. P. Dutton, 1940.

Gitlow, Benjamin. *The Whole of Their Lives: Communism in America: A Personal History and Intimate Portrayal of Its Leaders.* New York: Charles Scribner's Sons, 1948.

Hoyt, Franklin Chase. *Quicksands of Youth.* New York: Charles Scribner's Sons, 1921.

Leder, Mary M. *My Life in Stalinist Russia: An American Woman Looks Back.* Bloomington: Indiana University Press, 2001.

Masil, A. B., and Joseph North. *Steve Katovis: Life and Death of a Worker.* New York: International Pamphlets, 1930.

Proceedings of the Annual Convention of the Daughters of Union Veterans of the Civil War, 1929.

Reports of the Cases Heard and Determined in the Appellate Division of the Supreme Court of the State of New York, 277, 1929.

Select Secondary Sources

Allen, Julia M. *Passionate Commitments: The Lives of Anna Rochester and Grace Hutchins.* New York: SUNY Press, 2013.

Andrews, Thomas G. *Killing for Coal: America's Deadliest Labor War*. Cambridge, MA, Harvard University Press, 2008.

Ball, Alan. "State Children: Soviet Russia's Besprizornye and the New Socialist Generation." *Russian Review* 52, no. 2 (1993): 64–83.

Ball, Alan. "Survival in the Street World of Soviet Russia's "Besprizornye." *Jahrbücher für Geschichte Osteuropas* 39, no. 1 (1991): 228–247.

Banes, Sally. *Writing Dancing in the Age of Postmodernism*. Middletown, CT: Wesleyan University Press, 2011.

Barnard, John. *American Vanguard: The United Auto Workers during the Ruether Years, 1935–1970*. Detroit: Wayne State University Press, 2005.

Barker, William J. "Muscular Marxism and the Chicago Counter-Olympics of 1932." In *The New American Sport History: Recent Approaches and Perspectives*, ed. S. W. Pope, 284–289. Urbana: University of Illinois Press, 1997.

Bayard, Charles J. "The 1927–1928 Colorado Coal Strike." *Pacific Historical Review* 32, no. 3 (1963): 235–250.

Biehly, Janet. *Ecology or Catastrophe: The Life of Murray Bookchin*. New York: Oxford University Press, 2015.

Bornet, Vaughn Davis. *Labor Politics in a Democratic Republic: Moderation, Division, and Disruption in the Presidential Election of 1928*. Washington, DC: Spartan Books, 1964. Reprint: London: Palgrave Macmillan, 2015.

Boyce, Travis D., and Winsome M. Chunnu, eds. *Historicizing Fear, Ignorance, Vilification, and Othering*. Boulder: University of Colorado Press, 2019.

Carleton, William G. "The Politics of the 1920s." *Current History* 47, no. 278 (1964): 210–215.

Carr, E. H. *Twilight of the Comintern, 1930–1935*. New York: Pantheon Books, 1982.

Chalberg, John C. "The Spirit of the 1920s." *OAH Magazine of History* 20, no. 1 (2006): 11–14.

Chatterjee, Choi. "Imperial Subjects in the Soviet Union: M. N. Roy, Rabindranath Tagore, and Re-Thinking Freedom and Authoritarianism." *Journal of Contemporary History* 52, no. 4 (2017): 913–934.

Cohen, Ronald D. "Review." *History of Education Quarterly* 40, no. 1 (2000): 103–104.

Cornell, Tom. "The Catholic Worker, Communism and the Communist Party." *American Catholic Studies* 125, no. 1 (2014): 87–101.

Cupers, Kenny. "Governing through Nature: Camps and Youth Movements in Interwar Germany and the United States." *Cultural Geographies* 15, no. 2 (2008): 173–205.

D'Alessandro, Mark. "Free Lunch after All? An Historical Review of Implementation of School Meals in New York Public Schools." *Journal of Child Nutrition and Management* 43, no. 1 (2019).

Dale, Timothy M., and Joseph J. Foy. *Homer Simpson Marches on Washington: Dissent through American Popular Culture*. Lexington: University of Kentucky Press, 2010.

Diner, Hasia R. *Hungering for America: Italian, Irish, and Jewish Foodways in the Age of Migration*. Cambridge, MA: Harvard University Press, 2003.

Draper, Theodore. *The Roots of American Communism*. New York: Viking Press, 1957.

DuRocher, Kristina. *Raising Racists: The Socialization of White Children in the Jim Crow South*. Lexington: University of Kentucky Press, 2011.

Estraikh, Gennady, Kerstin Hoge, and Krutikov Mikhail. *Children and Yiddish Literature: From Early Modernity to Post-Modernity*. Cambridge: Taylor & Francis, 2016.

Fein, Gene. "For Christ and Country: The Anti-Semitic Anticommunism of Christian Front Street Meetings in New York City." *US Catholic Historian* 22, no.4 (2004): 37–56.

Fox, Craig. *Everyday Klansfolk: White Protestant Life and the KKK in 1920s Michigan*. East Lansing: Michigan State University Press, 2011.

Franklin, Vincent P. *African Americans and Jews in the Twentieth Century: Studies in Convergence and Conflict*. Columbia: University of Missouri Press, 1998.

Goldstein, Robert J., ed., *Little Red Scares: Anti-Communism and Political Repression in the United States, 1921–1946*. Burlington, VT, Ashgate, 2014.

Goodman, Walter. *The Committee: The Extraordinary Career of the House Committee on Un-American Activities*. London: Specker and Warburg, 1964.

Green, James, ed., *Workers' Struggles, Past and Present: A "Radical America" Reader*. Philadelphia: Temple University Press, 1983.

Haas, Britt. *Fighting Authoritarianism: American Youth Activism in the 1930s*. New York: Fordham University Press, 2018.

Haynes, John Earl, and Harvey Klehr. *Verona: Decoding Soviet Espionage in America*. New Haven, CT: Yale University Press, 1999.

Hodgson, Jack. "From the Bronx to Stalingrad: Harry Eisman and the Young Pioneers of America in New York City." *New York History* 103, no. 1 (2022): 68–84.

Hodgson, Jack. "'The Santy Claus Myth': The Politicisation of Santa Claus during the Great Depression." *Comparative American Studies: An International Journal* 20, no. 2–3 (2023): 291–307.

Homberger, Eric. "Proletarian Literature and the John Reed Clubs, 1929–1935." *Journal of American Studies* 13, no. 2 (1979): 221–244.

Honeck, Mischa. *Our Frontier Is the World: The Boy Scouts in the Age of American Ascendancy*. Ithaca, NY: Cornell University Press, 2018.

Hunt, Jonathan. "Communists and the Classroom: Radicals in U.S. Education, 1930–1960." *Composition Studies* 43, no. 2 (2015): 22–42.

Huyssen, David. *Progressive Inequality: Rich and Poor in New York, 1890–1920*. Cambridge, MA: Harvard University Press, 2014.

Keeran, Roger. "National Groups and the Popular Front: The Case of the International Workers Order." *Journal of American Ethnic History* 14, no. 3 (1995): 23–51.

Kelly, Catriona. "'The Little Citizens of a Big Country': Childhood and International Relations in the Soviet Union." *Trondheim Studies on Eastern European Cultures & Societies*, no. 8 (2008).

Klehr, Harvey. *The Heyday of American Communism: The Depression Decade*. New York: Basic Books, 1984.

Kosek, Joseph Kip. *Acts of Conscience: Christian Nonviolence and Modern American Democracy*. New York: Columbia University Press, 2009.

Kuhr, Corinna. "Children of 'Enemies of the People' as Victims of the Great Purges." *Cahiers du Monde russe* 39, no. 1/2 (1998): 209–220.

Levin, Murray B. *Political Hysteria in America: The Democratic Capacity for Repression*. New York: Basic Books, 1971.

Levine, Susan A. *School Lunch Politics: The Surprising History of America's Favorite Welfare Program*. Princeton, NJ: Princeton University Press, 2010.

Lindey, Sara. "Boys Write Back: Self-Education and Periodical Authorship in Late-Nineteenth-Century Story Papers." *American Periodicals* 21, no. 1 (2011): 72–88.

Logan, Gabe. "C'mon, You Reds: The US Communist Party's Workers' Soccer Association, 1927–1935." *Journal of Sport History* 44, no. 3 (2017): 384–385.

Logan, Gabe. "Playing for the People: Labor Sports Union Athletic Clubs in the Lake Superior/Iron Range ,1927–1936." *Upper Country: A Journal of the Lake Superior Region*,4 (2016): a3.

Lundin, Anne H., and Wayne Wiegand. *Defining Print Culture for Youth: The Cultural Work of Children's Literature*. Westport, CT: Libraries Unlimited, 2003.

Macleod, David I. "Review." *Canadian Journal of History* 35, no. 3 (2000): 598–599.

Marquit, Erwin. "Review." *Nature, Society, and Thought* 11, no. 1 (1998): 117.

Maynard, W. Barksdale. "An Ideal Life in the Woods for Boys: Architecture and Culture in the Earliest Summer Camps." *Winterthur Portfolio* 34, no. 1 (1999): 3–29.

McColloch, Mark. "Review." *ILR Review* 54, no. 4 (2001): 905.

McDuffie, Erik S. *Sojourning for Freedom: Black Women, American Communism, and the Making of Black Left Feminism*. Durham, NC: Duke University Press, 2011.

Messer-Kruse, Timothy. *The Trial of the Haymarket Anarchists: Terrorism and Justice in the Gilded Age*. New York: Palgrave Macmillan, 2011.

Mickenberg Julia L., and Philip Nel, eds. *Tales for Little Rebels: A Collection of Radical Children's Literature*. New York, 2010.

Mishler, Paul C. *Raising Reds: The Young Pioneers, Radical Summer Camps, and Communist Political Culture in the United States*. New York: Columbia University Press, 1999.

Moran, Rachel L. "Consuming Relief: Food Stamps and the New Welfare of the New Deal." *Journal of American History* 97, no. 4 (2011): 1001–1022.

Murray, Robert K. *Red Scare: A Study in National Hysteria, 1919–1920*. Minneapolis: University of Minnesota Press, 1955.

Naison, Mark. *Communists in Harlem during the Depression*. Urbana: University of Illinois Press, 1983.

Orleck, Annelise. *Common Sense and a Little Fire: Women and Working-Class Politics in the United States, 1900–1965*. Chapel Hill: University of North Carolina Press, 1995.

Palmer, Bryan D. "Rethinking the Historiography of United States Communism." *American Communist History* 2, no. 2 (2003): 139–173.

Palmer, Niall. *The Twenties in America: Politics and History*. Edinburgh: Edinburgh University Press, 2006.

Pasco, Allan H. "Literature as Historical Archive." *New Literary History* 35, no. 3 (2004): 373–394.

Péteri, György, ed. *Imagining the West in Eastern Europe and the Soviet Union*. Pittsburgh: University of Pittsburgh Press, 2010.

Pinar, William F. "White Women in the Ku Klux Klan." *Counterpoints* 163 (2001): 555–619.

Price, Wayne. "From Shachtmanite to Trotskyism to Anarchism." *The Utopian* 15, no. 2,(2016): 59–74.

Raymond, Boris. "A Sword with Two Edges: The Role of Children's Literature in the Writings of N. K. Krupskaia." *Library Quarterly* 44, no. 3 (1974): 206–218.

Reiss, Steven A. *Sports and the American Jew*. Syracuse, NY: Syracuse University Press, 1998.

Ribeiro, Julia. "'Knowing you will understand': The Usage of Poetry as a Historical Source about the Experience of the First World War." *Alicante Journal of English Studies* 31 (2018): 109–124.

Robbins, Michael W., and Wendy Palitz. *A Brooklyn State of Mind*. New York: Workman Publishing, 2001.

Romerstein, Herbert. *Communism and Your Child*. New York: Bookmailer, 1962.

Rosenzweig, Roy. "Organizing the Unemployed: The Early Years of the Great Depression." In *Workers' Struggles, Past and Present: A "Radical America" Reader*, ed. James Green. Philadelphia, Temple University Press, 1983.

Rouleau, Brian. "Children Are Hiding in Plain Sight in the History of US Foreign Relations." *Modern American History* 2, no. 3 (2019): 367–387.

Ruis, A. R. "'The Penny Lunch Has Spread Faster than the Measles': Children's Health and the Debate over School Lunches in New York City, 1908–1930." *History of Education Quarterly* 55, no. 2 (2015): 190–217.

Schmidt, Regin. *Red Scare: FBI and the Origins of Anticommunism in the United States, 1919–1943*. Copenhagen: Museum Tusculanum Press, University of Copenhagen, 2000.

Seymour, Harrold. *Baseball: The People's Game*. New York: Oxford University Press, 1990.

Siener, William H. "The Red Scare Revisited: Radicals and the Anti-Radical Movement in Buffalo, 1919–1920." *New York History* 79, no. 1 (1998): 23–54.

Smith, Michael B. "The Ego Ideal of the Good Camper' and the Nature of Summer Camp." *Environmental History* 11, no. 1 (2006): 70–101.

Solomon, Mark. *The Cry Was Unity: Communism and African Americans, 1917–1936*. Jackson: University of Mississippi Press, 1998.

Stansby, Janet F. "In Re Gault: Children Are People." *California Law Review* 55, no. 4 (1967): 1204–1218.

Stolee, Margaret K. "Homeless Children in the USSR, 1917–1957." *Soviet Studies* 40, no. 1 (1988): 64–83.

Strong, Tracy B., and Helene Keyssar. *Right in Her Soul: The Life of Anna Louise Strong*. New York: Random House, 1983.

Tanehaus, David S. *The Constitutional Rights of Children: In re Gault and Juvenile Justice*. Lawrence: University Press of Kansas, 2017.

Teitelbaum, Kenneth, and William J. Reese. "American Socialist Pedagogy and Experimentation in the Progressive Era: The Socialist Sunday School." *History of Education Quarterly* 23, no. 4 (1983): 429–454.

Van Slyck, Abigail A. "Kitchen Technologies and Mealtime Rituals: Interpreting the Food Axis at American Summer Camps, 1890–1950." *Technology and Culture* 43, no. 4 (2002): 668–692.

Van Slyck, Abigail A. *Manufactured Wilderness: Summer Camps and the Shaping of American Youth, 1890–1960*. Minneapolis: University of Minnesota Press, 2006.

Wald, Alan M. *Trinity of Passion: The Literary Left and the Antifascist Crusade*. Chapel Hill: University of North Carolina Press, 2007.

Wallace, Robert, H. Keith Melton, and Henry R. Schlesinger. *Spycraft: Inside the CIA's Top Secret Spy Lab*. London: Bantam Books, 2009.

Webb, Shelia. "Dorothy Day and the Early Years of the 'Catholic Worker': Social Action through the Pages of the Press." *US Catholic Historian* 21, no. 3 (2003): 71–88.

Weigand, Kate. *American Communism and the Making of Women's Liberation*. Baltimore: Johns Hopkins University Press, 2002.

Zaagsma, Gerben. *Jewish Volunteers, The International Brigades, and the Spanish Civil War*. London: Bloomsbury, 2017.

Zimmer, Kenyon. *Immigrants against the State: Yiddish and Italian Anarchism in America*. Urbana: University of Illinois Press, 2015.

INDEX

African American communists, 18, 33, 42, 47, 132–138, 165
all-American anti-imperialist league, 60
American cinema, 18, 130
American Civil Liberties Union, 82, 107, 124, 145
American communism: attitudes to childhood, 14, 55–58; historiography, 4–6
American Defense Society, 19
American Legion, 119, 122–123
Americanization, 99–101
anti-Christmas parties, 36–39
anti-Communism: among children, 58 89, 100; among historians 4–6; in Congress, 50–51, 94–96; violence, 92, 119–121, 123–124, 126. *See also* Fish Committee, police brutality, Red scares
antisemitism, 37, 92, 107

Bachman, Carl G, 96, 144. *See also* Fish Committee
baseball, 42–43
basketball, 40–41
Better America Foundation, 125–126
Blumkins, Perry, 141, 145. *See also* police brutality, violence perpetrated by YPA

Board of Education (New York), 80, 87–89, 93–97, 100
Board of Estimates, 86
Bookchin, Murray, 18–19
bootblacks, 73–74
Boyd, Leslie, 47–48
Boy Scouts of America, 33, 45, 49, 130–132,133, 159
Broun, Heywood, 27
Buitenkant, Jacques, 61–63

capitalist attitudes to childhood, 26, 63, 131
capitalist children's books, 130
capitalist school curriculum, 77, 80–83
child labor: legislation, 25; support of, 59–60; YPA opposition to, 20, 25–27, 32, 57–58, 110–113
children's poems, 31–32, 111–115
children's rights
Christian communists, 36, 38–39
CIA, 155
Clarke, Henry, 42
Communist Party (USA): headquarters, 21; relationship with YCL, 17; relationship with YPA, 17, 46, 55, 72; sports, 40, 68. *See also* May Day, Rebecca Grecht, Robert Minor, William Z. Foster

communist Sunday schools, 46–47
corporal punishment, 80, 102, 144
Coney Island, 43, 63, 100

Daughters of the American Revolution, 50–51, 109
Daughters of Union Veterans of the Civil War, 51
deaf children, 87
desecration of the American flag, 119–120, 122–123, 125–126
diplomacy, 5, 137, 146–147

Eisman, Alexander, 92, 96, 143–144
Eisman, Harry: arrests, 61, 133–134; early childhood, 91–92, 152; campaigns for, 120, 134–136, 143–146, 158–159, 168; court appearances, 63, 134; death and commemoration, 156–157; electioneering, 15, 55–56; hunger strike, 135; in custody, 15, 62, 134–136, 143–144; in schools, 69, 91–102, 107; in Soviet Press, 136, 146; in Soviet Union, 148–156, 168–169; Order of the Red Star, 154, 157; racial justice, 42, 149–150; speeches 55–56, 97, 140, 149, 151; Stalingrad, 154
Engdahl, John Louis, 151
espionage: by the Soviet Union, 73; by the United States, 155

FBI, 155
Finnish Americans, 3, 19, 35, 41, 47, 118, 121, 127
Fish Committee, 51, 94, 105, 131
Fish, Hamilton III, 51, 94, 107, 125. See also Fish Committee, antisemitism
Foster, William Z., 38, 82, 107–108, 142, 147
freedom of speech: at school, 82, 95; children's right to, 25, 82, 95, 140; suppression of, 25 106–107, 126, 140. See also anticommunism, children's rights, Red Scares

Gershonowitz, William, 31–32
Gitlow, Benjamin, 42–43, 82

Gorbait, Irving, 81
Granoff, Leo: attitude to religion, 39; at school, 20, 26, 29, 59; communist organizing, 21, 24, 69; interview, 27; publicity, 22–23, 25–26; speeches, 21, 28, 29; tactical influence, 30, 59, 63, 95, 97, 107–110, 134, 158; 1923 court appearance, 23–26
Grecht, Rebecca, 55–56, 66
Grossman, Joe, 82, 88

Haymarket Affair, 61
Herrick, William, 62, 157
Holmes, Ailene, 118–119, 121–124
Husa, Mabel, 118–119, 121–124

International Children's Congress, 132, 136, 146–147
International Labor Defense, 61, 66, 95, 120, 124–125, 145–146
International Workers Order, 3, 117

Jewish communists, 19, 36, 38, 91, 99, 154
John Reed clubs, 32, 34
Johnny and Rosie Red, 32, 108

Kahn, Thelma, 29, 39, 131
Kaplan, Bernard, 72, 93–94, 168
Kaplan, Lebe, 93–94, 98, 168
Kaplan, Nat, 14, 22, 27, 108–110
Kessler, Sam, 88
Kittredge, Mabel Hyde, 85–87
KKK, 68, 107–108, 119–121, 122–125, 161
Kroons, Victoria, 120. See also Patriotic Order of America
Krupskaya, Nadezhda, 137–138

Labor Sports Union, 40–43
Lemlich, Clara, 18, 72–73
Limpus, Lowell, 105
Lincoln brigades, 62, 157
Little Billy Worker, 83

malnutrition, 85, 112
May Day, 60–64, 166–167
McCarthyism, 4, 107, 155

McDonald, Elmer, 132, 138
McGuire, Edward, 93–95, 98, 168
McKela, Jack, 119–120, 122–123
messenger boys, 73–74
miners' relief funds, 70–72
Minor, Robert, 1–2, 56, 66, 108, 142

National Security League, 28
Nazism: protests against, 38, 150; persecution of Communists, 150; sympathizers, 95, 107. See also Hamilton Fish III
newspaper boys, 71–72, 73
New York Chamber of Commerce, 101
NYPD: leadership, 140–141, 142; in schools, 88, 94; radical bureau, 78, 79, 94; surveillance, 33, 37, 98, 161. See also police brutality

O'Shatz, Morris, 89
Overman Committee, 106–107

Patriotic Order of America, 119–123. See also anti-communists
playgrounds, 4, 33, 158
Plotkin, Rose, 66–67, 69, 158
police brutality, 72, 126–127, 128, 133, 140, 141–142
political cartoons, 1–2, 35–36, 83, 109. See also Little Billy Worker, Ryan Walker
punch ball, 43–44
Prohibition, 101

Red scares: Cold War era, 107; First Red scare, 5–6, 8–9, 166; historiography of, 7–8, 8–9, 160–161; Palmer Raids, 22; Wall Street bombing, 9; YPA experience of, 9–10, 22–30, 88–90, 93–101, 121–125, 126–130, 160–62. See also anti-communism, Hamilton Fish III, McCarthyism
Reggie van Sucker, 109
Rosenfeld, Gussie, 81–82

Santa Claus, 26, 36–39
Schachtman, Max, 108–110
school buildings, 79

school lunch, 78, 84–90, 158
School Lunch Committee, 85–87
school strikes, 61, 64
Scottsboro case, 18,130, 149–150,153
segregation, 18, 33, 47, 113
Shavelson, Irving, 17–18, 72–73, 131
soccer, 39–40
Socialist Sunday schools, 13–14
Society for the Prevention of Cruelty for Children, 62–66, 135, 150
Soviet cinema, 132, 153
Spartakiad, 44
Spector, Morris, 44, 47, 56–60, 158–159
strikes, 67–68, 70, 132
Strickland, Shelley, 132, 137–138
Stromberg, Yetta, 125–126

Taft, Jessie, 2, 61, 72, 98, 132, 138–139, 147, 157
tenement housing, 39, 110

Unconditional Service League of America, 58–59
United Council of Working Women, 55, 97

Valentine, Frank, 81

Walker, Jimmy, 141, 145
Walker, Ryan, 83
Warwick, Walter, 122–123
Weiss, Max, 99–100, 144
Wellman, Saul, 18, 62, 72, 100, 144, 157
Workers International Relief, 66, 118–120

YMCA, 33, 45
Young Communist Leage: election candidates, 2, 29; relationship with YPA, 29, 32, 60, 98, 108; sports, 40–42
Young Pioneers of America: closure, 3–4, 33; conventions, 70–72, 78, 132; establishment,13; ethnicity, 19; finances, 16–17; growth, 19, 105; in Baltimore, 113; in California, 123, 125–126; in Chicago, 66; in Cleveland, 8, 126; in Massachusetts, 68; in Michigan, 125; in Minneapolis–St Paul, 77; in New Jersey,

Young Pioneers of America (*continued*) 31–32, 68, 112; in Ohio, 126–129; in schools, 59 70–72, 77–79, 91–102, 167–168; recruitment, 14–15, 18; rules and regulations, 16, 165–166; sports, 39–44, 50; summer camping, 66–67, 118–121, 129; theatre, 21, 34–35; violence perpetrated by, 62–64, 100, 116–117, 131–132, 140–141

Zam, Herbert, 2, 29

Jack Hodgson, Lecturer in History at the University of Roehampton, London, specializes in American Communism and youth movements. His work has been featured in *Qualitative Inquiry*, *New York History*, *Rethinking History*, and *The Journal of American Studies*. Hodgson is also a recipient of the Ellen Craft Prize from the Scottish Association for the Study of America.

EMPIRE STATE EDITIONS SELECT TITLES FROM EMPIRE STATE EDITIONS

Salvatore Basile, *Fifth Avenue Famous: The Extraordinary Story of Music at St. Patrick's Cathedral*. Foreword by Most Reverend Timothy M. Dolan, Archbishop of New York

William Seraile, *Angels of Mercy: White Women and the History of New York's Colored Orphan Asylum*

Andrew J. Sparberg, *From a Nickel to a Token: The Journey from Board of Transportation to MTA*

New York's Golden Age of Bridges. Paintings by Antonio Masi, Essays by Joan Marans Dim, Foreword by Harold Holzer

Daniel Campo, *The Accidental Playground: Brooklyn Waterfront Narratives of the Undesigned and Unplanned*

John Waldman, *Heartbeats in the Muck: The History, Sea Life, and Environment of New York Harbor, Revised Edition*

John Waldman (ed.), *Still the Same Hawk: Reflections on Nature and New York*

Joseph B. Raskin, *The Routes Not Taken: A Trip Through New York City's Unbuilt Subway System*

Phillip Deery, *Red Apple: Communism and McCarthyism in Cold War New York*

Stephen Miller, *Walking New York: Reflections of American Writers from Walt Whitman to Teju Cole*

Tom Glynn, *Reading Publics: New York City's Public Libraries, 1754–1911*

R. Scott Hanson, *City of Gods: Religious Freedom, Immigration, and Pluralism in Flushing, Queens*. Foreword by Martin E. Marty

Dorothy Day and the Catholic Worker: The Miracle of Our Continuance. Edited, with an Introduction and Additional Text by Kate Hennessy, Photographs by Vivian Cherry, Text by Dorothy Day

Mark Naison and Bob Gumbs, *Before the Fires: An Oral History of African American Life in the Bronx from the 1930s to the 1960s*

Robert Weldon Whalen, *Murder, Inc., and the Moral Life: Gangsters and Gangbusters in La Guardia's New York*

Sharon Egretta Sutton, *When Ivory Towers Were Black: A Story about Race in America's Cities and Universities*

Britt Haas, *Fighting Authoritarianism: American Youth Activism in the 1930s*

David J. Goodwin, *Left Bank of the Hudson: Jersey City and the Artists of 111 1st Street*. Foreword by DW Gibson

Nandini Bagchee, *Counter Institution: Activist Estates of the Lower East Side*

Susan Celia Greenfield (ed.), *Sacred Shelter: Thirteen Journeys of Homelessness and Healing*

Elizabeth Macaulay-Lewis and Matthew M. McGowan (eds.), *Classical New York: Discovering Greece and Rome in Gotham*

Susan Opotow and Zachary Baron Shemtob (eds.), *New York after 9/11*

Andrew Feffer, *Bad Faith: Teachers, Liberalism, and the Origins of McCarthyism*

Colin Davey with Thomas A. Lesser, *The American Museum of Natural History and How It Got That Way*. Forewords by Neil deGrasse Tyson and Kermit Roosevelt III

Wendy Jean Katz, *Humbug: The Politics of Art Criticism in New York City's Penny Press*

Lolita Buckner Inniss, *The Princeton Fugitive Slave: The Trials of James Collins Johnson*

Mike Jaccarino, *America's Last Great Newspaper War: The Death of Print in a Two-Tabloid Town*

Angel Garcia, *The Kingdom Began in Puerto Rico: Neil Connolly's Priesthood in the South Bronx*

Jim Mackin, *Notable New Yorkers of Manhattan's Upper West Side: Bloomingdale–Morningside Heights*

Matthew Spady, *The Neighborhood Manhattan Forgot: Audubon Park and the Families Who Shaped It*

Marilyn S. Greenwald and Yun Li, *Eunice Hunton Carter: A Lifelong Fight for Social Justice*

Jeffrey A. Kroessler, *Sunnyside Gardens: Planning and Preservation in a Historic Garden Suburb*

Elizabeth Macaulay-Lewis, *Antiquity in Gotham: The Ancient Architecture of New York City*

Ron Howell, *King Al: How Sharpton Took the Throne*

Phil Rosenzweig, *"12 Angry Men": Reginald Rose and the Making of an American Classic*

Jean Arrington with Cynthia S. LaValle, *From Factories to Palaces: Architect Charles B. J. Snyder and the New York City Public Schools*. Foreword by Peg Breen

Boukary Sawadogo, *Africans in Harlem: An Untold New York Story*

Alvin Eng, *Our Laundry, Our Town: My Chinese American Life from Flushing to the Downtown Stage and Beyond*

Stephanie Azzarone, *Heaven on the Hudson: Mansions, Monuments, and Marvels of Riverside Park*

Ron Goldberg, *Boy with the Bullhorn: A Memoir and History of ACT UP New York*. Foreword by Dan Barry

Peter Quinn, *Cross Bronx: A Writing Life*

Mark Bulik, *Ambush at Central Park: When the IRA Came to New York*

Matt Dallos, *In the Adirondacks: Dispatches from the Largest Park in the Lower 48*

Brandon Dean Lamson, *Caged: A Teacher's Journey Through Rikers, or How I Beheaded the Minotaur*

Raj Tawney, *Colorful Palate: Savored Stories from a Mixed Life*

Edward Cahill, *Disorderly Men*

Joseph Heathcott, *Global Queens: An Urban Mosaic*

Francis R. Kowsky with Lucille Gordon, *Hell on Color, Sweet on Song: Jacob Wrey Mould and the Artful Beauty of Central Park*

Jill Jonnes, *South Bronx Rising: The Rise, Fall, and Resurrection of an American City, Third Edition*

Barbara G. Mensch, *A Falling-Off Place: The Transformation of Lower Manhattan*

David J. Goodwin, *Midnight Rambles: H. P. Lovecraft in Gotham*

Felipe Luciano, *Flesh and Spirit: Confessions of a Young Lord*

Maximo G. Martinez, *Sojourners in the Capital of the World: Garifuna Immigrants*

Jennifer Baum, *Just City: Growing Up on the Upper West Side When Housing Was a Human Right*

Davida Siwisa James, *Hamilton Heights and Sugar Hill: Alexander Hamilton's Old Harlem Neighborhood Through the Centuries*

Annik LaFarge, *On the High Line: The Definitive Guide, Third Edition*. Foreword by Rick Dark

Marie Carter, *Mortimer and the Witches: A History of Nineteenth-Century Fortune Tellers*

Alice Sparberg Alexiou, *Devil's Mile: The Rich, Gritty History of the Bowery*. Foreword by Peter Quinn

Carey Kasten and Brenna Moore, *Mutuality in El Barrio: Stories of the Little Sisters of the Assumption Family Health Service*. Foreword by Norma Benítez Sánchez

Kimberly A. Orcutt, *The American Art-Union: Utopia and Skepticism in the Antebellum Era*

Jonathan Butler, *Join the Conspiracy: How a Brooklyn Eccentric Got Lost on the Right, Infiltrated the Left, and Brought Down the Biggest Bombing Network in New York*

Nicole Gelinas, *Movement: New York's Long War to Take Back Its Streets from the Car*

For a complete list, visit www.fordhampress.com/empire-state-editions.

www.ingramcontent.com/pod-product-compliance
Lightning Source LLC
Chambersburg PA
CBHW020409080526
44584CB00014B/1240